Voices of Christ

Reflections on Applied Christianity

Robert C. Fischer, *ed.*

Leo Tolstoy

Bayard Rustin

Hugh Hollowell

J.C. Kumarappa

Magdalene Harrison

2014
Enfranchised Mind Press
Durham, North Carolina, USA

He that will fly without wings must fly in his dreams: and til he awakes,
will not find out, that to fly in a dream is but to dream of flying.
Samuel Taylor Coleridge

Death is not an event in life: we do not live to experience death. If we take
eternity to mean not infinite temporal duration but timelessness, then
eternal life belongs to those who live in the present. Our life has no end in the
way in which our visual field has no limits.
Ludwig Wittgenstein

A great value of antiquity lies in the fact that its writings
are the only ones that modern men still read with exactness.
Friederich Nietzsche

Those who do not have power over the story that dominates their lives,
the power to retell it, rethink it, deconstruct it, joke about it,
and change it as times change, truly are powerless, because they
cannot think new thoughts.
Salman Rushdie

Virtus iunxit mors non separabit.

Short Contents

Contents

Activist Writings
by Bayard Rustin

Selected Internet Writings
by Hugh Hollowell

Clothe Yourself in Righteousness (But First, Get Naked!)
by Magdelene Harrison

Conclusion

Forward

This is a seeking era. Progressives are seeking for a future while conservatives seek to recreate the past, and mystics seek change within themselves while activists seek change beyond themselves. Our world society is tumultuous and uncertain as it seeks truth and justice. The environment is demanding that we seek a sustainable way to exist. In this seeking era, the church is seeking to identify its relationship to the world and to its own past. If we are honest with ourselves, each of us are also seeking our owne relationships with this world. It is obvious that this is a seeking era, but it is easy to forget that this is not the only seeking era.

Two millenia ago, there was another seeking era. Scholars call that era the "Apocalyptic Age". In the Apocalyptic Age, like now, there is a charge to the air and tension in society. People sense that things are about to change. What people do not know is what this change will be: how will the world look on the other side of the transformation? What will the new kingdom be?

Jesus came to answer the questions of that Apocalyptic Age. He told all who had ears to hear what the new kingdom could be for them. He told them about the kind of character required to enter that new kingdom. He told them about the suffering that is part of birthing this new kingdom. Most frequently, however, he told of the way people would treat one another in the new kingdom. These messages took deep root and transformed the world for two millenia.

Yet our seeking age still needs to hear the message of Jesus. However, that message is easily lost in the din of church politics, denominational strife, and secular bombardment. Those who heard Jesus' earthly ministry heard with their own ears, and such a cutting voice could not be mistaken or ignored. We, however, are trying to hear that message as an echo two thousand years old. The message gets to us only through translations of translations of stories about the message. Even with the guidance of the Spirit, the message of Jesus is a struggle for our age to hear and comprehend. Yet we do have an advantage over those who lived two millennia ago.

Over the last two millennia, the message has not laid dormant. It is not only the voice of Jesus which carried the message. There have also been those who remind us of that message. We have been blessed with talented impersonators of Jesus: those who the Spirit recognizes as bearing the image of Jesus and carrying the same message. These people live into the new kingdom and bring that promised future into our present. They are grounded in reality, and so they cannot escape the difficulties and the pain that are in the world; yet, they continue to represent and share the love of God in a way that is unmistakably divine.

While others strain to hear Jesus' message in the distant echo, I have found it much easier to hear the message from those speaking it anew. The Bible and its traditional witness to Christ are still my canon, but the relevance of Jesus' message is proven in the contemporary witness of the image of Christ. It is easy for some to dismiss the echo of Jesus as a message meant for different ears and a different age, but the message cannot be denied when it is a living witness in the here and now.

That living witness is a witness through living. It cannot be communicated solely through a lecture or through sermons: it must be communicated through the pattern of living and through an entire way of relating to others. In this way, becoming one who bears the image of Christ is a transformation not just of the mind, but of the whole being.

This anthology is an effort to capture some of that lived message into writing. This anthology is certainly not the entirety of the message: Jesus may be the Word become flesh, but attempting to put that flesh back into words is extremely difficult. Through these select writings, however, I hope that you can glimpse the image of Christ that the authors carry. I hope that you get a new and deep appreciation for the message of Jesus. And I hope that you can join those following their models to move into the new kingdom.

These texts were all written in a spirit of love for the reader. They are provided so that they might do some good in your life, nurture the growth of your spirit, and bolster your expressions of God's peace. Please read them in love, and hopefully they will do well for your soul.

What I Believe
by Leo Tolstoy

Editor's Forward

Tolstoy is best known as an existentialist and nihilist. However, near the end of his life, he became a very devout Christian. Many of his biographers view this period of his life as one of increasing insanity, because Tolstoy abandons his hyper-rational viewpoint and adopts a creed that would have been laughably ridiculous to his younger self.

In this way, Tolstoy perfectly represents what it is to follow Christ: namely, to abandon worldly rationality for deeper and more loving understanding. Living into the new kingdom does not make any sense by the standards of the old kingdom. In the old kingdom, there is nothing higher than the self, perhaps extended slightly to include the nuclear family. The concerns of the self certainly extend no farther than that, and so the only rational thing in that worldview is servng yourself and working to better your own situation. In the new kingdom, however, the self is extended over all of humanity and subjugated to everyone we encounter. When the problems of your neighbors become your problems, then a different lifestyle begins to make sense. This is what Tolstoy realized late in his life: the new kingdom suddenly made sense to him, and he understood the core of Jesus' message.

Tolstoy had not heard this core Christian message from his church while growing up. He did not hear it from his family or from his nominally Christian nation. It was not until he was an old man that this message came to him, and this is his account of how that message arrived, what it was, and how he responded at first. This account provides a thorough and accurate description of the message of Jesus, but it is not included solely for that description. This account is included because of the earnest, grounded, and realistic way in which Tolstoy describes his compulsion to bear the image of Christ. Tolstoy's account is included not as a theological treatise, but as an account which sounds so familiar to those who hear that echo of Jesus and are moved by the Spirit to obey it.

Here are the confessions of a frustrated, confused, limited, but ultimately faithful Christian. Hearing these confessions can remind us all that we are not alone and that our frustrations are not new: we have a cloud of witnesses and a college of saints who have known our suffering, and who have their wisdom to share with us.[1]

License

Although the text is in the public domain, the digital copy of the text of *What I Believe* by Leo Tolstoy (translated by Constantine Popoff) was provided courtesy of

---

[1] By the way, you may have encountered Tolstoy's more popular Christian tract, *The Kingdom of God is Within You*. Tolstoy begins that Tract by discussing the reaction to a suppressed yet popular text. This is account is that suppressed yet popular text.

Introduction

I am fifty-five years old and, with the exception of the fourteen or fifteen years of my childhood, I have been until recently a "Nihilist" in the proper signification of that term. I have not been a Socialist or Revolutionist, but a Nihilist in the sense of being completely without faith.

Five years ago I began to believe in the doctrine of Christ, and in consequence a great change has been wrought in me. I now no longer care for the things that I had prized, and I have begun to desire things concerning which I had formerly been indifferent. Like a man who, going out on business, on his way suddenly becomes convinced of the futility of that business and turns back; and all that stood to the right now stands to the left, and all that was to the left is now to the right; his wish to be as far from home as possible is changed to the desire of being as near home as possible — so, I may say, the whole aim and purpose of my life has been changed; my desires are no more what they have been. For me, good and evil have changed places. This experience came through my apprehending the doctrine of Christ in an altogether different way, and seeing it in quite a new light.

It is not my intention to interpret the doctrine of Christ, but simply to relate how I came to understand the simplest, clearest, and most intelligible point in that doctrine; and how, when once I had clearly grasped His meaning, it gave a new direction to all my thoughts.

I have no wish to interpret the doctrine of Christ, but I should like to prevent others from interpreting it wrongly. Christian churches generally acknowledge that all men, however they may differ from each other in knowledge or mental capacity, are equal before God; and that the truth revealed to man is accessible to all. Christ Himself has told us that the Father has hidden some things 'from the wise and prudent, and revealed them to babes.'

All men cannot be initiated into the mysteries of dogmatic, homiletic, and patristic theologies, and so on, but all can understand what Christ taught and still teaches to simple and ignorant men. The teachings of Christ were incomprehensible to me until recently, but I understand them now, and what I have found I desire to explain to others.

The thief on the cross believed in Christ and was saved. Would it have harmed anybody if the thief had not died on the cross, but had come down to tell us how he believed in Christ?

Like the thief on the cross, I, too, believed in the doctrine of Christ, and found my salvation in it. This is not a far-fetched comparison; it worthily describes the condition of anguish and despair I was once in at the thought of life and of death, and it also indicates the peace and happiness that now fill my soul.

Like the thief, I knew that my life was full of wickedness; I saw that the greater part of those around me were morally no better than I was. Like the thief, too,

I knew that I was unhappy, and that I suffered; and that all around me were unhappy and suffering likewise, and I saw no way out of this state of misery but through death.

Like the thief, I was nailed, as it were by some invisible power, to this life of suffering and evil; and the same dreadful darkness of death that awaited the thief, after his useless suffering and enduring of the evils of life, awaited me.

In all this I was like the thief, but there was this difference between us: he was dying, and I still lived. The thief could believe that his salvation would be realized beyond the grave, but I could not; because, putting aside the life beyond the grave, I had yet to live on earth. I did not, however, understand life. It seemed awful to me until I heard the words of Christ and understood them; and then life and death no longer seemed to be evils; instead of despair I felt the joy of possessing a life that death has no power to destroy.

Can it harm anyone if I relate how it was that this change was effected in me?

Chapter I

I have endeavored to explain the reason why I had not properly understood the doctrine of Christ in my two works, *A Criticism on Dogmatic Theology* and *A New Translation and Comparison of the Four Gospels, with a commentary*. In these works I examine all that conceals the truth from the eyes of men, and also retranslate and compare the four gospels verse by verse.

I have been engaged for some six years upon this work. Every year, every month, I find new solutions and suggestions, and I am enabled to correct the defects that creep in through haste or impulse. My life will perhaps end before the work is complete, but I am sure that it is a much needed labor I have imposed on myself, and therefore I shall do what I can while my life lasts.

This is my outward work on the theology of the gospel. But the inner working of my soul, which I wish to speak of here, was not the result of a methodical investigation of doctrinal theology, or of the actual texts of the gospel; it was a sudden removal of all that hid the true meaning of the Christian doctrine — a momentary flash of light, which made everything clear to me. It was something like that which might happen to a man who, after vainly attempting, by a false plan, to build up a statue out of a confused heap of small pieces of marble, suddenly guesses at the figure they are intended to form by the shape of the largest piece; and then, on beginning to set up the statue, finds his guess confirmed by the harmonious joining in of the various pieces.

I wish to tell in this work how I found the key to the doctrine of Christ, by the help of which the truth was disclosed to me so clearly and convincingly.

I made the discovery in the following manner. Almost from the first years of my childhood, when I began to read the gospel for myself, the doctrine that teaches love, humility, meekness, self-denial, and returning good for evil was the doctrine that touched me most. I always considered it as the basic teaching of Christianity and loved it as such; but it was only after a long period of unbelief that its full meaning flashed upon me, that I understood 'life' as our unlettered working classes understand it, and accepted the same creed that they profess, the creed of the Greek Orthodox Church. But I soon observed that I should not find in the teaching of the Church the confirmation of my idea that love, humility, meekness, and self-denial were the essential principles of Christianity. I saw that this, which I regarded as the basis of Christianity, did not form the main point in the public teaching of the Church. At first I did not attach much importance to this. "The Church," I said to myself, "acknowledges, besides the doctrine of love, humility, and self-denial, a dogmatic and ritualistic doctrine. This estranges my heart; it is even repulsive to me, but there is no harm in it."

While, however, submitting to the teaching of the Church, I began to see more and more clearly that this peculiarity was not as unimportant as I had at first regarded it. I was drawn away from the Church by various singularities in its dogmas; by its approval of persecution, capital punishment, and war; and also by its intolerance of all other forms of worship than its own; but my faith in the teaching of the Church was shaken still more by its indifference to what seemed to me the very basis of the teaching of Christ, and by its evident partiality for what I could not consider an essential part of that doctrine. I felt that there was something wrong, but I could not make out distinctly what it was, because the Church did not deny what seemed to me the main point in the doctrine of Christ, though it failed to give it its proper position and influence.

I only passed from 'Nihilism' to the Church because I felt the impossibility of living without faith — without a knowledge of what is good and evil, resting on something more than my animal instincts. I hoped to find this 'something' in Christianity. But Christianity, as it appeared to me then, was only a certain disposition of mind — a very vague one. I turned to the Church for obligatory precepts of life, but the Church gave me only such as did not draw me nearer to the Christian state of mind I longed for, but rather alienated me from it. I turned away from the Church. For the precepts that were given to me by the Church concerning belief in dogmas, observance of the sacraments, fast-days, and prayers, I did not care; and precepts really founded on the teachings of Christ were wanting.

Moreover, the precepts of the Church weakened, and sometimes even destroyed, that Christian state of mind that alone seemed to me to be the true aim of life.

What perplexed me most of all was that all the evil things that men do, such as condemning private individuals, whole nations, or other religions; and the inevitable results of these condemnations — executions and wars — were justified by the Church. I saw that the doctrine of Christ, which teaches us humility, tolerance, forgiveness, self-denial, and love, was extolled by the Church, but that at the same time she sanctioned what was incompatible with such teachings.

Could the doctrine of Christ be so weak and inconsistent? That I could not believe. Besides, it had always perplexed me to find that the texts upon which the Church has grounded her dogmas are of an obscure character, whereas those that teach us how to live are the most simple and clear. While the Church specifies the dogmas, and the duties derived from them, in the most forcible manner, the practice of the 'doctrine' is urged only in obscure, dim, and mystical expressions. Is it possible that this was what Christ desired for His teaching? I could only find the solution of my doubts in the perusal of the gospels, and I read them over and over again. Of all the gospels, the Sermon on the Mount was the portion that impressed me most, and I studied it more often than any other part. Nowhere else does Christ speak with such solemnity; nowhere else does He give us so many clear and intelligible moral precepts, which commend themselves to everyone. If there are any clear and definite precepts of Christianity, they must have been expressed in this sermon; and, therefore, in those three chapters of St. Matthew's gospel I sought the solution of my doubts.

Many and many a time I read over the sermon, and every time I felt the same emotion on reading the texts about "turning my cheek to the one who strikes me," "giving up my cloak to him who takes my coat," "being at peace with all men," and "loving my enemies," — and yet there remained in me the same feeling of dissatisfaction. The words of God were not as yet clear to me. They seemed to enjoin an impossible self-denial that annulled life itself, and therefore it seemed to me that such self-denial could not be the requirement on which man's salvation depended.

But, then, if that were not the express condition of salvation, there was nothing fixed and clear! I not only read the Sermon on the Mount, but the rest of the gospels, and various commentaries upon them. Our theological explanations tell us that in the teachings of the Sermon on the Mount an indication is given of the perfection after which man must strive; that man, being full of sin, cannot attain this perfection by his own unaided strength, and that the salvation of a man lies in faith, prayer, and the gifts of the grace of God; but these explanations did not satisfy me.

Why should Christ have given to us such clear and good precepts, applicable to us all, if He knew beforehand that the keeping of them was impossible by man in his own unaided strength?

On reading over these precepts, it always seemed that they applied to me, and that I was morally bound to obey them. I even felt convinced that I could, immediately and from that very hour, do all that they enjoined.

I wished and tried to do so, but as soon as any difficulty arose in the way of my keeping them, I involuntarily remembered the teaching of the Church, that 'man is weak, and can do no good thing by himself,' and then I became weak.

I had been told that it was necessary to believe and to pray, but I felt that my faith was weak and that I could not pray. I had been told that it was necessary to pray for faith—for that faith without which prayer is of no avail. I was told that faith comes through prayer and that prayer comes through faith, which, to say the least, was certainly bewildering. Such statements commended themselves neither to reason nor experience.

After much useless study of the works that have been written in proof of the divinity or non-divinity of this doctrine, and after many doubts and much suffering, I was left alone with the mysterious Book, in which the doctrine of Christ is taught. I could not interpret it as others did, I could not abjure the Book, and yet I could not find a new and satisfying interpretation. It was only after losing all faith in the explanations of learned theology and criticism, and after laying them all aside in obedience to the words of Christ (Mark 10:15), that I began to understand what had until then seemed incomprehensible to me. It was not by deep thought, or by skillfully comparing or commenting on the texts of the gospel, that I came to understand the doctrine. On the contrary, all grew clear to me for the very reason that I had ceased to rest on mere interpretations. The text that gave me the key to the truth was the thirty-ninth verse of the fifth chapter of St. Matthew, "You have heard that it has been said, an eye for an eye, and a tooth for a tooth. But I say to you, do not resist evil..." The simple meaning of these words suddenly flashed full upon me; I accepted the fact that Christ meant exactly what He said; and then, though I had found nothing new, all that had hitherto obscured the truth cleared away, and the truth itself arose before me in all its solemn importance.

I had often read the passage, but these words had never until now arrested my attention: "I say to you, do not resist evil."

In my conversations since with many Christian people, who know the gospels well, I have observed the same indifference to the force of this text that I had felt. Nobody specially remembered the words; and, while conversing with persons upon the text, I have known them to take up the New Testament in order to assure themselves that the words were really there.

The words, "Whoever shall strike you on your right cheek, turn to him the other also," had always presented themselves to me as requiring endurance and self-mastery such as human nature is hardly capable of. They touched me. I felt that to act thus would be to attain moral perfection; but I felt, too, that I should never be able to obey them if they entailed nothing but suffering. I said to myself, "Well, I will turn my cheek---I will let myself be struck again. I will give up my coat---they shall take my all. They shall even take away my life. Yet, life is given to me. Why should I thus lose it? This cannot be what Christ requires of us." Then I said to myself, "Perhaps in these words Christ only purposes to extol suffering and self-denial, and in doing so He speaks exaggeratingly and His expressions are therefore to be regarded as illustrations rather than precise requirements." But as soon as I comprehended the meaning of the words, "do not resist evil," it became clear to me that Christ does not exaggerate, that He does not require suffering for the mere sake of suffering, and that He only expresses clearly and definitely what He means. He says, "Do not resist evil," and if you do not resist evil, you may meet with some who, having struck you on one cheek, and meeting with no resistance, will strike you on the other; after having taken away your coat, will take away your cloak also; having profited by your work, will oblige you to work on; will take, and will never give back. "Nevertheless, I say to you, do not resist evil. Still do good to those who even strike and abuse you."

Now I understood that the whole force of the teaching lay in the words "do not resist evil," and that the entire context was but an application of that great precept. I saw that Christ does not require us to turn the other cheek, and to give away our cloak, in order to make us suffer; but He teaches us not to resist evil, and warns us that doing so may involve personal suffering. Does a father, on seeing his son set out on a long journey, tell him to pass sleepless nights, to eat little, to get wet through, or to freeze? Will he not rather say to him, "Go, and if on the road you are cold or hungry, do not be discouraged but go on"? Christ does not say "Let a man strike your cheek, and suffer," but He says, "Do not resist evil. Whatever men may do to you, do not resist evil." These words, "do not resist evil" (the wicked man), thus apprehended, were the clue that made all clear to me, and I was surprised that I could have hitherto treated them in such a different way. Christ meant to say, "Whatever men may do to you, bear, suffer, and submit; but never resist evil." What could be clearer, more intelligible, and more indubitable that this? As soon as I understood the exact meaning of these simple words, all that had appeared confused to me in the doctrine of Christ grew intelligible; what had seemed contradictory now became consistent, and what I had deemed superfluous became indispensable. All united in one whole, one part fitting into and supporting the other, like the pieces of a broken statue put together again in their proper places.

This doctrine of 'non-resistance' is commended again and again in the gospels. In the Sermon on the Mount Christ represents His followers — i.e., those who follow this law of non-resistance — as liable to be persecuted, stoned, and reduced to beggary. Elsewhere He tells us that the disciple who does not take up His cross, who is not willing to renounce all, cannot be His follower, and He thus describes the man who is ready to bear the consequences that may result from the practice of the doctrine of non-resistance. Christ says to His disciples, "Be poor, be ready to bear persecution, suffering, and even death, without resisting evil." He prepared for suffering and death Himself without resisting evil; He reproved Peter, who grieved over Him because He proposed to yield in this way; and He died, forbidding others to resist evil, remaining true to His own doctrine and His own example. All His first disciples obeyed the same law of the non-resistance of evil, and passed their lives in disability and persecution.

We may bring forward, as an objection, the difficulty of always obeying such a law; we may even say, as unbelievers do, that it is a foolish doctrine, that Christ was a dreamer, an idealist who gave precepts that are impossible to follow. But, whatever our objections may be, we cannot deny that Christ expresses His meaning most clearly and distinctly; and His meaning is that man must not resist evil; he who fully accepts His teaching cannot resist evil.

Chapter II

When I at last clearly comprehended that the words 'do not resist evil' do really mean that we are never to resist evil, my former ideas concerning the teaching of Christ underwent a complete change. I wondered, not so much at my eyes being opened to the truth at last, but at the strange darkness that had, until then, enveloped my understanding. I knew — we all know — that the foundation requirement of the Christian doctrine is love toward all men. Isn't all Christianity summed up in the words, 'Love your enemies'? I had known that from my earliest childhood. How was it, then, that I had not hitherto taken in these words in all their simplicity, but rather had sought for some allegorical meaning in them? 'Do not resist evil' means never to resist evil, i.e., never offer violence to anyone. If a man reviles you, do not revile him in return; suffer, but do no violence. While believing, or at least endeavoring to believe, that He who gave us this commandment was God, how did I come to say that I could not obey it in my own strength? If my master were to say to me, 'Go and cut wood,' and I were to answer that I could not do it in my own strength, would it not show that either I had no faith in my master's words, or that I did not choose to obey him? God has given to us a commandment that He requires us to obey; He says that only those who keep His commandments shall enter life eternal; He fulfilled this commandment Himself, as offering us His example; and how could I then say that, though I never really tried to fulfill it, this injunction was one that it was impossible for a man to keep in his own strength, and without supernatural aid?

God became man for the securing of our salvation. Salvation lies in the fact that the second person of the Trinity, God the Son, suffered for us men, redeemed us from sin, and gave us the Church through which the grace of God is transmitted to all believers. Moreover, God the Son has left us this doctrine (teaching), and His own example, to show us the way of salvation. And yet, I said that the rule of life given to us by Christ was not only a hard one, but also an impossible one, apart from supernatural aid. Christ does not consider it as such. On the contrary, He says definitely that we are to fulfill His commandments, and that he who does not shall not enter the kingdom of God. He does not say that it is hard to keep this law; He says, on the contrary, "My yoke is easy and My burden is light." St. John the Evangelist says, "His commandments are not grievous." How was it, I said, that the express and positive commandment of God, which He Himself speaks of as being easy, the commandment which He Himself obeyed as a man, and which His first followers also fulfilled, was too hard for me, and even impossible for me, without supernatural aid?

If a man were to set all the faculties of his mind to the annulling of a given law, what more forcible argument could he use for its suppression than that it was an impracticable law, and that the legislator's own opinion of it was that it could not be kept without supernatural aid? And yet, this was exactly what I had thought about the commandment 'not to resist evil.' I tried to remember when and how the strange idea had first come into my mind, that the doctrine of Christ was divine in authority but impossible in practice. On reviewing my past life, I discovered that this idea had never been transmitted to me in all its nakedness, for then it would have repelled me; but that I had imperceptibly imbibed it from my earliest childhood, and that the associations of my life had confirmed the strange error.

I was taught from my childhood that Christ is God and that His teaching is divine and authoritative; while, on the other hand, I was also told to respect those institutions that, by means of violence, secured my safety from evil; I was taught to honor those institutions as being sacred. I was taught to resist evil; and it was instilled into me that it was humiliating and dishonorable to submit to evil and to suffer from it; and that it was praiseworthy to resist evil. I was taught to condemn and to execute. I was taught to make war, i.e., to resist evil by murder. The army, a member of which I was, was called a 'Christ-loving' army, and the Church consecrated its mission. I was taught to resist an offender by violence and to avenge a private insult, or one against my native land, by violence. All this was never regarded as wrong, but, on the contrary, I was told that it was perfectly right and in no way contrary to Christ's doctrine.

All surrounding interests, such as the peace and safety of my family, my property, and myself were based on the law that was rejected by Christ — on the law of a 'tooth for a tooth.'

Ecclesiastical teachers told me that the doctrine of Christ was divine, but that its observance was impossible on account of the weakness of human nature; and that the grace of God alone could enable us to keep this law. Secular teachers told me, and the whole order of life proved, that the teaching of Christ was impracticable and ideal, and that we must, in fact, live contrary to His doctrine. I imbibed such a notion of the practical impossibility of following the divine doctrine gradually and almost imperceptibly. I was so accustomed to it, it coincided so well with all my animal feelings, that I had never observed the contradiction in which I lived. I did not see that it was impossible to admit the Godhead of Christ — the basis of whose teaching is non-resistance of evil — and, at the same time, to work consciously and calmly for the institutions of property, courts of law, kingdoms, the army, and so on. It could not be consistent for us to regulate our lives contrary to the doctrine of Christ, and then pray to the same Christ that we might be enabled to keep His commandments — to 'forgive,' and not to 'resist evil.' It did not then occur to me, as it does now, that it would be much simpler to regulate our lives according to the doctrine of Christ; and then, if courts of law, executions, and war were found to be indispensably necessary for our welfare, we might pray to have them too.

And I understood from where my error arose. It arose from my professing Christ in words and denying Him in deed.

The precept 'not to resist evil' is one that contains the whole substance of Christ's doctrine, if we consider it not only as a saying, but also as a law we are bound to obey. It is like a latchkey that will open any door, but only if it is well inserted into the lock. To consider this rule of life as a precept that cannot be obeyed without supernatural aid is to annihilate the whole doctrine of Christ completely. How can a doctrine, the fundamental law of which is cast aside as impracticable, be considered practicable in any of its details?

This is what was done with Christ's doctrine when we were taught that it was possible to be a Christian without fulfilling His law not to resist evil.

A few days ago I was reading the fifth chapter of St. Matthew to a Hebrew rabbi. "That is in the Bible — that is in the Talmud too," he said at almost each saying, pointing out to me, in the Bible and the Talmud passages very much like those in the Sermon on the Mount. But when I came to the verse that says, 'do not resist evil,' he did not say that is also in the Talmud; but only asked me with a smile, "Do Christians keep this law? Do they turn the other cheek to be struck?" I was silent. What answer could I give, when I knew that Christians, in our days, far from turning the other cheek when struck, never let an opportunity escape of striking a Hebrew on both cheeks. I was greatly interested to know if there was any law like this in the Talmud, and I inquired. He answered, "No, there is nothing like it; but pray tell me, do Christians ever keep this law?" His question showed me clearly that the existence of a precept in the law of Christ, which is not only left unobserved, but of which the fulfillment is considered impossible, is superfluous and irrational.

Now that I comprehend the true meaning of the doctrine, I see clearly the strange state of contradiction within my own self that I had permitted to arise. I was confessing Christ as God, and His teaching as divine, and at the same time I was ordering my life contrary to His teaching. What was left for me to do but to acknowledge the teaching as an impracticable one? In word I acknowledged the teaching of Christ as sacred; but I did not carry out that teaching in deed, for I admitted and respected the unchristian institutions that surrounded me.

Throughout the Old Testament we find it said that the misfortunes of the Israelites arose from their believing in false gods, and not in the true God. In the eighth and twelfth chapters of the first Book of Samuel, the prophet accuses the people of having chosen, instead of God, who was their King, a human king who, according to their opinion, was to save them. "Do not believe in [toga] vain things," says Samuel to the people (1 Samuel 12:21). "They will not help you and will not save you, for they are [toga] vain. In order not to perish with your king, believe in God alone."

My faith in these 'toga,' in these empty idols, hid the truth from my eyes. In my way to Him these 'toga,' which I did not have the strength to renounce, stood before me, obscuring His light.

One day, as I was passing through Borovitzki gate, I saw a crippled old beggar with his head bound up in a ragged cloth and sitting in a corner. I had just taken out my purse to bestow a trifle upon him, when a bold, ruddy-faced young grenadier in a government fur coat came running down the Kremlin slope. On seeing the soldier, the beggar sprang up with a look of terror and ran limping down toward the Alexander Garden. The grenadier pursued him, but, not succeeding in overtaking him, stopped short and began to abuse the poor fellow for having dared to sit down near the entrance-gate in defiance of orders. I waited until the grenadier came up to where I stood, and then asked if he could read.

"Yes; what of that?" was the answer. "Have you ever read the gospel?" "I have." "Do you know these words: 'He who feeds the hungry...'?" I repeated the text to him. He listened attentively. Two passers-by stopped. It was evidently disagreeable to the grenadier that, while conscientiously discharging his duty by driving people away from the entrance-gate, as he was ordered to do, he unexpectedly found himself in the wrong. He looked puzzled, and seemed to be searching for some excuse. Suddenly his dark eyes brightened up with a look of intelligence, and, moving away as if about to return to his post, he asked, "Have you read the military code?" I told him that I had not. "Well, then, do not talk of what you do not understand," he said, with a triumphant shake of his head; and muffling himself up in his overcoat, he went back to his post.

He was the only man I have met in all my life who strictly, logically, solved the problem of our social institutions, which had stood before me, and still stands before each who calls himself a Christian.

Chapter III

To affirm that the Christian doctrine refers only to personal salvation and has no bearing upon state affairs is a great error. To say so is but to assert an audacious, groundless, most evident untruth, which a moment's serious reflection suffices to destroy. "Well," I say to myself, "I will not resist evil; as a private man, I will let myself be struck; but what am I to do if an enemy invades my native land, or other nations oppress it? I am called upon to take part in a struggle against evil — to go and kill." The question immediately arises: which will be serving God, and which will be serving 'toga'? To go, or not to go? Suppose I am a peasant. I am chosen as the senior member of my village, as judge, as juryman. I am bound to take an oath, to judge, and to punish. Fellow-creature, what am I to do? I have again to choose between the law of God and the law of man. Or let us say I am a monk and live in a monastery; the neighboring peasants have taken possession of the hay we had mown for our own use. I am sent to take part in a struggle against evil — to prosecute these men. I have again to choose between the laws of God and the laws of man. None of us can evade the demand for such a decision. To say nothing of the class of society that I belong to — military men, judges, administrators, whose whole lives are passed in resisting evil — there is not a single private individual, be he ever so insignificant, who has not had to choose between serving God by fulfilling His commandments, or serving the 'toga' in the government institutions of his country. Our private lives are interwoven with the organization of the state, and the latter requires unchristian duties of us, contrary to the commandments of Christ. At the present time, the military service, which is obligatory on all, and the participation of each, as jurymen, in the courts of law, place this dilemma with striking clarity before all. Each man is called upon to take up an instrument of murder — a gun, a sword — even if he does not kill a fellow-creature; he loads the gun and sharpens the sword, i.e., he is ready to commit murder. Each citizen is called upon to enter the courts of law, to take part in judging and punishing his fellow-creature; i.e., each must renounce the doctrine of Christ that teaches us not to resist evil.

The grenadier's question: the gospel or the military code, the law of God or the law of man? It still stands before all of us, as it did in the time of Samuel. It stood before Christ and His disciples. It now stands before all those who wish to be Christians; it stood before me.

The doctrine of Christ, which teaches love, humility, and self-denial, had always attracted me. But I found a contrary law, both in the history of the past and in the present organization of our lives — a law repugnant to my heart, my conscience, and my reason, but one that flattered my animal instincts. I knew that if I accepted the doctrine of Christ, I should be forsaken, miserable, persecuted, and sorrowing, as Christ tells us His followers will be. I knew that if I accepted that law of man, I should have the approbation of my fellow-men; I should be at peace and in safety; all possible sophisms would be at hand to quiet my conscience and I should 'laugh and be merry,' as Christ says. I felt this, and therefore I avoided a closer examination of the law of Christ, and tried to comprehend it in a way that should not prevent my still leading my animal life. But, finding that impossible, I desisted from all attempts at comprehension.

This led me into a state of mental obscurity, which now seems surprising to me. For instance, let me recall my former interpretation of the words, 'Do not judge, and you shall not be judged' (Matthew 7:1). 'Do not judge, and you shall not be judged; do not condemn, and you shall not be condemned' (Luke 6:37). The court of law of which I was a member, and which guarded my property and my personal safety, seemed to me so unquestionably sacred that it never came into my mind that the words 'do not condemn' could have any higher meaning than that we were not to speak evil of our fellow-men. The idea never occurred to me that these words could have any reference to courts of law, district courts, criminal courts, assizes, courts of peace, etc. When I at last took in the real meaning of the words 'do not resist evil,' the question arose in my mind, "What would Christ's opinion be of all these courts of law?" And seeing clearly that He would reject them, I asked myself, "Do these words mean that we are not only never to speak ill of our brethren, but that we are not to condemn them to punishment by our human institutions of justice?"

In the gospel of St. Luke, chapter 6, verses 37–39, these words come immediately after the commandment not to resist evil, and to return good for evil. After the words, "Be merciful, even as your Father in heaven is merciful," we read, "Do not judge, and you shall not be judged; do not condemn, and you shall not be condemned." "Doesn't it mean that we are not only never to condemn our brother in word — i.e., speak evil of him — but that we are not to institute courts of law for the condemnation of a fellow-creature to punishment?" I said to myself; and no sooner did this question arise, than both my heart and my reason answered in the affirmative.

I know how greatly this way of understanding the words surprises everyone at first. I was surprised, too. To show how far I formerly was from the true interpretation of these words, I may here mention a foolish saying of mine, of which I am now heartily ashamed. Even after having become a believer, and having recognized the divinity of the gospel, I used to say, jokingly, on meeting with a friend who was an attorney or a judge, "So, you go on judging, and yet isn't it said, 'Do not judge, and you shall not be judged'?" I was so firmly convinced that these words had no other meaning than that we were not to speak ill of one another, that I did not see the blasphemy of my own words. So sure was I that the words were not to be taken in a literal sense, that I used them — jokingly — in their true application.

I shall give a circumstantial account of the way in which all my doubts as to the real sense of these words were dispersed, and how it became evident to me that Christ forbids all human institutions of justice, and that He could mean nothing else.

The first point that struck me, when I understood the commandment, 'Do not resist evil,' in its true meaning, was that human courts were not only contrary to this commandment, but in direct opposition to the whole doctrine of Christ, and that therefore He must certainly have forbidden them.

Christ says, 'Do not resist evil.' The sole object of courts of law is — to resist evil. Christ enjoins us to return good for evil. Courts of law return evil for evil. Christ says, 'Make no distinction between the just and the unjust.' Courts of law do nothing else. Christ says, 'Forgive all. Forgive not once, not seven times, but forgive without end.' 'Love your enemies.' 'Do good to those who hate you.' Courts of law do not forgive, but they punish; they do not do good, but evil, to those whom they call the enemies of society. So, the true sense of the doctrine is that Christ forbids all courts of law. "This cannot be the case," I said to myself, "Christ had nothing to do with human courts of law, and never considered them." But I soon saw that this supposition was impossible. From the day of His birth, Christ had to submit to the jurisdiction of Herod, the Sanhedrin, and the high priests. Indeed, we find that Christ speaks more than once of tribunals as being an evil. He tells His disciples that they will have to be cited before the tribunals, and teaches them how they are to behave in courts of law. He says that He Himself will be condemned, and sets us all an example of the way in which we are to treat the laws of man. There can be no doubt that Christ meant the human courts of law, which were to condemn Him and His disciples; which have always condemned, and still continue to condemn, millions of men. Christ must have seen this evil, for He distinctly points it out. In the case of the adulteress He positively rejects human justice and proves that, on account of each man's own sinful nature, he has no right to judge another. We find the same doctrine repeated several times, as when He says, for instance, that the one who has a beam in his own eye cannot see the mote in his neighbor's eye; and that the blind cannot lead the blind.

"But, perhaps," I said to myself, "this applies only to the judgment of the adulteress, and the parable of the mote is only intended to show us the frailty of human nature in general. Christ does not intend to forbid our having recourse to human justice for our protection against evil men." But I saw that this would not hold true either.

In the Sermon on the Mount, addressed to all men, He says, "And if anyone sues you at the law for your coat, let him have your cloak also." Therefore He forbids our going to law.

But perhaps this applies only to the relations between private individuals and public courts of law. Perhaps Christ does not deny justice itself, and admits in Christian societies the existence of persons chosen for the purpose of administering justice. I see that this hypothesis is likewise inadmissible. In His prayer Christ enjoins all men, without any exception, to forgive as they hope to be forgiven. We find the same precept repeated many times. Each man must forgive his brother when he prays, and before bringing his gift. How, then, can a man judge and condemn another when, according to the faith he professes, he is bound to forgive? Thus I see that, according to the doctrine of Christ, a judge who condemns his fellow-creature to death is no Christian.

But perhaps the connection between the words, 'do not judge, do not condemn,' and those that follow proves that they do not refer to human courts of law? This is likewise false. On the contrary, the connection between these words and those that follow proves clearly that the words 'do not judge' are directed precisely against the institutions of courts of law. According to the gospels of Matthew and Luke, the texts, 'Do not judge; do not condemn,' are preceded by the words, 'Do not resist evil, suffer evil, do good to all.' In the gospel according to Matthew the words of the Hebrew criminal law are repeated, 'An eye for an eye, a tooth for a tooth.' And after citing the criminal law, Christ says, 'But you are not to act thus; do not resist evil.' Then He goes on to say, 'Do not judge.' So Christ's words refer precisely to our human criminal law, and by the words 'do not judge' He clearly rejects it.

Besides this, we find in St. Luke that He not only says, 'Do not judge,' but also adds, 'and do not condemn.' The latter word, almost synonymous with the former, must have been added with some purpose, and it could have been with no other than that of showing clearly the sense in which the first word is to be taken.

Had He wished to say, 'Do not judge your neighbor,' i.e., 'do not speak evil of him,' He would have said so; but He says plainly, 'Do not condemn,' and then adds, 'and you shall not be condemned; forgive, and you shall be forgiven.'

But perhaps Christ's words do not apply to courts of law at all, and I give them an interpretation of my own that is foreign to them.

I tried to discover how the first followers of Christ, His disciples, considered human courts of law, and whether they approved of them.

In chapter 4, verses 11 and 12, the disciple James says, 'Do not speak evil of one another, brethren. He who speaks evil of his brother, and judges his brother, speaks evil of the law, and judges the law; but if you judge the law, you are not a doer of the law, but a judge. There is one lawgiver, who is able to save and to destroy. Who are you to judge another?'

The word that is translated as 'do not speak evil' is the word καταλαλεω. Even without consulting the dictionary, it is evident to all that this word can mean nothing but 'to accuse.' That is the only true meaning of the word, as anyone can find by consulting the dictionary. The translation of the passage in question is as follows: 'He who speaks evil of his brother speaks evil of the law,' and the question involuntarily arises, 'How so?' In speaking evil of my brother, I do not speak evil of the law of man. No; but if I accuse and sit in judgment over my brother, I evidently condemn the doctrine of Christ; i.e., I look upon the doctrine of Christ as insufficient, and thus judge and condemn the law of God. It clearly follows that I do not fulfill this law, but I myself become a judge. 'A judge,' Christ says, 'is he who can save.' Then how can I, being unable to save, be a judge and punish?

This whole text speaks of human judgment, and rejects it. The whole of this epistle is penetrated with the same idea. In the same epistle of James (2:1-13) he says, 'My brethren, do not have the faith of our Lord Jesus Christ, the Lord of glory, together with a respect of persons. For if there comes into your assembly a man with a gold ring in fine clothes, and there comes in also a poor man in shabby clothes; and you have respect for him who wears the fine clothing, and if you say to him, "Sit here in a good place," and say to the poor man, "Stand there," or, "Sit here under my footstool," are you not then being partial, and have you not become judges with evil thoughts? Hearken, my beloved brethren, hasn't God chosen the poor of this world to be rich in faith and heirs of the kingdom, which He has promised to those who love Him? But you have despised the poor. Don't rich men oppress you, and draw you before the judgment seat? Don't they blaspheme that worthy name by which you are called? If you fulfill the royal law according to the Scripture, "You shall love your neighbor as yourself" (Leviticus 19:18), you do well. But if you have respect to persons, you commit sin, and are convicted by the law as transgressors. For whoever shall keep the whole law, and yet offend in one point, he is guilty of all. For He who said, "Do not commit adultery," also said, "Do not kill." Now if you commit no adultery, yet if you kill, you have become a transgressor of the law (Deuteronomy 22:22; Leviticus 28:17–25). So speak and act as those who shall be judged by the law of liberty. For he who has shown no mercy shall have judgment without mercy; mercy triumphs over the law.' (The last words, 'mercy triumphs over the law,' have often been translated as, 'Mercy is extolled in judgment,' and are cited as meaning that the existence of human judgment may be admitted, provided that it is merciful.)

James exhorts his brethren to make no difference between men. If you make any difference, then you διεκρίνετε, become partial, and are like judges with evil thoughts. You judge the beggar as being less worthy than the rich man. On the contrary, the rich man is the less worthy one. It is he who oppresses you and draws you before the judgment seat. If you live according to the law of love and mercy (which James calls the royal law to distinguish it from the other), you do well. But if you have respect of persons, and make a distinction between rich and poor, you are transgressors of the law of mercy. James, bearing in mind the case of the adulteress who was brought before Christ to be stoned, or perhaps speaking of adultery in general, says that he who punishes an adulteress with death is guilty of murder, and transgresses the eternal law, because the same eternal law that forbids adultery also forbids murder. He says, 'And act like men who are judged by the law of liberty; because there is no mercy for him who is himself without mercy, and therefore mercy destroys judgment.'

Can anything be more clear and definite? Every distinction between men is forbidden, every judgment by which we consider the one as good and the other as bad; human justice is distinctly pointed out as being evil; it is clearly shown that judgment sins by punishing for crime, and that all judgment is annihilated by the law of God—mercy.

I read the epistle of Paul the apostle, who had himself suffered from courts of law, and in his first chapter to the Romans he warns them against their vices and errors, and speaks against their courts of law (Romans 1:32). 'Who, knowing the judgment of God, that they who commit such things are worthy of death, not only do the same, but have pleasure in those who do them.'

Romans 2:1–4: 'Therefore you are without excuse, you who judge; for when you judge another, you condemn yourself; for you who judge do the same things. But we are sure that the judgment of God is according to truth against those who commit such things. And do you think that when you judge those who do such things, and do the same things yourself, that you shall escape the judgment of God? Or do you despise the riches of His goodness and forbearance and longsuffering; not knowing that the goodness of God leads you to repentance?'

The apostle Paul says, while fully aware of the just judgment of God, men act unjustly themselves, and they teach others to do the same; therefore the man who judges another cannot be justified. Such is the opinion I find in the epistles of the apostles in reference to courts of law. We all know that, during the whole course of their lives, human courts of law could never have been considered by them as anything but evil—a trial that was to be endured with firmness and submission to the will of God.

On reviewing the position of the early Christians amidst the heathens, we clearly perceive that men who were themselves persecuted by human courts of law could never have dared openly to forbid them. They could only occasionally allude to them as an evil, the basis of which they could not admit.

I examine the writings of the earliest teachers of Christianity, and I find that they all consider the precept never to use force, never to condemn or execute, as the one that distinguishes their doctrine from all others (Athenagarus, Origen). They only submit to the tortures inflicted upon them by human justice. The martyrs all confessed the same, not only in word, but also in deed.

I find that all true Christians, from the disciples up to the time of Constantine, regarded courts of law as evils that had to be endured with patience; and the possibility of a Christian's taking any part in judging another never occurred to any one of them.

All this convinced me that the words 'do not judge and do not condemn' apply to courts of law; and yet these words are so generally understood as meaning only 'speak no evil of your neighbor,' that courts of law flourish, so boldly and with such assurance, in all Christian states, and are openly upheld by the Church. It was some time before I could feel quite convinced that my interpretation was the right one.

'If all have until now interpreted the words as referring to evil speaking, and have, consequently, instituted these courts of law, they must have some good grounds for acting thus,' I said to myself, 'and I must be in the wrong.'

And I turned to the commentaries of the Church. In all of them, from the fifth century to the present day, I found that these words are considered as signifying to condemn in word — i.e., to speak evil of our neighbor. Now if these words are understood as meaning nothing else, doesn't the question immediately arise, 'How can we help judging others?' We must condemn (blame) what is evil? Thus the point on which all comments turn is: what may we condemn, and what may we not condemn? We are told that these words cannot be considered as forbidding the servants of the Church to judge — that the apostles themselves judged (Chrysostom and Theopilactus). We are told that these words of Christ probably applied to the Hebrews, who often used to accuse their neighbors of trifling sins while committing greater ones themselves.

But nowhere is there a word said about our human institutions of courts of law, or of the reference that this precept not to judge might have to them. Does

Christ forbid them, or does He approve of them? This question, which arises so naturally in our minds, is left unanswered, as if there could not be the slightest doubt that, when once a Christian has taken his seat in the judgment hall, he has a right, not only to judge his neighbor, but also even to condemn him to death.

I consulted the Greek, Catholic, and Protestant theologians, as well as the works of the Tubingen school, and found that even the most liberal interpreters considered these words as meaning 'not to speak evil of.' Not one of them solves the question why so narrow an interpretation is given, and why they are not considered as prohibiting the institution of courts of law; or why Christ, while forbidding our speaking evil of a fellow-creature — which each of us may often do inadvertently — does not consider as wrong, and does not forbid, the same condemnation when given consciously and accompanied by violence against the condemned man. That the word 'condemn' may apply to judiciary condemnation, from which millions suffer, is not even hinted at. Nor is this all. By means of these very words, 'do not judge and do not condemn,' the form of judiciary condemnation is set altogether apart, and fenced round. Our theological interpretations say that the existence of courts of law in Christian states is necessary, and is not contrary to the law of Christ.

This made me doubt the sincerity of these interpretations, and I applied myself to a closer examination of the translation of the words 'judge' and 'condemn,' which is the thing I ought to have begun with. In the original these words are κρινω and καταδικαζω. The incorrect rendering of the word καταλαλεω in the epistle of James, which is translated as 'do not speak evil,' confirmed my doubts of the correctness of the translation.

I consulted the translation of the words κρινω and καταδικαζω in the gospels in various languages, and I found that the word 'to condemn' is translated in the Vulgate and in French by the word condemnare; in Slavonic, осуждатъ; by Luther, verdammen — to damn, to doom.

The different renderings of these words increased my doubts, and I asked myself what the Greek word κρινω, used in both the above-mentioned gospels, could really mean, and what was the true signification of the word καταδικαζω, which is used by Luke the Evangelist, who wrote, according to the opinion of all able scholars, in good Greek? If a man, who knew nothing about the gospel and the interpretations given to it were to have this saying placed before him, how would he translate it?

I consulted the common dictionary, and I found that the word κρινω has many different meanings, and among others is very often used in the sense of 'condemning by judgment' — executing — but never in that of 'evil-speaking.' I consulted the glossary of the New Testament, and I found that this word is often used there in the sense of condemning by judgment. It is sometimes used as meaning 'to choose,' but never as 'to speak evil of.' And so I saw that the word κρινω may be rendered in several ways, but that a translation that renders it as 'speaking evil of' is the furthest from the original.

I looked for the word καταδικαζω and added to it the word κρινω, which has several meanings, for the purpose of explaining the sense in which the writer himself takes the first word. I looked in the common dictionary for the word καταδικαζω and I found that this word never had any other meaning than to 'condemn by judgment' or to 'execute.' I consulted the glossary of the New Testament, and I found that this word is used in the New Testament four times, and every time in the sense of 'condemn', 'execute.' I consulted the context, and I found that this word is used in the epistle of James, chapter 5, verse 6, in which it is said, 'You have condemned and killed the just.' The word 'condemned' is the same word, καταδικαζω, which is used in reference to Christ, who was condemned to death; and in no other way and in no other meaning is this word used, either in the whole New Testament or in any Greek dialect.

What can this mean? What a state of idiocy have I fallen into! All of us, when reflecting on the destiny of man, have been struck with terror at the sufferings and evils that our human criminal laws have brought into our lives — evils both for those who judge and for those who are judged, from the executions of Tshingis-Han in the second half of the 12th century and the revolutions to those of the present day.

No man of feeling has escaped the impression of horror and doubt concerning 'good,' produced by the recital, if not by the sight, of men executing their fellow-men by rods, the guillotine, or the gallows.

In the gospels, every word of which we esteem sacred, it is said clearly and distinctly, 'You have the criminal law — a tooth for a tooth; and I give you a new one — do not resist the evil man. Fulfill this commandment all of you; do not return evil for evil; always do good to all; forgive all.'

And farther on we read, 'Do not judge.' Then, in order to render all doubt impossible as to the meaning of His words, Christ adds, 'do not condemn to punishment by courts of law.' My heart says clearly and distinctly, 'Do not execute.' Science says, 'Do not execute; the more you execute, the more evil there will be.' Reason says, 'Do not execute; you cannot put a stop to evil by evil.' The Word of God, which I believe in, says the same. I used to read the whole doctrine. I read these words, 'Do not judge and you shall not be judged; do not condemn and you shall not be condemned; forgive and you shall be forgiven.' I acknowledged that these were God's words, and I thought they meant that we are not to gossip or slander, and I continued to consider courts of law as Christian institutions, and myself as a judge and a Christian! I was shocked at the grossness of the error I was indulging.

Chapter IV

Now I understood what Christ meant when He said, 'You have heard that it has been said, "An eye for and eye, and a tooth for a tooth." And I say to you, do not resist evil.' Christ means, 'You have been taught to consider it right and rational to protect yourselves against evil by violence, to pluck out an eye for and eye, to institute courts of law for the punishment of criminals, and to have a police and an army to defend you against the attacks of an enemy; but I say to you, do no violence to any man, take no part in violence, never do evil to any man, not even to those whom you call your enemies.'

I now understood that, in this doctrine of non-resistance, Christ not only tells us what the natural result of following His doctrine will be, but by placing this same doctrine in opposition to the Mosaic Law, the Roman law, and the various codes of the present time, He clearly shows that it ought to be the basis of our social existence and should deliver us from the evil we have brought on ourselves. He says, 'You think to amend evil by your laws, but they only aggravate it. There is one way by which you can put a stop to evil; it is by indiscriminatingly returning good for evil. You have tried the other law for thousands of years; now try Mine, which is the very reverse.' Strange to say, I have had frequent opportunities lately of conversing with men of diverse opinions on this doctrine of non-resistance. I have met with some who agreed with me, though these have been few. But there are two orders of men who always refuse to admit, even in principle, a direct understanding of this doctrine, and warmly uphold the justice of resisting evil. They are men belonging to two extreme poles: our Christian conservative patriots, who consider their Church as the true orthodox one, and our revolutionary atheists. Neither the former nor the latter will give up their right to resist by violence what they consider as evil. Even their cleverest, most learned men close their eyes to the simple, self-evident truth, that if we admit the right of one man to resist what he considers as evil by violence, we cannot refuse another the right to resist by violence what he in his turn may consider as evil. A short time ago I met with a correspondence particularly instructive as bearing on this very point. It was carried on between an orthodox Slavophil and a Christian revolutionist. The former excused the violence of war in the name of his oppressed Slavonian brethren, and the latter vindicated the violence of the revolution in the name of his oppressed brethren, the Russian peasants. Both admit the necessity for violence, and both ground their reasoning on the doctrine of Christ.

Each of us gives the doctrine of Christ an interpretation of his own, but it is never the direct and simple one that flows out of His words.

We have grounded the conduct of our lives on a principle that He rejects; we do not choose to understand His teaching in its simple and direct sense. Those who call themselves 'believers' believe that Christ-God, the second Person of the

Trinity, made Himself man in order to set us an example how to live, and they strictly fulfill the most complicated duties, such as preparing for the sacraments, building churches, sending out missionaries, naming pastors for parochial administration, etc.; they forget only one trifling circumstance — to do as He tells them. Unbelievers, on the other hand, try to regulate their lives somehow or other, but not in accordance with the law of Christ, feeling convinced beforehand that it is worthless. Nobody ever tries to fulfill His teaching. Nor is that all. Instead of making any effort to follow His commandments, both believers and unbelievers decide beforehand that to do so is impossible.

Christ says that the law of resistance by violence, which you have made the basis of your lives, is unnatural and wrong; and He gives us instead the law of non-resistance, which, He tells us, can alone deliver us from evil. He says, 'You think to eradicate evil by your human laws of violence; they only increase it. During thousands and thousands of years you have tried to annihilate evil by evil, and you have not annihilated it; you have but increased it. Follow the teaching I give you by word and deed, and you will prove its practical power.'

Not only does He speak thus, but He also remains true to His own doctrine not to resist evil in His life and in His death.

Believers take all this in with their ears and hear it read in churches, calling it the Word of God. They call Him God, and then they say, 'His doctrine is sublime, but the organization of our lives renders its observance impossible; it would change the whole course of our lives, to which we are so used and with which we are so satisfied. Therefore, we believe in this doctrine only as an ideal that mankind must strive after — an ideal that is to be attained by prayer, by believing in the sacraments, in redemption, and in the resurrection of the dead.' Others, unbelievers, the free interpreters of Christ's doctrine, the historians of religion — Strauss, Renan, and others — adopting the interpretation of the Church, that this doctrine has no direct application to life and is only an ideal teaching that can only serve to console the weak-minded, say, very seriously, that the doctrine of Christ was all very well for the savage population of the deserts of Galilee, but that we, with our civilization, can only consider it as a lovely reverie 'du charmant Docteur,' as Renan calls Him. According to their opinion, Christ could not attain the height of understanding all the wisdom of our civilization and refinement. If He had stood on the same scale of civilization as these learned men, He would not have uttered those pretty trifles about the birds of the air, about letting one's cheek be struck, and about taking no care for tomorrow. Learned historians judge Christianity according to what they see in our Christian society. Now the Christian society of our times considers our life as a good and holy one, with its institutions of solitary imprisonment, of fortresses, sweatshops, journals, brothels, and parliaments, while it only borrows from the doctrine of Christ what is not against these habits of life. And, as Christ's teaching is in direct opposition to all this, nothing is taken from that teaching but its mere words. The learned historians see this, and not having the same interest in concealing the fact as the so-called believers have, they subject this, for them, meaningless doctrine of Christ to a profound analysis, argue against it, and prove on good grounds that Christianity never was anything but the dream of an idealist. And yet it seems to me that before pronouncing an opinion upon the doctrine of Christ, we ought clearly to understand what it is, and in order to decide whether His teaching is rational or not, it is necessary first of all to believe that He meant exactly what He said. This is just what neither the interpreters of the Church nor free-thinkers do, and the reason why is not hard to see.

We know very well that the teaching of Christ, as we have received it, embraces all the errors into which humanity has fallen, all the 'toga,' empty idols, the existence of which we try to justify by calling them church, government, culture, science, arts, and civilization, thinking thus to exclude them from the rank of errors. But Christ warns us against them all, without excluding any 'toga.'

Not only Christ's words, but those of all Hebrew prophets, of John the Baptist, and of all the truly wise men who have ever lived, have referred to this same church, this same government, culture, civilization, etc., calling them evils and the causes of man's perdition.

For instance, suppose an architect were to say to the owner of a house, 'Your house is in a bad state; it must be wholly rebuilt,' and were then to go on giving all the necessary details about the kinds of beams that would be required, how they were to be cut, and where placed. If the owner were to turn a deaf ear to the architect's words about the ruinous condition of the house and the necessity for its being rebuilt, and were only to listen with a feigned interest to the secondary details concerning the proposed repairs, the architect's counsels would evidently appear but so much useless talk; and if the owner happened to feel no great respect for the builder, he would call his advice foolish. This is exactly what occurs with the teaching of Christ.

I used this simile for want of a better one, and I remember that Christ, while preaching His doctrine, used one very like it. He said, 'I will destroy your temple, and within three days I will build up another.' He was crucified for these words. His doctrine is crucified for the same reason up to the present time.

The least that can be required of those who judge another man's teaching is that they should take the teacher's words in the exact sense in which he uses them. Christ does not consider His teaching as some high ideal of what mankind should be but cannot attain to, nor does He consider it as a chimerical, poetical fancy, fit only to captivate the simple-minded inhabitants of Galilee; He considers His teaching as work — a work that is to save mankind. His suffering on the cross was no dream; He groaned in agony and died for His teaching. And how many people have died, and will still die, in the same cause? Such teaching cannot be called a dream.

Every doctrine of truth is a dream for those who are in error. We have come to such a state of error that there are many among us who say, as I did myself formerly, that this doctrine of Christ is chimerical because it is incompatible with the nature of man. It is incompatible with the nature of man, they say, to turn the other cheek when he has been struck; it is incompatible with the nature of man to give up his property to another — to work, not for himself, but for others. It is natural to man, they say, to protect himself, his own safety, that of his family, and his property — in other words, it is the nature of man to struggle for life. Learned lawyers prove scientifically that the most sacred duty of a man is to protect his rights — i.e., to struggle.

We need only for one moment to cast aside the idea that the present organization of our lives, as established by man, is the best and most sacred, and then the argument that the teaching of Christ is incompatible with human nature immediately turns against the arguer. Who will deny that it is repugnant and harrowing to a man's feelings to torture or kill, not only a man, but also even a dog, a hen, or a calf? I have known men, living by agricultural labor, who have ceased entirely to eat meat only because they had to kill their own cattle. And yet our lives are so organized that for one individual to obtain any advantage in life another must suffer, which is against human nature. The whole organization of our lives, the complicated mechanism of our institutions, whose sole object is violence, are but proofs of the degree to which violence is repugnant to human nature. No judge will ever undertake to strangle with his own hands the man whom he has condemned to death. No magistrate will himself drag a peasant from his weeping family in order to shut him up in prison. Not a single general, not a single soldier, would kill hundreds of Turks or Germans, and devastate their villages — no, not one of them would consent to wound a single man, were it not in war, and in obedience to discipline and the oath of allegiance. Cruelty is only exercised (thanks to our complicated social machinery) when it can be so divided among a number that none shall bear the sole responsibility, or recognize how unnatural all cruelty is. Some make laws, others apply them; others, again, drill their fellow-creatures into habits of discipline — i.e., of senseless passive obedience; and these same disciplined men, in their turn, do violence to others — killing without knowing why or wherefore. But let a man even for a moment shake off in thought the net of worldly institutions that so ensnares him, and he will see what is really incompatible with his nature.

If once we cease to affirm that the evil we are so used to, and profit by, is an immutable divine truth, we may see clearly which is the more natural to man — violence, or the law of Christ. Which is better — to know that the comfort and safety of my family and myself, all my joys and pleasures, are obtained at the price of the misery, depravity, and suffering of millions, by yearly executions, by hundreds of thousands of suffering prisoners, and by millions of soldiers, policemen and sergeants (урядниковъ) torn from their homes and half stupefied by military discipline, who protect my idle pleasures by keeping starving men at a distance with their loaded pistols; to know that every dainty morsel I put into my mouth, or give my children, is obtained at the price of all this suffering, which is inevitable, in order to obtain these dainties; or to know that my fare is my own, that nobody suffers for the want of it, and that nobody has suffered in procuring it for me?

It is sufficient to comprehend, once and for all, that, in our present organization of life, every joy and every moment of peace is bought at the cost of the privations and sufferings of thousands, who are only restrained by violence, in order to see clearly what is natural to man; i.e., not only to the animal nature of man, but to his rational nature as well. It is sufficient to understand the doctrine of Christ in all its high significance and with all the consequences it entails, to see that it is not inconsistent with human nature, but that, on the contrary, His whole doctrine throws aside what is inconsistent with human nature — the delusive human teaching of resistance of evil, which is the chief cause of all human misery.

The doctrine of Christ, which teaches us not to resist evil is — a dream! But the sight of men in whose breasts love and pity are innate, spending their lives in burning their brethren at the stake, scourging them, breaking them on the wheel, lashing, slitting their nostrils, putting them to the rack, keeping them fettered, sending them to the galleys or the gallows, shooting them, condemning to solitary confinement, imprisoning women and children, organizing the slaughter of tens of thousands by war, bringing about periodical revolutions and rebellions, the sight of others passively fulfilling these atrocities, the sight of others again writhing under these tortures or avenging them — this is no dream!

When once we clearly understand the teaching of Christ, we see that it is not the world given by God to man for his happiness that is a dream, but the world such as men have made it for their own destruction that is a wild terrifying dream — the delirium of a madman — a dream from which it is enough to awake once, never to return to it.

God came down from heaven — the Son of God, the Second Person of the Holy Trinity — and became man to redeem us from the punishment entailed by the sin of Adam. We think that this God must speak in some mysterious, mystical way, difficult to be understood; indeed, that His Word can only be understood through faith and God's grace; and yet God's words are so simple and so clear. He says, 'Do no evil to each other, and there will be no evil.' Is it possible that the revelation of God is so simple? Can this be all? All this is so familiar to us.

The prophet Elijah, having fled from the haunts of men and concealed himself in a rock, had it revealed to him that he should see God at the entrance of the cavern. A tempest arose — the trees were rent asunder. Elijah thought God was there and looked, but God was not there. The earth quaked, fire issued out of it, the rock was split in two, and the mountains fell. Elijah looked, but God was not there. Then all grew still and calm, and a light breeze wafted the fragrance of the freshened fields toward him. Elijah looked, and God was there! It is thus with the simple words of God, 'Do not resist evil.'

They are very simple, but they contain in themselves the sole and eternal law of God and man. This law is eternal, and if in history we find any progress made toward the annihilation of evil, it is due to those who truly understood the doctrine of Christ, who suffered evil without resisting by violence. The progression of mankind toward good is brought about by martyrdom, not by tyranny. Fire cannot extinguish fire, no more than evil can extirpate evil. Good, meeting with evil and remaining untainted by it, can alone conquer evil. There is a law in the heart of each man that is as immutable as the law of Galileo — still more immutable. Men may turn aside from it or conceal it from others; nevertheless it is the only path that leads to true happiness. Each step that has brought us nearer to this great end was taken in the name of the doctrine of Christ: 'Do not resist evil.' It is with greater confidence even than Galileo that the follower of Christ can say, in defiance of all the temptations around him and the threats held out to him, 'It is not by violence but by doing good that you will eradicate evil.' And if the progress is made slowly, it is only because the clarity, simplicity, and rationality of the teaching of Christ and its inevitable absolute necessity are concealed from the eyes of men in the most crafty and dangerous manner; concealed under a spurious teaching, falsely called His.

Chapter V

Everything tended to convince me that I had now found the true interpretation of Christ's doctrine. But it was a long while before I could get used to the strange thought that after so many men had professed the doctrine of Christ during 1,800 years, and had devoted their lives to the study of His teachings, it was given to me to discover His doctrine as something altogether new. It seemed strange, nevertheless so it was. Christ's doctrine of 'non-resistance' seemed to rise before me as something hitherto unknown and unfamiliar to me. And I asked myself how this could be. Had some false conception of Christ's doctrine prevented my understanding it?

When I first began to read the gospel I was not in the position of one who heard the teaching of Christ for the first time. I already had a complete theory concerning the sense in which it was to be taken. Christ did not appear to me as a prophet, come to reveal the law of God to man, but rather as an expounder and amplifier of the indubitable divine law well known to me. I already possessed a complete, definite, and very complicated doctrine concerning God and the creation of the world and of man, as well as concerning the commandments of God, as transmitted to us through Moses.

In the gospel I found the words, 'You have been told, "An eye for and eye, and a tooth for a tooth," but I say to you, do not resist evil.' The precept, 'An eye for an eye, and a tooth for a tooth,' was the commandment given by God to Moses. The precept, 'I say to you, do not resist evil,' was a new commandment that reversed the first.

Had I considered the doctrine of Christ simply, without the theological theory I had imbibed from my earliest childhood, I should have understood the true sense of these simple words. I should have seen that Christ sets aside the old law and gives a new one. But it had been instilled into me that Christ did not reject the Law of Moses — that, on the contrary, he confirmed it to the least jot and tittle, and amplified it. The seventeenth and eighteenth verses of the fifth chapter of St. Matthew, which seem to confirm that assertion, had, in my former studies of the gospel, struck me by their obscurity, and had raised doubts in my mind.

On reading the Old Testament, especially the last books of Moses, in which so many trivial, useless, and even cruel laws are laid down, each preceded by the words, 'And God said to Moses,' it seemed passing strange to me that Christ should have confirmed such laws; His doing so seemed incomprehensible. But I then left the problem unsolved. I blindly believed the teaching of my childhood: that these commandments were inspired by the Holy Ghost, that they were in perfect harmony with each other, that Christ confirmed the Law of Moses, and that He amplified and completed it. I could, indeed, never clearly explain to myself wherein the amplification lay, nor how the striking opposition, so obvious to all, between the verses 17–20 and the words 'but I say to you' could be harmonized. But when I at last really understood the clear and simple meaning of Christ's doctrine, I saw that these two commandments were in direct opposition to each other; that there could be no question of harmony between them, or of the one being an amplification of the other; that it was necessary to accept either the one or the other, and that the interpretation of verses 17–20 of the fifth chapter of St. Matthew, which, as I have already said, had struck me by their want of clarity, was erroneous.

On a second reading of the same verses 17–20, which had seemed so unintelligible to me, their meaning flashed full upon me.

This again was not the result of my having discovered anything new, or having made any alteration of the words; it was due solely to my having cast aside the false interpretation that had been given to them.

Christ says (Matthew 5:17–19), 'Do not think that I have come to destroy the law or (the teaching of) the prophets. I have not come to destroy, but to fulfill. For truly I say to you, until heaven and earth pass, one jot or one tittle (the least particle) shall in no way pass from the law, until all is fulfilled.'

And (verse 20) he adds, 'Except your righteousness shall exceed the righteousness of the scribes and Pharisees, you shall in no case enter the kingdom of heaven.'

Christ means by these words, 'I have not come to destroy the eternal law, for the fulfillment of which your books and prophecies are written; but I have come to teach you how to fulfill that eternal law. I do not speak of the law that your teachers, the Pharisees, call the law of God, but of the eternal law, which is less liable to change than heaven and earth.'

I here give the meaning of the text in other words, solely for the purpose of drawing the mind away from the incorrect interpretation usually offered. If this incorrect interpretation did not exist, we should see that the idea of Christ could not be better or more definitely expressed than by these words.

The interpretation that Christ does not reject the Mosaic Law is based on the fact that in this passage, without any ostensible reason (except the comparison of the jot of the written law) and contrary to the true sense, the word 'law' is treated as meaning the 'written law,' and not the eternal law. But Christ does not speak here of the written law. If Christ, in this passage, had spoken of the written law, He would have used the words 'the law and the prophets,' as He always does in speaking of the written law; but He uses a very different expression: 'the law or the prophets.' Had Christ meant to speak of the written law, He would have used the words 'the law and the prophets' in the next verse, which is but the continuation of the preceding one; but there He uses the word 'law' alone.

Moreover we find, in the gospel according to St. Luke, that Christ uses the same words in a manner that leaves no doubt as to their true meaning (Luke 16:15). Christ says to the Pharisees, who thought to justify themselves by the written law, 'You are those who justify themselves before men; but God knows your hearts, for that which is highly esteemed among men is an abomination in the sight of God. The law and the prophets were until John. Since that time the kingdom of God is preached, and every man presses into it.' And immediately after this, in the 17th verse, we read, 'And it is easier for heaven and earth to pass, than one tittle of the law to fail.' The words 'the law and the prophets, until John,' annul the written law. The words 'it is easier for heaven and earth to pass, than for one tittle of the law to fail,' confirm the eternal law. In the first text Christ says 'the law and the prophets,' i.e. the written law; in the second He uses the word 'law' alone, i.e. the eternal law. It is obvious, therefore, that the eternal law is here set in opposition to the written law, and that exactly the same occurs in the context of the gospel of St. Matthew, where the eternal law is expressed by the words 'the law or the prophets.'

The history of the different renderings of this text (v.17–18) is very curious. In most of the transcripts the word 'law' is not followed by the words 'and the prophets.' In this case there can be no doubt of its signifying 'the eternal law.' In other transcripts, as, for instance, in those of Tischendorf and the canonical transcripts, the word 'prophets' is added — not with the conjunction and, but with the disjunctive or — 'the law or the prophets,' which likewise excludes the meaning of 'the written law,' and confirms that of the 'eternal law.'

In some transcripts again, which are not adopted by the Church, we find the word 'prophets' preceded by the conjunction and, and not by or; in these transcripts, after the repetition of the word 'law,' the words 'and the prophets' are again added. Thus the meaning given to the whole saying, by this remodeling, is that Christ's words refer only to the written law.

These variations give us the history of the various interpretations to which this passage has been subjected. One point is obvious: Christ speaks here, as He does in the gospel according to St. Luke, of the eternal law; but we find men among the transcribers of the gospels who have added the words 'and the prophets' to the word 'law,' with the design of rendering the Mosaic Law obligatory, and have thus altered the sense of the text.

Other Christians, again, who reject the Mosaic Law, either leave out the word completely, or substitute the word η (or), for the word καὶ (and). And thus the passage enters the canon with the disjunctive or. Yet though the text adopted by the canon is so indubitably clear, our canonical commentators continue to expound on the passage in the spirit of the alterations that have not been adopted.

Countless commentators have treated this passage, and as the expounder agrees less with the simple, direct sense of the doctrine of Christ, the further his commentary must necessarily be from the true sense of that doctrine. The majority of expounders retain the apocryphal sense, which the text rejects.

In order to be convinced that Christ speaks in this verse only of the eternal law, it will suffice to fully understand the word that has given rise to these false interpretations. In Russian, it is 'законъ' (law); in Greek νομος; in Hebrew, 'tora.' This word has two principal meanings in the Russian, Greek, and Hebrew languages: the one, the unexpressed, unwritten law; the other, the written expression of what certain men call the law. Indeed, the difference exists in all languages.

In Greek, in the epistles of Paul, the difference is sometimes marked by the use of the article. In speaking of the written law, the apostle omits the article before the word law, and when he speaks of the eternal law, the article is prefixed.

The ancient Hebrews, the prophets, and Isaiah always use the word 'tora' (the law) to indicate the eternal, unwritten, but revealed law of God. This same word 'tora' (the law) was first used by Ezra, and later we find it in the Talmud, as signifying the five books of Moses, which bear the general title of 'tora' in the same sense as our word 'Bible,' with this difference, however, that we distinguish the Bible from the law of God by two different denominations, while in the Hebrew language there is but one word for both.

Therefore Christ, using the word 'tora,' takes it in the two different accepted meanings of the word — either confirming it, as Isaiah and the other prophets do, in the sense of the law of God, which is eternal, or rejecting it, when He refers to the Mosaic Law. But in order to make a distinction between the different meanings of the word, he always adds 'and the prophets,' and the pronoun 'your,' in speaking of the written law.

When Christ says, 'As you would want men to treat you, also treat them likewise; this is the whole law and the prophets,' He refers to the written law. He tells us that the whole written law may be reduced to this sole expression of the eternal law; and, by these His words, He annuls the written law.

When He says (Luke 16:16), 'The law and the prophets until John the Baptist,' He refers to the written law, and by these words asserts that it is no longer obligatory.

When He says (John 7:19), 'Didn't Moses give you the law, and yet none of you keeps the law?' or (John 8:17), 'Isn't it said in your law?' or again (John 15:25), 'The word that is written in their law,' He refers to the written law — the law that He rejects — the law by which He was, soon after, sentenced to death. John 19:7: 'The Jews answered Him, "We have a law, and by our law He ought to die".' It is obvious that this law of the Hebrews, by which Christ Himself was sentenced to death, was not the law that He taught. But when Christ says, 'I come, not to destroy the law, but to teach you to fulfill it, for nothing can be altered in the law, but all must be fulfilled,' He does not speak of the written law, but of the divine, eternal law.

It may be said that these proofs are controvertible; that I have skillfully assorted the contexts, and have carefully concealed all that could contradict my interpretation; that the commentaries given by the Church are very clear and convincing, and that Christ did not destroy the Law of Moses, but that He left it in full force. Let us suppose this to be the case. What, then, does Christ teach?

According to the commentaries of the Church, He taught men that He was the Second Person of the Trinity, the Son of God the Father, and that He had come down from heaven to redeem mankind from the sin of Adam. But whoever has read the gospel knows that Christ says nothing of this, or, at least, alludes to it in very ambiguous terms; the passages in which Christ speaks of Himself as being the Second Person of the Trinity, and of His redeeming mankind, are the shortest and least perspicuous in the gospels. In what, then, does the rest of Christ's teaching consist?

It is impossible to deny, what all Christians have always acknowledged, that the main point in Christ's doctrine consists in His rules of life — how men are to live together. Now, if we admit that Christ taught a new system of life, we must form some definite idea of the men among whom He taught.

Take, for instance, the Russians, the English, the Chinese, the Hindus, or even any wild insular tribe, and you will be sure to find that they all have their own rules of life, their own laws; and that no teacher could introduce new laws of life without destroying the former ones; he could not teach without infringing them. Such would be the case everywhere. The teacher would inevitably have to begin by destroying our laws, which have grown precious and almost sacred in our eyes.

Perhaps in our days it might happen that the teacher of a new doctrine of life would only destroy our civil laws, our government, and our customs without interfering with the laws that we call divine, though this is hardly probable. But the Hebrews had only one law — a divine law that embraced life in its minutest details. What could a preacher teach them if he began by declaring that the entire law of the people to whom he preached was inviolable?

But let us assume that this is not regarded as a proof. Then let those who assert that Christ's words confirm the Mosaic Law explain to themselves who they were whom Christ denounced during His whole life; who did He speak against, calling them Pharisees, lawyers, and scribes? Who was it that refused to follow the doctrine of Christ, and crucified Him?

If Christ acknowledged the Mosaic Law, where were the true followers of the law, whom Christ must have approved of? Is there a single one? We are told that the Pharisees were a sect. The Hebrews do not say so. They call the Pharisees the true fulfillers of the law. But let us suppose they were a sect. The Sadducees were also a sect. Where, then, were the true believers — those who did not belong to any sect?

In the gospel according to St. John, all the enemies of Christ are called Hebrews. They do not assent to Christ's doctrine; they oppose it only because they are Hebrews. But in the gospel the Pharisees and Sadducees are not the only enemies of Christ; the lawgivers, who keep the Mosaic Law, the scribes, who study it, and the elders, who are considered as the representatives of the popular wisdom, are likewise called the enemies of Christ.

Christ says, 'I did not come to call the righteous to repentance,' to a change of life, μετανοια, 'but sinners.' Where were the righteous, and who were they? Surely Nicodemus was not the only one? And even Nicodemus is described as being a good man, but one who had gone astray.

We have grown so used to the singular interpretation given to us, that the Pharisees and some wicked Hebrews crucified Christ, that the simple question never occurs to us, 'Where were the true Hebrews, who kept the law and who were neither Pharisees nor wicked men?' No sooner does the question arise than all grows clear. Christ, be He God or man, brought His doctrine to a people who already had a law that gave them definite rules of life, and which they called the law of God. In what light could Christ have considered that law?

Every prophet — teacher of a faith — on revealing the law of God to a people, will find that they already possess a law that they consider as the divine law, and he cannot avoid a twofold application of the word, as referring either to what men wrongly consider the law of God (your law) or as referring to the true eternal law of God. Moreover, not only is the preacher of the new doctrine unable to avoid the two-fold use of the word, but it often happens that he does not even endeavor to do so, and purposely unites both ideas, in order to point out that the law confessed by those he tries to convert, though defective as a whole, is not devoid of some divine truths. And it is just these truths, so familiar to his hearers, which every preacher will take as the basis of his preaching. Christ does so in addressing the Hebrews, who have the same word 'tora' for both laws. Referring to the Mosaic Law, and more often still to the prophets, especially the prophet Isaiah, whom he often quotes, Christ acknowledges that in the Hebrew law, and in the prophets, there are eternal truths, divine truths, which coincide with the eternal law; and He bases His doctrine upon them, as for instance in the saying 'Love God and your neighbor.'

Christ expresses this idea on many occasions, e.g., Luke 10:26: 'What is written in the law? How do you read it?' We may find the eternal truth in the law, if we can read. And He points out more than once that the precept contained in their law of love to God and their neighbor was a precept of the eternal law.

After the parables by which he explains His doctrine to His disciples, Christ says, as if in reference to all that had preceded, 'Therefore every scribe (i.e. every man who can read and has been taught the truth) is like a householder who brings forth out of his treasure (indiscriminately) things old and new.' (Matthew 13:52)

It is thus that St. Irenaus understands these words, and so does the Church, and yet, arbitrarily transgressing the true sense of the saying, they attribute to these words the meaning that the whole ancient law is sacred. The obvious meaning of the text is that he who seeks for what is good, takes not only what is new, but what is old too, and that its being old is not a sufficient reason for throwing it aside. Christ means, by this saying, that He does not deny what is eternal in the ancient law. But when questioned concerning the law or its forms, He says, 'We do not pour new wine into old bottles.' Christ could not confirm the whole law, neither could He completely deny the law and the prophets; He could neither deny the law that says, 'Love your neighbor as yourself,' nor the prophets, in whose word He often clothes His thought.

And so, instead of our understanding these clear and simple words as they were said, and in the sense that the whole doctrine of Christ confirms, an obscure interpretation is given to us, which introduces inconsistency where there is none, and thus destroys the true sense of the doctrine, leaving nothing but words, and in reality re-establishing the Mosaic teaching with all its barbarous cruelty.

According to the commentaries of the Church, and those of the fifth century in particular, Christ did not destroy the written law, but confirmed it. But we are not told how He confirmed it, or how the law of Christ and the Mosaic Law can be supposed to be united into one. We find nothing in these commentaries but a play upon words. We are told that Christ kept the Mosaic Law by the prophecies concerning Himself being fulfilled; and that Christ fulfilled the law through us, through the faith of men in Him. No effort is made to solve the only question that is of essential importance to every believer: how these two contradictory laws, referring to life, can be united into one. The inconsistency of the text, which says that Christ does not destroy the law, with the one in which we read, 'It has been said...but I say to you,' (indeed the contradiction between the whole spirit of the Mosaic Law and the doctrine of Christ) remains in all its force.

Let everyone who is interested in this question examine for himself the commentaries on this passage given to us by the Church, beginning from John Chrysostom to the present time. It is only after having read these that he will see clearly not only that no explanation of the contradiction is given, but also that a contradiction has been skillfully inserted where there was none before. The impossible attempts at uniting what cannot be united are clear proof that this was not an involuntary mental error, but was effected with some definite purpose in view; that it was found necessary; and the cause of its having been found necessary is obvious.

Let us see what John Chrysostom says in answer to those who reject the Mosaic Law.[1]

'On examining the ancient law that enjoins us to take an eye for an eye and a tooth for a tooth, the objection is raised, 'How can He who speaks thus be righteous? What answer can we give?' Why, that it is, on the contrary, the best token of God's love toward man. It was not that we should really take an eye for an eye that He gave us this law, but that we should avoid wronging others for fear of suffering the same at their hands. As, for instance, when threatening the Ninevites with destruction, His desire was not to destroy them (had He indeed decreed their destruction He would not have spoken of it); His purpose was only, by His menaces, to induce them to amend their lives and, by so doing, turn His wrath aside. Thus likewise the hot-tempered, who are ready to put out their neighbors' eyes, are threatened with punishment for the sole purpose of making their fears of punishment restrain them from injuring their fellow-creatures. If this is cruelty, there is cruelty likewise in the commandment that forbids murder, or the one that interdicts adultery. But such an argument would only prove a man to have reached the last stage of madness. And I so dread calling these commandments cruel, that I should rather be inclined to consider a contrary law as wrong, according to plain common sense. You call God cruel because He has enjoined taking an eye for an eye; but I say that many would have had a greater right to call Him cruel, as you do, had He not given this commandment.'

John Chrysostom plainly acknowledges the law of a tooth for a tooth to be the divine law, and the reverse of that law — i.e. Christ's doctrine of non-resistance — to be wrong.

Pages 322, 323: 'Let us suppose that the law is entirely cast aside,' says John Chrysostom further, 'that all fear of promised punishment is done away with, that the wicked are left to live according to their inclinations, without fear of punishment — adulterers, murderers, thieves, and perjurers. Wouldn't all be overthrown; wouldn't houses, marketplaces, cities, lands, seas, and the whole universe be full of iniquity? This is obvious. For if even the existence of laws, fear and threats of punishment, can hardly keep the evil intentioned with bounds, what would there then be to restrain men from evil deeds, if all obstacles were removed? What disasters would then rush in torrents into the lives of men! Cruelty does not lie in leaving the wicked free to act as they please, but in letting the innocent man suffer without defending him. If a man were to collect a crowd of miscreants

---

[1] Commentary of the gospel according to St. Matthew, vol. 1, pp. 320, 321.

around him, and having furnished them with weapons, were to send them forth into the town to kill all those they met in the streets, could anything be more barbarous? And if another were to bind these armed men and imprison them, releasing the victims these miscreants had threatened with death, could anything be more humane?'

But John Chrysostom does not tell us by what the other is to be guided in his definition of the wicked. May he not himself be a wicked man, and imprison the good?

'Now apply this example to the law. He who gave the commandment, "an eye for an eye" has bound the minds of the wicked in chains of fear, and may be compared to the man who bound the miscreants; but if no punishment were appointed for criminals, would it not be arming them with the weapons of fearlessness, and acting like him who gave weapons to the miscreants, and sent them forth into the town?'

If John Chrysostom does acknowledge the doctrine of Christ, he ought to have told us who is to take an 'eye for an eye,' or a 'tooth for a tooth,' and cast into prison. If He who gave the commandment, that is, God Himself, were to inflict the threatened punishment, there would be no inconsistency; but it must be done by men, the men who were forbidden to do so by the Son of God. God said, 'An eye of an eye.' The Son says, 'Do not act thus.' One of the two commandments must be acknowledged as just. John Chrysostom and the Church follow the commandments of the Father — i.e., the Mosaic Law — and reject the commandments of the Son, while ostensibly professing His doctrine.

Christ rejects the Mosaic Law, and gives His own in its stead. For him who believes in Christ there is no contradiction. He pays no heed to the Mosaic Law, believes in Christ's doctrine, and fulfills it. Neither is there any contradiction for him who believes in the Mosaic Law. The Hebrews do not consider the words of Christ valid, and they believe in the Mosaic Law. There is a contradiction only for those who, while choosing to live according to the Mosaic Law, try to persuade themselves and others that they believe in the doctrine of the Christ; only for those whom Christ calls, 'You hypocrites, you generation of vipers.'

Instead of acknowledging one of the two — either the Mosaic Law or the doctrine of Christ — we say that both are divine truths.

But no sooner does the question touch upon life itself, than the doctrine of Christ is straightway cast aside, and the Mosaic Law is acknowledged.

If we examine this false interpretation closely, we shall see in it one phase of the awful struggle between good and evil, light and darkness.

Christ appears amidst the Hebrews, who were entangled in countless minute rules, laid down by their Levites, and called by them the divine law, each of which was preceded by the words, 'And God said to Moses.'

Not only the relations in which man stands to God, but the sacrifices, feast days, fasts, the relations between men — public, civil, and family relations — all the details of private life, circumcision, ablution of themselves and their cups, their clothes, all — even in the most trifling details — were encompassed by rules, and these were acknowledged as the commandments of God, the law of God. What could a prophet do — I do not say Christ-God — but what could a prophet, a teacher do, when teaching such a people, without first destroying the obligations of a law by which everything, down to the smallest detail of life, was thus regulated? Christ does what any other prophet would do. He takes from the old law, considered by the people as divine, what is truly the law of God. He takes the basic principles, setting all the rest aside, and He adds to it His own revelation of the eternal law. Though all need not be cast aside, a law that is considered obligatory in all its minutest details must inevitably be violated. This is what Christ does, and He is accused of destroying the law of God; and He is crucified for this. But His teaching remains among His disciples, and passes on to other peoples. Yet, in the course of ages, and among the new peoples who receive Christ's truth, the same human interpretations and explanations shoot up. Again the shallow precepts of man appear in place of the divine revelation. Instead of the words, 'And God said to Moses,' we now read, 'By the revelation of the Holy Spirit.' Again the letter rather than the spirit of the doctrine is preferred. It is a striking fact that the doctrine of Christ is united to all this 'tora,' which He rejected. This 'tora' is said to be the revelation of the Spirit of Truth — i.e., of the Holy Ghost — and so Christ is taken in the meshes of His own revelation.

And now, after 1800 years, the strange duty has fallen to my lot to discover the sense of Christ's doctrine as something new.

It was no small discovery that I had to make. I had to do what all those who seek to know God and His law have to do: to find out the eternal law of God from amidst the precepts that men call His law.

Chapter VI

Now it has grown clear to me that Christ's law is truly His law, and not the mixed Law of Moses and Christ. The claim of His doctrine distinctly repudiates the claim of the Mosaic Law; and, consequently, instead of the obscurity, diffuseness, and inconsistency that I had previously found in the gospels, they now combine to form an indissoluble whole; and the basis, or central maxim, of the entire doctrine is expressed in the simple, clear, and perfectly intelligible five commandments of Christ (Matthew 5:21–48), which I had hitherto failed to apprehend.

Mention is made in all the gospels of the 'commandments of Christ,' and their fulfillment is enjoined. All theologians speak of the commandments of Christ, but I never knew what these commandments were.

I supposed the commandment of Christ to be the exhortation to love God, and our neighbor as ourselves. I did not see that this could not be the commandment of Christ, seeing that it was a commandment given to the ancient Hebrews (see Deuteronomy and Leviticus). On reading the words, 'Whoever, therefore, shall break one of these commandments, and shall teach men so, he shall be called the least in the kingdom of heaven; but whoever shall do and teach them, the same shall be great in the kingdom of heaven (Matthew 5:19),' I thought they referred to the Mosaic Law. It never occurred to me that the new commandments of Christ were clearly and distinctly expressed in verses 21–48 of the fifth chapter of St. Matthew. Nor did I notice that by the words, 'You have heard that is has been said...but I say to you,' Christ gives us new and most definite commandments; annexed to the five quotations of the Mosaic Law (reckoning the two quotations that refer to adultery as one), we find five new and definite commandments of Christ.

I had often heard about the Beatitudes, and had met with the enumeration and explanation of them in the course of the religious instruction given to me in my youth; but I never heard a word about the commandments of Christ. To my great surprise I had to discover them.

I shall now point out what led me to the discovery. In Matthew 5:21–26, we read, 'You have heard that it was said to the people long ago, "You shall not kill; and whoever shall kill shall be in danger of the judgment." (Exodus 20:23) But I say to you, that whoever is angry with his brother without a cause shall be in danger of the judgment; and whoever shall say to his brother, raca, shall be in danger of the judgment; but whoever shall say, "You fool!" shall be in danger of hell-fire. Therefore, if you bring your gift to the altar, and there remember that your brother has something against you; leave your gift there before the altar, and go your way; first be reconciled to your brother, and then come and offer your gift. Agree with your adversary quickly, while you are on the way with him, lest at any time the adversary deliver you to the judge, and the judge deliver you to the officer, and you be cast into prison. Truly I say to you, you shall by no means come out from there until you have paid the last kopeck.'

On a clear comprehension of the doctrine of 'non-resistance,' it seemed to me that the text quoted above must have the same application to life as that doctrine. I had formerly considered these words as meaning that we were to avoid all anger against a fellow-creature, that we were never to use abusive language, and that we were to live at peace with all, not excepting any; but there stood a clause in the text which excluded all possibility of thus understanding it. It is said, 'whoever is angry with his brother without a cause,' and the idea of unconditional peace is annulled by the last, italicized words. They puzzled me. I sought for a solution of my doubts in theological commentaries; but to my surprise I found that the interpretation of the Fathers of the Church were especially directed toward defining the cases in which anger may be excused and cannot be excused. Laying particular stress on the words 'without a cause,' commentators tell us the meaning of the text is that we are never to wound a man's feelings causelessly, nor use abusive language; but add that anger is not always unjust, and in support of that opinion they cite instances of the anger of the apostles and the saints.

I was obliged to acknowledge that, though contrary to the whole spirit of the gospel, the interpretation of the Fathers, by which anger is accounted justifiable when, to use their own expression, it is 'to the glory of God,' was consistent, being based on the words 'without a cause,' which we find in verse 22. This clause entirely altered the sense of the saying.

Do not be angry without a cause. Christ exhorts us to forgive all, to forgive without end; Christ Himself forgave, and when led away to be crucified, reproved Peter for defending Him against Malchus; and yet it would seem that Peter had good cause for anger. And the same Christ exhorts all men not to be angry without a cause, thus justifying anger if there is a reason for it, if it is not causeless! Isn't it as if Christ, who came to preach peace to all simple-minded men, had, on second thoughts, added the words 'without a cause' to show that this precept did not apply to all cases indiscriminately — that anger might sometimes be justifiable? Commentators tell us that anger may be justifiable. 'But,' I said to myself, 'can any man be a fit judge of the reasonableness of his anger? Never yet have I seen an angry man who did not consider himself perfectly just in his anger. Each thinks his anger both lawful and necessary.' The words 'without a cause' seemed entirely to destroy the meaning of the text. But they were in the gospel, and I could not set them aside. And yet it came to much the same as if, to the saying 'Love your neighbor,' were added the words 'your neighbor who pleases you.'

The words 'without a cause' destroyed the significance of the whole text for me. Verses 23 and 24, in which we read that before praying we must be at peace with him who has something against us, which would have had a direct, obligatory sense without the words 'without a cause,' now acquired a conditional meaning.

It seemed to me that Christ must have meant to forbid all anger, all ill-will, and in order to suppress it, had enjoined each person, before he brings his gift to the altar — i.e., before he draws near to God — to think upon whether there is any man who is angry with him. And if there is someone, he must be reconciled to him first, and then he may bring his gift to the altar or pray. It seemed thus to me, but, according to all commentaries, the sense of the passage was conditional.

In all commentaries we are told that we must try to be at peace with all men; but if that is impossible, on account of the perversity of our adversary, we must be at peace with him in mind, in our thoughts, and then his enmity will be no barrier to our prayer. Moreover, the words that declare that whoever shall say 'raca,' or 'you fool,' commits a great sin, always seemed most strange and unintelligible to me. If the words forbid abusive language, why are such weak epithets chosen, which can hardly be reckoned terms of abuse? And why was there so awful a threat against one who might, perhaps inadvertently, use as inoffensive a word as raca — i.e., a worthless fellow? This seemed incomprehensible to me.

I felt sure that there was the same misunderstanding here as I had found in the words 'do not judge.' I felt sure that a simple, definite, and highly important commandment, which all have it in their power to fulfill, had been perverted, as in the preceding instance, into something almost incomprehensible. I felt sure that Christ had not used the words, 'be reconciled to your brother,' in the sense now given to them by our commentators: 'be reconciled to your brother in mind.'

Reconciled in mind! What can that mean? I thought that Christ meant exactly what He expressed in the words of the prophet, 'I will have mercy' — i.e., love to all men — 'and not sacrifice.' And therefore, if you wish to find favor in God's sight, before repeating your morning and evening prayer, or before attending public worship, reflect whether anyone is angry with you; and if such a one can be found, go and be reconciled to him first, and then you may come and pray. Let your reconciliation no be 'in mind' only. I saw that the interpretation, which destroyed the direct and clear meaning of the text, was based on the words 'without a cause.' Their omission would render the whole perfectly clear; but the canonical gospel, in which stand the words 'without a cause,' and all commentaries upon it, were contrary to my interpretation.

Had I chosen arbitrarily to alter the sense of this passage, I might have done so with any other text as well; and might not other interpreters have done so too? All the difficulty lay in one little clause. If this clause were removed, all would be clear. So I endeavored to find some philological explanation of the words that should not destroy the sense of the text.

On consulting the dictionary, I saw the Greek word is εἰχῃ, and that it likewise means 'purposelessly, thoughtlessly.' I again read the text over attentively, to see if any other meaning could be given to it, but found that the clause was evidently correct. I consulted the Greek dictionary, and the meaning given to the word was the same. I consulted the context, but the word is only used once in the gospels: in the passage in question. We find it several times in the epistles. In the first epistle to the Corinthians (15:2) it is used in the same sense. Therefore, there seemed to be no other possible rendering of the text, and I found myself obliged to believe that Christ said, 'Do not be angry without a cause.' I must confess that, to believe in Christ's having uttered so indefinite a saying — which admits of an interpretation that reduces it to a mere nothing — seemed to me equivalent to an entire renunciation of the gospel itself. A last hope was left to me: was this clause to be found in all the transcripts of the gospel? I examined various translations.

I looked in Griesbach's edition of the gospels, in which he enumerates all the transcripts in which a similar expression is used; and I found, to my great joy, that there were several references attached to this particular text. I examined them, and found that they referred to the very words, 'without a cause.' In the greater number of the transcripts of the gospel, and in the commentaries of the Fathers of the Church, these words are omitted. Thus, the majority understood the text as I do. I then consulted the first transcript of Tischendorf, but the words are not there. The shortest way to solve the problem would have been to look in Luther's translation of the gospel; but the words are not to be found there either.

The clause, which so entirely destroys the sense of Christ's doctrine, was an addition made in the fifth century, and it is not to be found in any of the most trustworthy transcripts of the gospel. Someone had inserted the clause, and others had approved of it, and then tried to explain it.

Christ never could have added so monstrous a clause; and the simple, direct meaning of the text, which had first struck me, and must strike others, is the true one.

Nor is this all; for, no sooner did I understand that Christ's words forbade anger against any person whatever, than the command not to call a fellow-creature 'raca,' or 'you fool,' struck me in a new light, and I could no longer consider it as being intended to forbid the use of abusive language. The untranslated word raca opened my eyes to the true sense. The word raca means 'trampled upon, set at naught, made of no account.' The word rac is a word very generally used, and it signifies 'excepting,' 'only not.' Raca, therefore, means a man unworthy of the title of man. We find the plural, rakim, used in the Book of Judges (9:4) in the sense of 'lost.' So this is the word we are forbidden by Christ to use in speaking of a fellow-creature. In the same manner He forbids our saying 'you fool,' words by which we may consider ourselves justified in setting aside our duty toward our neighbor. We give way to anger, wrong others, and allege for our justification that the man who has excited our anger is a lost man or a fool. And these are the epithets that we are forbidden by Christ to apply to any man. He forbids our giving way to anger against our fellow-creatures; He forbids our justifying our anger by calling its object a lost man or a fool.

And now, in the place of an indistinct, indefinite, and insignificant expression, subject to countless arbitrary interpretations, the first simple, clear, and distinct commandment of Christ arose before me, as contained in verses 21–26: 'Be at peace with all men, and never consider your anger as just. Never look upon any man as worthless or a fool, neither call him such. Not only shall you never think yourself justified in your anger, but also you shall never consider your brother's anger as causeless; and therefore, if there is one who is angry with you, even if it is without a cause, go and be reconciled to him before praying. Endeavor to destroy all enmity between yourself and others, that their enmity may not grow and destroy you.'

And now the second commandment of Christ, which also begins with a reference to the ancient law, grew clear to me also.

Matthew 5:27–32: 'You have heard that it was said to the people long ago, "You shall not commit adultery." (Exodus 20:14–28) But I say to you that whoever looks on a woman to lust after her has committed adultery with her already in his heart. And if your right eye offends you, pluck it out and cast it from you; for it is profitable for you that one of your members should perish, and not that your whole body should be cast into hell. And if your right hand offends you, cut it off and cast it from you; for it is profitable for you that one of your members should perish, and not that your whole body should be cast into hell. It has been said, "Whoever shall put away his wife, let him give her a writing of divorcement." (Deuteronomy 24:1) But I say to you that whoever shall put away his wife, saving for the cause of fornication, causes her to commit adultery; and whoever shall marry a divorced woman commits adultery.'

I understood these words to signify that no man must ever admit, even in thought, the possibility of leaving the woman he was first united to for another, a thing that is permitted by the Mosaic Law.

As in His first commandment against anger, we are advised to stifle the feeling in its birth — the advice being further exemplified by the comparison of the man delivered up to the judge — so here Christ says that fornication is the consequence of men and women letting their thoughts dwell on sexual relations; and, to avoid this, we must set aside all that can excite such thoughts; and, when once united to a woman, we must never leave her, under any pretext whatever, because this opens the door to sinful indulgence.

I was struck by the wisdom of the saying. It tends to do away with all the evils resulting from sexual relations. Men and women are to avoid all that can excite sensuality, being fully aware that nothing is more conducive to dissensions in the world than carnal pleasures, and knowing also that the law of nature is that the race should live together in couples, united in bonds that cannot be dissolved.

In the Sermon on the Mount the words, 'saving for the cause of fornication,' which had always seemed strange to me, struck me still more forcibly when I saw that they were considered as permitting divorce if the wife had committed adultery.

Besides there being something unworthy in the very way the idea is expressed, and in this strange exception standing side by side with the most important principles that the sermon contained — like a regulation in some code — the exception itself was in direct opposition to the fundamental idea of Christ's teaching.

I consulted the commentators of the gospels, and all of them (John Chrysostom, page 365), and even theological critics like Reuss, affirm that these words mean that Christ permits divorce if the wife has committed adultery; that in Christ's prohibition of divorce, in Matthew 19:9, where we read 'saving for the cause of fornication,' the words have that meaning. I read the thirty-second verse over and over again, and came to the conclusion that this interpretation of the words was erroneous. In order to verify my opinion, I examined the context, and found, earlier in the chapter 19 of the gospel according to St. Matthew, in Mark 10, in Luke 16, and in the first epistle of Paul to the Corinthians, a similar declaration of the indissolubility of the marriage tie, without exception of any kind.

In the gospel according to St. Luke 16:18, we read, 'Whoever puts away his wife, and marries another, commits adultery; and whoever marries a woman who is put away from her husband commits adultery.'

In the gospel according to St. Mark 10:4–12, we read, 'For the hardness of your heart he wrote you this precept. But from the beginning of the creation God made them male and female. For this cause a man shall leave his father and mother, and cleave to his wife; and the two of them shall be one flesh; so then they are no longer two, but one flesh. Therefore, what God has joined together, do not let man put asunder.' And in the house His disciples asked Him again of the same matter. And He said to them, 'Whoever shall put away his wife, and marry another, commits adultery against her. And if a woman shall put away her husband, and be married to another, she commits adultery.'

We find the same teaching in the gospel according to St. Matthew 19:4–8.

In the epistle of Paul to the Corinthians, 7:1–12, the statement that depravity may be prevented by husbands and wives never forsaking each other, nor defrauding each other for their rights, is enlarged upon; and it is distinctly said that neither shall the husband in any case forsake his wife for another woman, nor the wife leave her husband for another man.

Thus we see that, according to the gospels of Mark and Luke and the epistle of Paul, divorce is wholly forbidden. According to the interpretation that husband and wife are one flesh, joined together by God, which we find repeated in two of the gospels, divorce is forbidden. According to the sense of the whole doctrine of Christ, who exhorts us to forgive all, not excluding the wife who has gone astray, it is forbidden. According to the sense of the whole text, which clearly points out that a man's leaving his wife brings depravity into the world, it is forbidden.

From where, then, is the conclusion drawn that a wife who has committed adultery may be divorced, and on what is it grounded? It is grounded on the very words of Matthew 5:32, which had so strangely struck me. It is alleged that these words prove that Christ permits divorce if the wife has committed adultery; and they are also repeated in the nineteenth chapter in numerous transcripts of the gospel, and by many of the Fathers of the Church, instead of the words, 'except it be for fornication.'

I read the words over and over again, and it was long before I could understand them. I saw that there was probably something incorrect in the translation and interpretation, but could not for some time make out what it was. That there was a mistake was obvious. Placing his commandment in opposition to that of the Mosaic Law, which says that if a man hates his wife he may put her away, giving her a writing of divorcement, Christ says, 'But I say to you, that whoever puts away his wife, saving for the cause of fornication, causes her to commit adultery.' There is no opposition in these words, and no mention made of the possibility or impossibility of divorce. We are only told that he who puts away his wife causes her to commit adultery. And then comes a clause that excepts the wife guilty of adultery. This exception is altogether strange and unexpected; it is indeed absurd, as it destroys even the dubious sense of the words. It is stated that the putting away of a wife causes her to commit adultery, and then the husband is exhorted to put away his wife if she is guilty of adultery; as if the wife who was guilty of adultery would not commit adultery!

Moreover, on a closer examination of the text, I saw that it was even grammatically incorrect. It is said, 'Whoever puts away his wife, saving for the cause of fornication, causes her to commit adultery,' or, if we translate the word παρεψτος literally, 'besides fornication, causes her to commit adultery.' The words refer to the husband who causes his wife to commit adultery by putting her away. Then why is the clause 'cause of fornication' inserted? If it were said that the husband who puts away his wife, besides being guilty of fornication, commits adultery, the sentence would be grammatically correct. But as the text stands, the noun 'husband' has one predicate — 'causes her,' etc. — and how does the phrase 'saving for the cause of fornication' refer to it? 'Cannot cause her to commit adultery, saving for the cause of adultery?' Even if the words 'wife' or 'her' were added, which is not the case, the words could have no reference to the predicate 'causes her.' According to the accepted interpretation, these words are considered as referring to the predicate 'puts away,' but the verb 'puts away' is not the predicate of the principal sentence, for that is 'causes her to commit adultery.' Therefore, for what purpose are the words 'saving for (or besides) the cause of fornication' inserted? Whether the wife is guilty of adultery or not, by putting her away the husband causes her to commit that sin.

The sentence would have a meaning if in the place of the word 'fornication' we found the words 'lasciviousness,' 'debauchery,' or some similar word expressing, not an action, but a quality or a state.

'Doesn't it mean,' I said to myself, 'that he who divorces his wife causes her to commit adultery, and is besides guilty of debauchery himself?' (For if a man divorces his wife, it is in order to take to himself some other woman.) If the word used in the text is found to mean 'debauchery,' then the sense will be clear.

And again, as in the preceding instances, the text confirmed my surmise in a manner that left no room for doubt. What first struck me on reading the text was that the word πορνεια, which is, in all translations except the English, rendered as 'adultery' in the same way as μοιχασθαι, is, in reality, quite another word. Perhaps the two words are synonymous, or are used in the gospel in the same sense, I thought. So I referred both to the common dictionary and to the evangelical glossaries, and found that the word πορνεια, which is equivalent to the Hebrew 'zono' the Latin 'fornicatio,' the German 'Hurerei,' the Russian 'распугство' (lewdness), has its own definite meaning, and in no dictionary is it considered as signifying adultery; 'adultère,' 'Ehebruch,' as it has been translated by Luther. It properly implies a depraved state or disposition, and not an action, and cannot therefore be translated by the word 'adultery.' Moreover, I saw that the word 'adultery' is always expressed in the gospel, and even in the above-named verses, by another word, μοιχεω. And no sooner had I corrected this evidently intentional perversion of the text than I saw that the sense given to the context of the nineteenth chapter, and by our commentators, was altogether impossible; I saw that there could be no doubt about the word πορνεια referring only to the husband.

Every Greek scholar will construe the passage thus: Παρεχτος (besides) λογου (the matter) πορνειας (of lewdness) ποιει (causes) αυτην (her) μοιχασθαι (to commit adultery). Therefore, the text stands word for word thus: 'He who divorces his wife, besides the sin of lewdness, causes her to commit adultery.'

We find exactly the same in the nineteenth chapter. No sooner is the incorrect translation of the word πορνεια amended, as well as that of the preposition επι, which has been translated 'for'; no sooner is the word 'lewdness' placed instead of 'adultery,' and the preposition 'by' instead of 'for'; than it grows perfectly clear that the words ει μη επι πορνεια can have no reference to the wife. And as the words παρεχτος λογου πορνειας can have no other meaning that 'besides the sin of lewdness of the husband,' so the words ει μη επι πορνεια, which we find in the nineteenth chapter, can have no reference to anything except the lewdness of the husband. It is said, ει μη επι πορνεια, which, being translated literally, is, 'if not by lewdness,' 'if not out of lewdness.' And thus the meaning is clear that Christ in this passage refutes the notion of the Pharisees that a man who put away his wife, not out of lewdness, but in order to live matrimonially with another woman, did not commit adultery; Christ says that the repudiation of a wife, even if it is not done out of lewdness, but in order to be joined in bonds of matrimony to another woman, is adultery. And thus the sense is simple, clear, perfectly consistent with the whole doctrine, and both logically and grammatically correct.

It was with the greatest difficulty that I at last discovered this clear and simple meaning of the words themselves, and their harmony with the whole doctrine of Christ. And, in truth, read the words in the German or French versions, where it is said, 'pour cause d'infidélité,' or 'à moins que cela ne soit pour cause d'infidélité,' and you will hardly be able to guess that the text has quite another meaning. The word παρεχτος, which according to all dictionaries means 'excepté,' 'ausgenommen,' is translated in the French by a whole sentence, 'à moins que cela ne soit.' The word πορνεια is translated 'infidélité,' 'Ehebruch,' 'adultery.' And on this intentional perversion of the text is based an interpretation that destroys the moral, religious, grammatical, and logical sense of Christ's words.

And once more I received a confirmation of the truth that the meaning of Christ's doctrine is simple and clear. His commandments are definite, and of the highest practical importance; but the interpretations given to us, based on a desire to justify existing evils, have so obscured His doctrine that we can with difficulty fathom its meaning. I felt convinced that had the gospel been found half burnt or half obliterated, it would have been easier to discover its true meaning than it is now; that it has suffered from such unconscientious interpretations, which have purposely concealed or distorted its true sense. In this last instance the special object of justifying the divorce of some Ivan the Terrible, which thus led to the misrepresentation of the Christian doctrine of matrimony, is more obvious than in the preceding cases to which reference has been made.

No sooner are all these interpretations thrown aside than vagueness and mistiness fade away, and the second commandment of Christ rises plainly before us: 'Take no pleasure in concupiscence; let each man, if he is not a eunuch, have a wife, and each woman a husband; let a man have but one wife, and a woman one husband, and let them never under any pretext whatever dissolve their union.'

Immediately after the second commandment we find a new reference to the ancient law, and the third commandment is given. Matthew 5:33–37: 'Again, you have heard that it has been said to the people long ago, you shall not swear falsely, but shall perform to the Lord your oaths (Leviticus 19:12; Deuteronomy 23:21).

But I say to you, do not swear at all; neither by heaven, for it is God's throne; nor by the earth, for it is His footstool; neither by Jerusalem, for it is the city of the great King. Neither shall you swear by your head, because you cannot make one hair white or black. But let your word be yes, yes, or no, no; for whatever is more than these comes from evil.'

In my former readings of the gospel this text had always puzzled me. Not by its obscurity, as the text referring to divorce did; nor by its inconsistency with other passages, as did the text that forbids anger only if it is 'without a cause'; nor, again, by the difficulty of fulfilling the commandment, like the text that enjoins our letting ourselves be struck. It puzzled me, on the contrary, by its evident clarity and simplicity. Side by side with precepts, the depth and importance of which filled me with awe, I found an apparently useless, insignificant precept, very easy of fulfillment, and comparatively unimportant in its bearing upon myself or upon others. I had never sworn by Jerusalem, or by God, or by anything; and had never found any difficulty in abstaining from doing so; besides, it seemed to me that my swearing or not swearing could be of no importance to anyone. And longing to find some explanation of a precept that puzzled me by its simplicity, I consulted the commentaries on the gospel. This once they helped me.

Commentators see in these words a confirmation of the third commandment of Moses, not to swear by God's name. They say that Christ, like Moses, forbids our taking God's name in vain. But they add besides that this precept given to us by Christ is not always obligatory, and that in no case does it refer to the oath of allegiance to the existing powers, which every citizen is obliged to take. They choose out texts from Holy Scripture, not with the purpose of confirming the direct meaning of Christ's precept, but in order to prove that it is possible and even necessary to leave it unfulfilled.

It is affirmed that Christ Himself sanctioned the taking of an oath in courts of law by His answer, 'You have said,' to the High Priest's words, 'I charge you under oath by the living God.' It is likewise affirmed that the apostle Paul called upon God to bear witness to the truth of his words, and that this was obviously an oath. It is affirmed that the Mosaic Law enjoined oaths, and that Christ did not abrogate them, and only set useless, pharisaically hypocritical oats aside.

And when I saw the meaning and the true object of the interpretation, it grew clear to me that Christ's law against swearing was not as insignificant and easy of fulfillment as I had thought before I had come to regard the 'oath of allegiance' as one of those that are forbidden by Christ.

And I said to myself, 'Doesn't it mean that the oath, which is so carefully fenced round by the Church commentaries, is also forbidden? Don't Christ's words oppose the very oath without which the division of men into separate governments would be an impossibility — the oath without which a military class would be impossible?' Soldiers are those who act by violence and they call themselves 'sworn men' (присяга). Had I asked the grenadier I mentioned in a preceding chapter how he solved the problem of the inconsistency between the gospel and the military code, he would have answered that he had taken an oath, i.e., sworn upon the gospel. All the military men I ever asked answered thus. Oaths are so essential in upholding the awful evils brought about by war and violence that in France, where Christ's doctrine is entirely set aside, the oath of allegiance remains in full force. Indeed, had Christ not said, 'Do not swear at all,' He ought to have said so. He came to destroy evil, and how great is the evil brought about in the world by the taking of oaths! Perhaps some may urge that this was an imperceptible evil in Christ's time. No assumption can be more gratuitous. Epictetus and Seneca enjoined all men to take no oaths. In the laws of Manou the same precept may be found. Why should I say that Christ did not see this evil, when He speaks of it so definitely and so forcibly?

He says, 'I say to you, do not swear at all.' The saying is as clear, as simple, and as indubitable as the words, 'do not judge, do not condemn,' and it gives as little scope for false interpretation, the less so because the words 'Let your communication be yes, yes, or no, no; for whatever is more than these comes from evil,' are added.

Now if Christ by this teaching exhorts us always to fulfill the will of God, how dare a man swear to obey the will of another man? The will of God may not always coincide with the will of man. Christ tells us so in this very text. He says (verse 36), 'Do not swear by your head, for not only your head but every hair on it is subject to the will of God.' We find the same thing taught in the epistle of James, who says (chapter 5, verse 12), 'But above all things, my brethren, do not swear, neither by heaven, neither by the earth, neither by any other oath; but let your yes be yes, and your no be no, lest you fall into condemnation.' The apostle tells us why we are not to swear. Though the taking of an oath may be no sin in itself, he who swears falls into condemnation, and therefore shall no man swear. Can any language be clearer than the words of Christ and of this apostle?

But my ideas on this point were in so confused a state that for some time I went on asking myself, with surprise, 'Does the precept really mean this? How is it that all swear by the gospel? It cannot be.'

But I had read the commentaries on the gospel, and saw that what I deemed impossible had, nevertheless, been done. The same remark has to be made in reference to this as to the texts, 'Do not judge,' 'Do not give way to anger,' 'Never break the union of husband and wife.' We have set up our own institutions; we love them, and choose to consider them sacred. Christ, whom we acknowledge to be God, comes, and He says that our rules of life are bad. We acknowledge Him to be God, yet we do not choose to set our rules of life aside. What is left then for us to do? When, by inserting the words 'without a cause,' we turn the commandment against anger into a meaningless sentence; when, like crafty lawyers, we interpret the sense of the commandment in a manner that gives it a contrary meaning to that designed by Him who spoke it, as we do if, instead of prohibiting altogether the putting away of a wife, we declare divorce to be lawful and just, we put our institutions in the place of truth. But if it is impossible to interpret the words otherwise than as I have indicated, in the treatment of the precepts 'Do not judge,' 'Do not condemn,' 'Do not swear at all,' then we boldly act in direct opposition to Christ's doctrine, while asserting that we strictly fulfill it, if we cleave to traditional interpretations.

The chief obstacle to our understanding that the gospel wholly forbids our taking an oath is that the so-called Christian teachers boldly insist upon men's taking oaths upon the gospel; and in this acting contrary to the gospel. How can it come into the head of a man who is made to take an oath on the gospel, or the crucifix, that that crucifix is sacred for the very reason that He who forbade our swearing was crucified upon it? He who takes the oath perhaps kisses the very passage that so clearly and definitely says, 'Do not swear at all.'

But such boldness no longer confounded me. I clearly saw that in the fifth chapter, verses 33–37, lay the third definite and practicable commandment of Christ, which may be stated: 'Never take an oath under any circumstances. Every oath is extorted from men for evil.'

After this third commandment stands a fourth reference to the Mosaic Law, and then the fourth commandment is presented. Matthew 5:38–42: 'You have heard that it has been said, an eye for an eye, and a tooth for a tooth. But I say to you, do not resist evil; but whoever shall strike you on your right cheek, turn to him the other also. And if any man will sue you at law, and take away your coat, let him have your cloak also. And whoever shall compel you to go a mile, go two miles with him. Give to him who asks you, and from him who would borrow from you do not turn away.'

I have already spoken of the direct meaning of these words, and of our having no foundation whatever for interpreting them otherwise. The various commentaries upon them, from John Chrysostom to the present time, are truly surprising. We all admire the words, and each one tries to find some profound hidden meaning in them; but we usually fail to see that they mean exactly what they express. Ecclesiastical commentators, unmindful of the authority of Him who they acknowledge as God, unhesitatingly limit the meaning of His words. They say, 'It is clearly understood that the precepts of long-suffering non-retaliation, being especially directed against the vindictiveness of the Hebrews, do not exclude either the right of setting limits to the progress of evil by the punishment of evil-doers, or private, individual endeavors to uphold the inviolability of truth, to amend the wicked, or to deprive evil-doers of the possibility of injuring others; the divine commandments of the Savior would otherwise be reduced to mere words, and would lead only to the progress of evil and the repression of virtue. The Christian's love should be like God's love; but since God's love limits and punishes evil only in proportion as it is more or less necessary for the glory of God or the salvation of our brethren, so is it the duty of those in authority to limit the progress of evil by punishments' (Exposition of the Gospel, by the Archim. Michael, based on the Commentaries of the Fathers of the Church).

Neither do learned and free-thinking Christians scruple to correct the sense of Christ's words. They affirm that His sayings are sublime, but impracticable; that the application of the precept of non-resistance would destroy the whole organization of life, which we have set up so well; such is the opinion of Renan, Strauss, and other free-thinking commentators.

Yet if we treat the words of Christ in the same way that we do the words of any man who may chance to speak to us, i.e., if we suppose that He says what He means, all profound interpretations will became unnecessary. Christ says, 'I find that the way you have regulated your lives is both foolish and bad. I propose another way.' And then He gives us His precepts in verses 38–42. Doesn't it seem right that, before correcting these words, they should at least be understood? And this is just what none of us choose to do. We decide beforehand that the present organization of our lives, which His words tend to destroy, is the sacred law of mankind.

I had not considered our way of living as either good or sacred, and therefore I came to understand this commandment before I did the others. And when I understood these words exactly in the sense in which they were uttered, I was struck by their truth, clarity, and force. Christ says, 'You think to destroy evil by evil. That is irrational. In order that there should be no evil, do no evil.' And then, after enumerating all that is evil in our social adjustments, Christ exhorts us to act otherwise.

The fourth commandment, I have said, was the one that I understood first, and it opened up to me the true meaning of all the rest. The fourth clear, simple commandment, which it is within the power of all to obey, says, 'Never resist evil by violence; never return violence for violence. If anyone strikes you, bear it; if anyone takes away what is yours, let him have it; if anyone makes you labor, do so; if anyone wants to have what you consider to be your own, give it up to him.'

And after this fourth commandment stands a fifth reference to the Mosaic Law, and the fifth commandment. Matthew 5:43–48: 'You have heard that it has been said, "You shall love your neighbor, and hate your enemy (Leviticus 19:17–18)." But I say to you, love your enemies, bless those who curse you, do good to those who hate you, and pray for those who despitefully use you and persecute you, that you may be the children of your Father who is in heaven; for He makes His sun to rise on the evil and on the good, and sends rain on the just and on the unjust. For if you love those who love you, what reward do you have? Don't even the publicans do the same? And if you salute your brethren only, what do you do more than others? Don't even the heathens do so? Therefore be perfect, even as your Father who is in heaven is perfect.'

I had formerly considered these words as explaining, amplifying, and giving more emphasis to, even exaggerating, the doctrine of non-resistance. But having already found the simple, definite, and applicable sense of each of the preceding texts, which begin with a reference to the ancient law, I had a sense that I should find some fresh meaning here also. I had observed that a commandment was annexed to each reference to the ancient law, and that each verse of the commandment had its own significance, and could not be turned aside; and I was sure that would prove to be the fact here also. The last words that we repeated in the gospel according to St. Luke say that, as God makes no distinction between men, but pours down His blessings upon all, so should we be like our Father in heaven and make no distinction between men; not acting as the heathen do, but loving all men, and doing good to all. These words were very clear; they seemed to me an explanation and commendation to some clearly defined precept, but what that precept precisely was I could not for a long time make out. 'Love one's enemy.' That was impossible. It was one of those beautiful utterances that cannot be considered otherwise than as presenting an unattainable moral ideal. It was either too much or it meant nothing. We may avoid wronging our enemy, but to love him is impossible. Christ cannot have commanded what we cannot fulfill.

Moreover, the very first words in reference to the ancient law, 'It has been said, Hate your enemy,' were dubious. In the preceding passages Christ quotes the exact, authentic words of the Mosaic Law; but in this one He cites words that were never used. He seems to knowingly make a false statement about the ancient law.

The various commentaries on the gospel, which I consulted, helped me no more than they had done in my former doubts. All commentators acknowledge that the words 'hate your enemy' do not stand in the Mosaic Law; but by none of them is there any explanation of the incorrect quotation given. They tell us that it is hard to love one's enemies — the wicked — and, commenting on Christ's words, they add that though a man cannot love his enemy, yet he may neither wish him evil, nor actually wrong or injure him. It is persistently instilled into us that it is our obligation and duty to denounce evil-doers, i.e., to oppose our enemy; and the various steps are mentioned by which this virtue may be attained; and thus, according to the interpretation given by the Church, the final conclusion is that Christ, without any ostensible reason, quotes the words of the Mosaic Law incorrectly, and has uttered many beautiful sayings that are, in themselves, useless and impracticable.

It seemed to me that this could not be a true statement of the case. I felt sure that there was as clear and definite a sense in these words as I had found in the first four commandments. In order to comprehend the real meaning of the text, I endeavored, first of all, to take in the sense of the incorrect reference to the Mosaic Law, 'You have been told, hate your enemy.' It is not without some distinct purpose that, before giving each of His own precepts, Christ quotes the words of the old law, 'You shall not kill,' 'You shall not commit adultery,' etc., and places His doctrine in opposition to them. Now, if we do not comprehend what meaning Christ attached to the words He quotes, neither can we comprehend the duty that He enjoins. It seemed to me that the first point it was necessary to make out was for what purpose Christ had cited words that are not found in the Mosaic Law.

Here we find two precepts set in opposition to each other: 'You have been told, you shall love your neighbor, and hate your enemy.' It is obvious that the basis of the new commandment must be the very difference between these two precepts of the ancient law. In order to see the distinction more clearly, I asked myself, 'What do the words "neighbor" and "enemy" mean, in the language of the gospel?' And on consulting the dictionary and other passages of the Bible, I found that the word 'neighbor' in the Hebrew language always signifies 'a Hebrew.' In the gospel, a similar definition of the word 'neighbor' is given in the parable of the Good Samaritan. According to the Hebrew lawyer's question, 'Who is my neighbor,' a Samaritan could not be his neighbor. The same definition of the word 'neighbor' is given in the Acts of the Apostles, 7:27. The word 'neighbor,' as used in the gospel, signifies a 'fellow-countryman,' one who belongs to the same nation. And I hence concluded that the antithesis used by Christ in this passage, when quoting the words of the law, 'You have been told, you shall love your neighbor, and hate your enemy,' places a 'fellow-countryman' in opposition to 'a stranger.' I then asked myself what the word 'enemy' meant, according to the Hebrews. It is almost always used, in the gospel, in the sense, not of a private, but a common enemy — a national enemy (Luke 1:71, Matthew 22:44, Mark 12:36, Luke 20:43, and elsewhere). The use of the word 'enemy' in the singular number, in the text, 'hate your enemy,' made it clear to me that the words referred to a national enemy. The singular expresses an enemy taken in a collective sense. In the Old Testament the word 'enemy,' when used in the singular, always implies a national enemy.

No sooner did I comprehend this than my difficulty in understanding how it was that Christ, who always quoted the original words of the law, in this instance inserts the words, 'You have been told, You shall hate your enemy,' which are not in the Mosaic Law, was solved. To remove all doubts as to the meaning of the passage, we have only to take the word 'neighbor' as meaning a 'fellow-countryman.' Christ speaks of the Mosaic regulations concerning a national enemy. He combines in the single expression 'to hate, to wrong an enemy,' all the various precepts dispersed through the scriptures by which the Hebrews are enjoined to oppress, kill, and destroy other nations. And He says, 'You have been told that you shall love your own people, and hate the enemies of your nation; but I say to you, that you love all, without distinction of their nationality.'

And no sooner had I understood this than the second and chief difficulty, i.e., how the words 'love your enemies' were to be understood, was removed. It is impossible to love our personal enemies. But we can love men of another nation as we do those of our own people. I saw clearly that by the words, 'You have heard that it has been said, love your neighbor, and hate your enemy; but I say to you, Love your enemies,' Christ asserts that all men are accustomed to consider their fellow-countrymen as their neighbors and men of other nations as their enemies, and this He forbids our doing. He says that, according to the Law of Moses, a distinction was made between him who was a Hebrew and him who was not, but was considered as a national enemy; and then He commands that no such distinction should be made between them. Indeed, in the gospels according to St. Matthew and St. Luke we find that, immediately after this precept, He says that all are equal before God, that the same sun shines on all, and that the same rain falls upon all. God makes no distinction between men, and does equal good to all; ought not men to do likewise, without recognizing distinctions of nationality?

Thus I again found ample confirmation of the simple and practicable sense of Christ's words. Instead of an indistinct and indefinite philosophy, I discovered a clear, definite precept, which all have it within their power to fulfill. To make no distinction between one's own and other nations, and so to avoid the natural results of these distinctions, such as being at enmity with other nations, going to war, taking part in war, arming for war, etc., and to treat all men, whatever nation they belong to, as we do our fellow-countrymen, was the requirement of Christ. All this was so simple and so clear that I was surprised I had not understood it at once.

The hindrance in my way was the same that had prevented my comprehending the prohibition of courts of law and oaths. It is difficult to conceive that the very courts of law, which are inaugurated with Christian prayer, and consecrated by those who regard themselves as the fulfillers of Christ's law, are incompatible with the Christian faith, and are in direct opposition to Christ's doctrine. Nor is it easier to conceive that the oath of allegiance, which all men are made to take by the keepers of Christ's law, is expressly forbidden by that very law. And it is hardest of all to conceive that, to uphold what is considered not only as necessary and natural, but even grand and glorious, as love of one's native land — its defense, its aggrandizement, war against an enemy, and so on — is not only sinning against the law of Christ, but even abjuring it. We have become so estranged from the doctrine of Christ that this very estrangement is now the chief obstacle to our understanding it. We have turned a deaf ear to His words, and forgotten all He taught us of the life we are to lead; how that we should not kill, nor even bear malice against a fellow-creature; that we should never defend ourselves, but turn our cheeks to be struck; that we should love our neighbor, etc. We have grown so used to calling the men who devote their lives to murder 'a Christ-loving army'; who put up prayers to Christ for victory over the enemy; whose pride and glory are in murder; and who have raised the symbol of murder, i.e., the sword, into something almost sacred, so that he who is deprived of that symbol is considered as having been disgraced; we have grown so used to all this, I repeat, that it now appears to us that Christ did not forbid war; and that, if He had intended to do so, He would have expressed His meaning more clearly.

We forget that Christ could never have thought it possible that men who believe in His doctrine of humility, love, and universal brotherhood would calmly and consciously institute the murder of their brethren. Christ cannot have supposed it possible, and therefore He could no more have forbidden a Christian to make war, than could a father, while admonishing his son to live honestly, without injuring or defrauding others, exhort him not to cut men's throats on the high road.

Not one of the apostles, not one of Christ's disciples, could have supposed it necessary to forbid a Christian's committing murder, which is misnamed war. See what Origen says in his answer to Celsus, chapter 63.

'Celsus exhorts you to help the sovereign with all your strength, to take part in his duties, to take up arms for him, to serve under his banner, if necessary to lead out his army to battle. Moreover, we may say, in answer to those who, being ignorant of our faith, require of us the murder of men, that even their high priests do not soil their hands in order that their god may accept their sacrifice. No more do we.' And concluding by the explanation that Christians do more good by their peaceful lives than soldiers do, Origen says, 'Thus we fight better than any for the safety of our sovereign. We do not, it is true, serve under his banners, and we should not, even were he to force us to do so.'

It was thus that the first Christians regarded war and thus their teacher spoke when addressing the great men of this world, at the time when hundreds and thousands of martyrs were perishing for the Christian faith.

But in our times the question whether a Christian ought to take part in war never seems to occur to any. Youths brought up according to the Church law, which is called the Christian law, go every autumn, at fixed periods, to the conscription halls, and, with the assistance of their spiritual pastors, there renounce the law of Christ. A short time ago a peasant refused to enter the military service, grounding his refusal on the words of the gospel. The clergy all tried to persuade the man that his view of the matter was erroneous; and as the peasant still believed in Christ's words, and not in theirs, he was cast into prison, and kept there until he denied Christ. And this takes place although we, Christians, received 1800 years ago a perfectly clear and definite commandment from our God, which said, 'Never consider men of another nation as your enemies; look upon all men as brethren, and behave toward all men as you do toward your fellow-countrymen; therefore you shall not kill those whom you call your enemies; love all and do good to all.'

And when I had understood these simple, definite commandments, which admit of no other interpretation, I asked myself, 'What would the world be if all Christians believed that these commandments must be fulfilled in order to attain happiness, instead of treating them only as commandments that must be sung or read in churches, in order that we may find favor in the eyes of God? What would the world be if people did but as firmly believe in the obligatory character of these commandments as they now do in the necessity of daily prayer; of attending public worship every Sunday; of fasting on Fridays, and receiving communion every year? What would the world be, if all men did but as firmly believe in these commandments as they do in the prescribed rules of the Church?' And I pictured to myself men and women, in Christian society, living up to these commandments, and instilling the same into new generations; ourselves and our children no longer taught, both by word and deed, that man must maintain his own dignity, must defend his own rights (which cannot be done without humbling or offending others), but, instead, taught that no man has any rights, that none can be superior or inferior to another, that only he who tries to rise above all others is lower and more degraded than others, that there is no feeling more debasing for a man to cherish than that of anger against another, that the seeming insignificance or foolishness of a man can never justify either anger or enmity. Instead of our present social adjustments — from the show-glasses of shops to theatres, novels, and millinery — whose tendency is but to sensuality, I pictured to myself that we, and our children, were taught, by word and deed, that the pleasures of sensational books, theatres, and balls was the basest kind of pleasure; that every action whose aim was the embellishing or showing-off of our persons was base and disgusting. Instead of our present social adjustments, by which it is considered necessary, and even in a sense right, that a young man should 'sow his wild oats' before marriage, instead of a life in which separation between husband and wife is regarded as an ordinary thing, instead of the acknowledged necessity for the existence of a class of women who serve to pamper depravity, instead of the permission and authorization of divorce, I pictured to myself that we were taught, both by precept and by example, that a single, unmarried state, for a man in all his virility, was an anomaly and a shame, that a man's leaving the woman he was united to, or taking another in her place, was not only as unnatural a proceeding as incest, but a cruel and inhuman deed. Instead of our lives being based upon violence, instead of each of us being either chastened himself or chastising others from childhood to old age, I pictured to myself that we were taught, both by precept and by example, that vengeance is but a base instinct; that violence is not only shameful, but deprives man of his true happiness; that the proper joys of life are only those that need no violence to protect them; that it is not he who despoils others, or keeps what is his own out of the hands of others, and makes others serve him, who is the most deserving of respect, but, rather, he who gives most, and who helps others most. Instead of considering it very right and lawful that each man should take an oath, and thus give away the most precious of his possessions, i.e., his whole life into the keeping of another, I pictured to myself that we were taught to regard the intelligent will of man as that 'holiest of holies' which no man can ever give away; and that to promise anything with an oath is to renounce one's own rational self, and is an outrage against all that is most holy in man. I pictured to myself that instead of the enmity toward other nations that is instilled into us under a semblance of patriotism, instead of the praise of murder or war, which we, from our childhood, look upon as a glorious thing, there was instilled into us the dread and scorn of all those diplomatic or military institutions that serve to disunite men; that to admit the existence of states, laws, frontiers, countries, etc., is but a proof of the most brutal ignorance; that to go to war, i.e., to kill men who are complete strangers to us, with out any reason, is the most horrid crime, of which only a lost and depraved man, degraded to the rank of a wild beast, is capable. I pictured to myself that all men believed in this, and I asked myself, 'What would the world be then?'

Formerly I had more than once asked myself what the fulfillment of the doctrine of Christ, as I then understood it, would lead to, and the involuntary answer had been, 'To nothing at all.' We shall all go on praying, receiving the Holy Sacrament, believing in our redemption and salvation, in the redemption and salvation of the whole world through Christ, and still this salvation will not be brought about by ourselves; but Christ will come again, in His appointed time, to judge the living and the dead, and then the kingdom of God will be established on earth, independently of the life that we have led. But the doctrine of Christ, as I now understand it, has another signification: the establishing of the kingdom of God on earth depends upon us. The fulfillment of Christ's doctrine, as expressed in the five commandments, establishes this kingdom of God. The kingdom of God on earth is peace among all men. Peace among men is the highest earthly bliss that man can attain. It was thus that the Hebrew prophets pictured the kingdom of God to themselves. And it is thus that each human heart ever has and ever will picture it.

The substance of the entire doctrine of Christ is the establishing of the kingdom of God on earth, and that brings peace to all men. In the Sermon on the Mount, in His conversation with Nicodemus, in the mission He gave to the disciples, in all His teachings, He speaks of what causes division among men and prevents their living in peace and entering the kingdom of God. All Christ's parables are definitions of the kingdom of God — they all seek to instill into us that it is only by loving our brethren, and being at peace with them, that we can enter the kingdom. John the Baptist, the precursor of Christ, says that the kingdom of God is at hand, and that Jesus Christ will give it to the world.

Christ says that He brings peace on earth (John 14:27); 'Peace I leave with you, my peace I give to you; I give it to you not as the world gives. Do not let your heart be troubled, neither let it be afraid.'

These five commandments of Christ do indeed give peace to men. The tendency of all the five commandments is to procure peace among men. Let men but believe in the doctrine of Christ, and obey it, and there will be peace on earth; not the peace established by man, which is fleeing and transitory, but general, inviolable, eternal peace.

The first commandment says: Be at peace with all men and do not consider any man as worthless or foolish (Matthew 5:22). If peace has been destroyed, use your utmost endeavors to re-establish it. The service of God is the annihilation of all enmity (Matthew 5:23–24). Let the least disagreement be followed by immediate reconciliation, lest you swerve from the true life. This commandment includes all in itself. But Christ foresees the temptations of the world that destroy peace among men, and gives a second commandment against the seductions of sexual relations that destroy peace: Do not consider carnal beauty to lust after it. Avoid the temptation (Matthew 5:28,30); let each man have one wife, and each woman one husband; and let them never leave each other, under any pretext whatever (Matthew 5:23). Another temptation is the taking of oaths, for it leads men into sin. Know, therefore, that to do so is to sin, and consequently never make any vow (Matthew 5:34,35). The third temptation is to vengeance, which is called human justice. Never take vengeance on any man, nor seek to excuse yourself by saying you have received injury at the hands of another; bear the wrong done to you, and do not return evil for evil (Matthew 5:38,42). The fourth temptation arises from the distinction made between nations, the enmity between races and states. Know that all men are brethren, and sons of the same God, and never destroy peace in the name of national interests (Matthew 5:43,48). Let men leave but one of these commandments unfulfilled, and peace will be destroyed. Let men fulfill all these commandments and the kingdom of peace will be established on earth. These commandments exclude all evil from the relationships of men.

The fulfillment of Christ's commandments will make the lives of men such as each human heart seeks and longs for. All men will be brethren, each will be at peace with the other, and each will be free to enjoy all the blessings of this world during the term of life allotted to him by God. Men will turn their 'swords into ploughshares and their spears into pruning hooks.' And on earth will be established the kingdom of God; the kingdom of peace that was promised by the prophets, which drew nearer with John the Baptist, and which Christ announced in the words of Isaiah, 'The Spirit of the Lord is upon me, because He has anointed me to preach the gospel to the poor; He has sent me to heal the broken-hearted, to preach deliverance to the captives, and recovering of sight to the blind; to set at liberty those who are bruised, and to preach the acceptable year of the Lord.'

The simple and clear commandments of peace, given by Christ, by which all causes of dissension are foreseen and turned aside, reveal the kingdom of God on earth to men. Thus Christ is truly the Messiah.

Chapter VII

Why does man not do the things that Christ enjoins and that can give him the highest earthly felicity — the felicity he has ever longed to attain? The answer as usually given, with slight variations of expression, is that the doctrine of Christ is indeed sublime, and its fulfillment would establish the kingdom of God on earth, but it is difficult and therefore impracticable.

It is in the nature of man to strive after what is best. Each doctrine of life is but a doctrine of what is best for man. If men have pointed out to them what is really best for them, how do they come to answer that they wish to do what is best, but cannot?

Human intellect, ever since man has existed, has been directed toward discovering what is best among all the demands that are made both in individual and in social life. Men struggle for land, for any object that they may want, and then end by dividing all among themselves, each calling what he may get his 'personal property.' They find that though difficult of adjustment, it is better arranged thus, and they keep to their own property. Men fight to get wives for themselves, and then come to the conclusion that it is better for each to have his own family; and though it may be hard to maintain a family, men keep to their property, their families, and all else they are said to possess. No sooner do men find it best for themselves to act in a particular way, than they proceed to act in that way, however hard it may be. Then what do we mean by saying the doctrine of Christ is sublime, a life in accordance with His doctrine would be a better one than the one we now lead, but we cannot lead the life that would be best for us because it is hard to do so?

If 'hard' means that it is hard to give up the momentary satisfaction of our desires for some great and good end, why do we not say, as well, that it is hard to plough the ground in order to have bread; to plant apple trees in order to have apples? Every being endowed with the least germ of reason knows that no great good can be attained without trouble and difficulty. And now we say that though Christ's doctrine is sublime, we can never put it into practice because it is hard to do so. Hard, because its observance would deprive us of what we have always possessed. Have we never heard that it may be better for us to suffer and to lose, than never to suffer and always to have our desires satisfied?

Man may be but an animal, and nobody will find fault with him for being such; but a man cannot reason that he chooses to be only an animal; no sooner does he reason than he admits himself to be a rational being, and, making this admission, he cannot help recognizing a distinction between what is rational and what is irrational. Reason does not command, it only enlightens.

While groping about in the darkness in search of the door, I bruise my hands and knees. A man comes with a light, and I see the door. I can no longer bruise myself against the wall now that I see the door, still less can I assert that, though I see the door and feel convinced the best plan would be to enter it, it is hard to do so, and I prefer bruising my knees against the wall.

There must evidently be some strange misconception in the argument that the doctrine of Christ is good, and conducive to good to the world, but man is weak, man is bad, and, while wishing to act for the best, he acts for the worst, and therefore he cannot do what he know is best for himself.

This notion must be the result of some false assumption. It is only by assuming that what is, is not, and that what is not, is, that man can have arrived at so strange a negation of the possibility of fulfilling a doctrine that, as he himself admits, would give him happiness.

The assumption that has brought mankind to accept this notion is based on the dogmatic Christian creed — the creed that is taught to all members of the Orthodox, Roman Catholic, and Protestant Churches from their earliest childhood.

This creed, according to the definition given by believers, is an acknowledgement of the existence of things that seem to be (a definition given by St. Paul and repeated in works on divinity and catechisms as the best definition of faith). It is this belief that has brought mankind to the singular conviction that the doctrine of Christ is good, but cannot be put in practice.

The doctrine of this creed is literally as follows: God eternal, Three Persons in one God, chose to create a world of spirits. The bountiful God created that world of spirits for their happiness; but it chanced that one of the spirits grew wicked, and therefore unhappy. Some time passed away, and God created another world, a material world, and created man, likewise for happiness. God created man happy, immortal, and sinless. Man was happy because he enjoyed all the blessings of life without labor; immortal, for he was always to live thus; sinless, for he did not know evil.

Man was tempted in Eden by the spirit of the first creation who had grown wicked; and from that time man fell, and other fallen men like him were born into the world; men labored, sickened, suffered, died, and struggled morally and physically; i.e., the imaginary man became the real man, such as we know him to be; and we have no grounds for imagining him ever to have been otherwise. The state of man who labors, suffers, strives after good, avoids evil, and dies; this state, which is real, and beyond which we can imagine no other, is not the true state of man, according to this orthodox belief, but it is a temporary, accidental state, unnatural to him.

And though, according to this teaching, this state of man has continued for all men from the expulsion of Adam out of Eden, i.e., from the beginning of the world to the birth of Christ, and has continued in the same way since that time, believers are bound to think that this is only an accidental, temporary state. According to this teaching the Son of God, God Himself, the Second Person of the Trinity, was sent down from heaven by God, and was made man, to save men from this accidental, temporary state, unnatural to them, to deliver them from the curse laid upon them by the same God for the sin of Adam, and to re-establish them in their former natural state of perfect happiness, i.e., of health, immortality, innocence, and idleness. According to this teaching, again, the Second Person of the Trinity redeemed the sin of Adam by the fact that men crucified Him, and thus put an end to the unnatural state of man, which has lasted from the beginning of the world. And from that time man believed in Christ, and became again such as he was before the fall, immortal, healthy, sinless, and idle.

The orthodox teaching does not dwell at any length upon the consequent results of the redemption, according to which, after the death of Christ, the earth should have begun to yield up her fruits to believers without labor, sickness should have ceased, and mothers should have given birth to their offspring without suffering; for, however great their faith is, it is difficult to instill into those who find labor hard, and sickness painful, that labor is not hard, and suffering is not painful. Great stress, however, is laid on that part of the teaching that says that 'death and sin are no more.'

It is confidently asserted that the dead live. And, as the dead cannot possibly tell us whether they are dead or alive, any more than a stone can tell whether it can speak or not, this absence of all denial is taken as a proof of the assertion that those who are dead are not dead. And with yet greater solemnity and assurance is it asserted that, after the coming of Christ on earth, man is delivered from sin by his faith in Him, i.e., that man has no need of reason to enlighten his path in life, and has no need to strive after what is best for himself; he only has to believe that Christ redeemed him from sin to become sinless, i.e., perfectly good. Thus, according to this doctrine, men must think their intellect impotent, and that therefore they are sinless, i.e., cannot err.

The true believer must fancy that ever since Christ came into the world, the earth yields fruit without labor; that children are brought into the world without suffering; that there is no sickness, no death, no sin — i.e., no errors. He must imagine that what is not, is, and what is, is not.

Such is the teaching of our strictly logical theory of theology.

This teaching seems innocent in itself. But a deviation from truth can never be innocent; it entails consequences, more or less important, according to the importance of the subject of the untruth. In this case the subject of the untruth is the whole life of man.

This teaching calls an individual blissful, sinless; and eternal life the true life, i.e., a life that nobody has ever seen, and that does not exist. And the life that is, the only one we know, which we lead, and which mankind has ever led, is, according to this teaching, a fallen, wicked life.

The struggle between the intellectual and animal nature of man, which lies in the soul of each, and is the substance of the life of each man, is entirely set aside. The struggle is made to refer to what befell Adam at the creation of the world. And the question, 'Am I to eat the apples that tempt me?' according to this teaching, no longer applies to man. Adam solved the question in the negative, once and forever, in the garden. Adam sinned, that is, Adam erred, and we all fell irrevocably, and all our endeavors to live rationally are useless, and even godless. I am irrevocably bad, and I must know it. My salvation does not lie in the fact that I can order my life by my reason, and, having learned to know good from evil, do what is best. No, Adam sinned once for all, and Christ has, once and for ever, set the evil right; and all that is left for me to do is to mourn over the fall of Adam, and rejoice in my salvation through Christ.

According to this teaching, not only are the loves of good and truth, which are innate in man, his endeavors to enlighten by his reason the various phenomena of life, and his spiritual life deemed unimportant, but they are all vainglory and pride.

Our life here on earth, with all its joys, with all its charms, with all its struggles between light and darkness, the lives of all those who lived before, my own life with its inward struggles and consequent victories of reason, is not the true life, but a hopelessly spoiled, fallen life; the true life, the sinless life, according to this teaching, lies only in faith, i.e., in fancy, i.e., in madness.

Let a man but set aside the teaching he has imbibed from his childhood, let him transfer himself in thought into a new man, not brought up in that doctrine, and then let him imagine in what light this teaching would appear to him. Would he not deem it complete insanity?

Strange and awful though it was to think thus, I was forced to admit that it was even so, for only thus could I explain to myself the strikingly inconsistent, senseless arguments, which I heard all around me, against the possibility of fulfilling the doctrine of Christ. 'It is good and would lead to happiness, but men cannot fulfill it.'

It is only the assumption that what does not exist, exists, and what exists, does not exist, that can have brought mankind to so surprising an inconsistency. And I found that false assumption in the so-called Christian faith, which has been preached during 1800 years.

Believers are not the only persons who say that the doctrine of Christ is good, but impracticable. Unbelievers, men who either do not believe, or think that they do not believe, in the dogmas of the fall and the redemption, say the same. Men of science, philosophers, and men of cultivated minds in general, who consider themselves perfectly free from superstition, likewise argue the impracticability of Christ's doctrine. They do not believe, or at least think that they do not believe, in anything, and therefore consider themselves as having nothing to do with superstition, with the fall of man, or with redemption. I thought so too, formerly. I also thought that these learned men had other grounds for denying the practicability of the doctrine of Christ. But, on closer examination of the basis of their negation, I clearly saw that unbelievers had the same false idea, that life is not what it is, but what it seems to be; and that this idea has the same basis as the idea of believers. Men who call themselves 'unbelievers' do not, it is true, believe in God, in Christ, or in Adam; but they believe in the fundamental false assumption of the right of man to a life of perfect bliss, just as firmly as theologians do.

However privileged science, with her philosophy, may boast of being the judge and the guide of intellect, she is, in reality, not its guide, but its slave. The view taken of the world is always prepared for her by religion; and science only works in the path assigned her by religion. Religion reveals the meaning of life, and science applies this meaning to the various phases of life. And, therefore, if religion gives a false meaning to life, science, reared in this religious creed, will apply this false meaning to the life of man.

The teaching of the church gave, as the basis of life, the right of man to perfect bliss — bliss that is to be attained, not by the individual efforts of man, but by something beyond his own control; and this view of human life became the basis of our European science and philosophy.

Religion, science, and public opinion all unanimously tell us that the life we lead is a bad one, but that the doctrine, which teaches us to endeavor to improve, and thus make our life itself better, is impracticable.

The doctrine of Christ, as an improvement of human life by the rational efforts of man, is impracticable because Adam sinned and the world is full of evil, says religion.

Philosophy says that Christ's doctrine is impracticable because certain laws, which are independent of the will of man, govern human life. Philosophy and science say, in other words, exactly the same as religion does in its dogmas of original sin and redemption.

In the doctrine of redemption there are two fundamental theses on which all is grounded: (1) man has a right to perfect bliss, but the life of this world is a bad one and cannot be amended by the efforts of man, and (2) we can only be saved by faith.

These two theses have become first truths, both for the believers and the unbelievers of our so-called Christian Society. Out of the second thesis arose the Church, with its institutions. Out of the first arose our social opinions, and our philosophical and political theories.

All the political and philosophical theories that justify existing order, Hegelism and its offspring, are based on this thesis.

Pessimism, which expects of life what it cannot give, and therefore denies life, is but the result of the same thesis.

Materialism, with its strange enthusiastic assertion that man is but a process, is the lawful child of this teaching, which acknowledges that the life here below is a fallen life.

Spiritism, with its learned partisans, is the best proof that scientific and philosophical views are not free, but are based on the principle, inculcated by religion, that a blissful eternal life is natural to man.

This erroneous idea of the meaning of life has perverted the whole activity of man. The dogma of the fall and of the redemption of man has closed the most important and lawful domain of man's activity to him, and has excluded from the whole sphere of human knowledge the knowledge of what man must do to be happier and better. Science and philosophy fancy themselves the adversaries of so-called Christianity, and pride themselves upon the fact, while they, in reality, work for it. Science and philosophy address everything except the one important point: how man is to improve his condition and lead a better life. The teaching of morality, called ethics, has quite disappeared from our so-called Christian society.

Neither believers nor unbelievers ask themselves how we ought to live, and how we must use the reason that is given to us; but they ask themselves, 'Why is

our life here not such as we fancied it to be, and when will it be such as we wish
it to be?'

It is only through the influence of this false doctrine that we can explain how
it is that man has forgotten that his whole history is but an endeavor to solve the
contradictions between his rational and animal nature.

The religious and philosophical teachings of all nations (except the philosophical teachings of the so-called Christian world), Judaism, Buddhism, Brahmanism,
the teaching of Confucius, and of the sages of ancient Greece have but one purpose in view — the regulation of life, and the solution of the problem of how
man must strive to improve his condition and lead a better life. The teaching of
Confucius deals with personal improvement; Judaism consists of man's following
the covenant made with God, and Buddhism teaches each how to escape the evils
of life. Socrates taught personal improvement in the name of reason. The Stoics
acknowledge rational liberty as the sole basis of the true life.

The rational activity of man has always lain in enlightening, by reason, his
striving after good. Free will, says philosophy, is an illusion; and it prides itself
on the audacity of the assertion. But free will is not only an illusion; it is a word
that has really no meaning. It is a word invented by theologians and legislators;
and to try to disprove its existence is but wrestling with a windmill.

Reason, which enlightens our life and forces us to modify our actions, is not
an illusion, and cannot possibly be explained away. The following after reason in
order to attain happiness was a doctrine taught to mankind by all true teachers,
and in it lies the whole doctrine of Christ.

The doctrine of Christ concerns the son of man, and is applicable to all men,
i.e., it concerns the striving of all men after good; and it concerns human reason,
which enlightens man in his search. (To prove that 'the Son of Man' signifies the
son of man is superfluous. In order to consider the words, 'the Son of Man' as
having any other meaning, it would be necessary to prove that Christ purposely
used words that have another meaning to express what He wished to say. But
even if, according to the positive teaching of the Church, the words, 'the Son of
Man,' signify 'the Son of God,' the words, 'the Son of Man,' still signify man, for
Christ calls all men 'the sons of God.')

The doctrine of Christ concerning the son of man, the Son of God, which is the
basis of the whole gospel, is expressed in the clearest manner in His conversation
with Nicodemus. 'Every man,' He says, 'in addition to his consciousness of an
individual life, through his human parents, must admit that His birth is from
above' (John 3:5–7). That which man acknowledges in himself as being free, is
just what is born of the Eternal Being, of Him Whom we call God. This Son of
God in man, born of God, is what we must exalt in ourselves in order to obtain
the true life. The son of man is of the same nature as God (not begotten of God).
He who exalts in himself the Son of God over all the rest that is in him, he who
believes that life is in himself alone, will not find himself in contradiction with
life. The contradiction only results from men not believing in the light that is in
them; the light of which John the Evangelist speaks when he says, 'In him is life,
and the life is the light of men.'

Christ teaches us to exalt above all else the son of man, who is the Son of God and the light of men. He says, 'When you lift up the son of man, you will know that I do not speak of myself' (John 8:28). The Hebrews do not understand His words, and they ask, 'The son of man must be lifted up. Who is this son of man?' (John 12:34). He answers thus (John 12:35): 'Yet a little while is the light in you. Walk while you have the light, lest darkness come upon you; for he who walks in darkness does not know where he goes.' On being questioned what the words, 'Lift up the son of man' signify, Christ answers, 'To live according to the light that is in man.'

The son of man, according to the answer given by Christ, is the light in which man must walk while the light is in them. Luke 11:35: 'Take heed that the light that is in you is not darkness.' Matthew 6:23: 'If the light that is in you is darkness, how great is the darkness?' Christ speaks thus to all men.

Both before Christ and after Him men have said the same: that there lives in man a divine light, sent down from heaven, and that light is 'reason,' and each must follow that light alone, seeking for good by its aid alone. This has been said by the Brahmin teachers, by the Hebrew prophets, by Confucius, Socrates, Marcus Aurelius, Epictetus, and by all truly wise men who were not compilers of philosophical theories, but who sought the truth for their own good and that of all men.

And now, according to the dogma of the redemption, we find that it is altogether unnecessary to think or speak of that light in man. Believers say it is necessary to consider the nature of each person of the Trinity, and which of the sacraments must be observed; for the salvation of man will come, not of his own efforts, but through the Trinity, and by a regular observance of the sacraments. We must consider, say unbelievers, by what laws the infinitesimal particle of substance moves in the endless expanse of endless time; but it is not necessary to consider what reason requires of man for his own good, because the improvement of his state will not proceed from his own efforts, but from the general laws that we shall discover.

I am persuaded that, in a few centuries, the history of the so-called scientific activity in Europe during these latter ages will form an inexhaustible subject of laughter and pity for still later generations, who will report somewhat in this style: 'During several centuries the learned men of the small Western part of the great hemisphere were in a state of epidemic insanity, fancying that a life of eternal bliss was to be theirs; and were plunged in laborious studies of all kinds as to how, and according to what laws, that life was to begin for them, meanwhile doing nothing themselves, and never thinking of improving themselves.' And still more touching will this seem to the future historian when he finds that these men had a teacher who clearly and definitely explained to them what they were to do in order to be happier, but that the teacher's words were taken by some to mean that He would come in a cloud to set all right, while others said that the words of the Teacher were perfect, but impracticable; for human life was not such as they wished it to be, and was not worth caring about; that human intellect was to be directed toward a study of the laws of this life, without any reference to the good of man.

The Church says that the doctrine of Christ is impracticable, because life here is but a suggestion of the true life; it cannot be good — it is all evil. The best way to live this life is to despise it, and to live by faith, i.e., by fancy, in a future life of eternal bliss. Philosophy, science, and public opinion say that the doctrine of Christ is impracticable because the life of man does not depend on the light of reason, but on general laws; and that there is no need to enlighten life by our reason or to seek to be guided by reason, for we must live as we can, firmly believing that, according to the laws of historical and sociological progress, after we have lived badly for a very long time, our life will grow very good of itself.

Men come to a farm, and find all they want there; a house with all necessary utensils, barns full of corn, cellars full of all kinds of provisions; in the yard are implements of husbandry, tools, harnesses, horses, cows, and sheep — in a word, all that is necessary for living contentedly. Men crowd in and begin to use what they find, each mindful of himself alone, never thinking of leaving anything either for those who are with him in the house, or for those who are to come after him. Each wishes to have all for himself. Each hastens to take as much as he can, and consequent destruction of everything ensues; all are struggling, fighting to possess the property themselves; milk cows and unshorn sheep about to kid are killed for meat; the ovens are heated with benches and carts; the men fight for milk and for corn; and thus spill, spoil, and waste more than they use. Not one of them can eat a morsel in peace, each is snarling at his neighbor; a stronger man comes and takes possession of all, and he is despoiled in his turn.

At last these men, all bruised and exhausted with fighting and hunger, leave the farm. The master again makes the farm ready so that men may live there in peace. Again plenty fills the yard, and again passers-by come in, and the struggling and fighting are renewed; all is wasted once more, and the worn-out, bruised, and angry men again leave the farm, abusing and hating their companions and the master too, for having so sparingly and so poorly provided for them. Once again the good master gets the farm ready, and the struggling returns over and over again. Now, one day, among the new comers there appears a teacher who says, 'Brethren, we are all wrong. See what plenty there is here; see how carefully all is provided. There will be enough, not only for us, but also for those who come after us, if we simply live wisely. Let us not despoil, but rather let us help each other. Let us sow, plough, and breed cattle, and it will be well for us all.' And it happened that some understood what the Teacher said, and they followed His advice; they ceased fighting and robbing each other, and they set to work. But some had not heard the Teacher's words, and others had heard, but did not believe Him, and they did not do what He enjoined, but continued to fight as before, and, after wasting the master's property, they too left the farm. Those who obeyed the Teacher said, 'Do not fight, do not waste the master's property; it will be better for you if you do not act thus. Do as our Teacher bids us.' But there were many who had not heard, or would not believe, and things went on in the old way. But it is said that the time came when all in the farm heard the Teacher's words, and not only understood them, but knew that God Himself spoke to them through the Teacher; that the Teacher was God; and all believed each word the Teacher said to be a true and sacred word. Yet it is reported that even after this, instead of all living according to the words of the Teacher, it came to pass that none turned away from violence; they all fell to struggling and fighting again. 'We are sure, now,' they said, 'that it must be so, that it cannot be otherwise.'

What could that mean? Even beasts know in what manner to eat their food without trampling it underfoot; and men who knew how to live better, who believed that God Himself had taught them how they were to live, lived worse, because, as they said, they could not live otherwise. These men must have fallen into some delusion. What could those men in the farm have imagined, to induce them to lead their former lives, despoiling each other, wasting their master's property, and ruining themselves while believing in the words of the Teacher? It was this: the Teacher had said to them, 'The life you lead here is a bad one, improve it and you shall be happy.' They fancied that the Teacher condemned their life in the farm, and promised them another and better life, in some other place, and not in that farm. Whereupon they concluded that the farm was but an inn, and that it was not worth while trying to live well in it; and that the only thing necessary was to endeavor not to lose the good life promised to them elsewhere. It is only thus that the strange conduct can be explained; for both those who believed that the Teacher was God, and those who acknowledged him to be a clever man and His words to be just, continued to live contrary to His instructions.

If men would but keep from ruining their own lives, and keep from expecting someone from outside to come and help them — either Christ on the clouds, with the flourish of trumpets, or some historical law, or the law of the differentiation and integration of power! No one will help them, if they do not help themselves. And that is easily done. Let them expect nothing, either from heaven or earth, and simply cease from ruining their own lives.

Chapter VIII

Granting, then, that the doctrine of Christ gives bliss to the world; granting that it is rational; and that man, as a rational being, has no right to renounce it; what can one man do alone, amidst a world of men who do not fulfill the law of Christ? If all would agree to practice the doctrine of Christ, its fulfillment would be possible; but what can the efforts of one man avail, if the whole world is against him? How often do we hear it said, 'If, amidst a whole world of men who do not fulfill the doctrine of Christ, I alone begin to follow it, by giving up what I love, by letting my cheek be struck, or even by refusing to take an oath, or to have any part in war, I shall be robbed, and, if I do not starve, I shall be either beaten to death, or imprisoned, or shot; and I shall have destroyed the happiness of my whole life, and even my life itself, in vain.'

We often hear men argue thus, and I said the same myself, until I had entirely set aside the influence of Church teaching, which had prevented my taking in the full meaning of Christ's doctrine about life.

Christ gives His doctrine as the means of salvation from the corrupt life that those who do not follow His teaching lead, and yet I say that I should like to follow it, but cannot make up my mind to ruin my life! It would seem, then, that I do not consider my life as corrupt, but as something real and good, and something that is my own. It is just in the conviction that this earthly, individual life is something real, and something that actually belongs to us, that the misunderstanding lies, which prevents our comprehending the doctrine of Christ. Christ knows the delusion by which men consider their own individual lives as something real, and something to which they have a personal right; and He shows them, in a series of sermons and parables, that they have no claims on life, that they have, indeed, no life at all, until they attain true life by renouncing the shadow of which they call their life.

In order to understand Christ's doctrine of salvation, we must, first of all, comprehend what the prophets Solomon, Buddha, and all the sages of the world have said concerning the individual life of man. We may, as Pascal says, live on without thinking of all this, holding a screen before our eyes, which hides from us the abyss of death, toward which we are all hastening; but we need only reflect upon what the individual life of man is to be convinced that his entire life, if it is only the individual life, is of no importance for each separate man.

In order to understand the doctrine of Christ, we must first of all consider ourselves and repent, so that in us may be fulfilled the μετανοια, which the precursor of Christ, John the Baptist, speaks of when preaching to men who, like ourselves, had gone astray. He says first of all, 'Repent,' i.e., consider yourselves, 'otherwise you shall all perish.' He says, 'The axe is already laid to the root of the tree to hew it down. Death and destruction are close at hand. Remember this, and alter your lives.' Christ begins His preaching with the same words, 'Repent, or you shall all perish.'

Luke 13:1–5: Christ hears of the destruction of the Galileans, killed by Pilate, and He says, 'Do you suppose that these Galileans were sinners above all the Galileans, because they suffered thus? I tell you, no, but unless you repent, you shall all likewise perish. Or do you think that those eighteen men, upon whom the tower of Siloam fell and killed them, were sinners above all men who lived in Jerusalem? I tell you, no, but unless you repent, you shall all likewise perish.'

If Christ lived in our days in Russia, He would have said, 'Do you suppose that those who were burnt in the circus at Berditche, or who perished on the embankment near Koukouevo, were sinners above all others? You shall likewise perish if you do not repent, if you do not find that which is imperishable. The death of those who were crushed by the tower, who were burnt in the circus, fills you with awe, but death, awful and inevitable, awaits you too. And you endeavor in vain to forget it. If it comes upon you unawares, it will be more awful still.'

He says (Luke 12:54–57), 'When you see a cloud rise out of the west, you immediately say there is a shower coming, and so it is. And when the south wind blows, you say there will be heat, and so it is. Hypocrites, you can discern the face of the sky and of the earth, but how is it that you do not discern this time? Why you yourselves not judge what must be?'

'You can judge, according to various signs, what the weather will be like. How is it then, that you cannot see what awaits you yourselves? You may try to escape peril; you may take the greatest care of your life, and still, if Pilate does not kill you, the tower will crush you, and if neither Pilate nor the tower destroys you, you will die in your bed in worse tortures.'

Make a simple calculation, as worldly men do when they begin any business, as, for instance, erecting a tower, going to war, or building a factory. They work with some rational end in view. Luke 14:28–31: 'For which of you, intending to build a tower, does not sit down first and count the cost, to see whether he has sufficient resources to finish it? Lest by chance after he has laid the foundation, and is not able to finish it, all that behold begin to mock him, saying, "This man began to build and was not able to finish." Or, what king going to make war against another king does not sit down first and consult whether he is able, with ten thousand, to meet him who comes against him with twenty thousand?'

'Isn't it senseless to work at what will never be finished, however hard you may try! Death will always come before you have built up the tower of your earthly happiness. And if you know beforehand that however you may struggle against death, it will conquer you, would it not be better, instead of struggling against it, not to put your whole soul into what shall surely perish, but to seek some work that cannot be destroyed by inevitable death?'

Luke 12:22–27: And He said to His disciples, 'Therefore I say to you, take no thought for your life, what you shall eat; neither for the body, what you shall put on. Your life is more than meat, and your body is more than clothing. Consider the ravens; for they neither sow nor reap; they neither have storehouse nor barn, and God feeds them; how much more are you better than they? And which of you by thinking about it can add to his stature even one cubit? If you are not able to do the very thing that is least, why do you take thought for the rest? Consider the lilies, how they grow; they do not toil, they do not spin; and yet I say to you that Solomon, in all his glory, was not arrayed like one of these.'

However much a man may care about body and food, he cannot add one hour to his life. Then isn't it foolish to trouble oneself about things that cannot be done?

While knowing that the end is death, you care only to assure your lives by gaining wealth. Life cannot be assured by wealth. Why will you not comprehend that you but delude yourselves with a ridiculous deception?

The purpose of life, Christ says, does not lie in what we possess, and in what we gain, what is not ourselves; it must lie in something else than that. He says (Luke 12:16–21) that the life of man, in spite of all his riches, does not depend upon his property. 'The ground of a certain rich man brought forth plentifully; and he thought within himself, "What shall I do? I have no room to store my fruits." And he said, "I will do this: I will pull down my barns and build larger ones, and there I will store all my corn and all my goods. And I will say to my soul, Soul! You have much goods laid up for many years; take your ease, eat, drink, be merry." But God said to him, "You fool, this night your soul shall be required of you; then whose shall those things be, which you have provided?" So it is with him who lays up treasure for himself, and is not rich toward God.'

Death stands every moment over you. (Luke 12:35–40) 'Therefore, stay dressed and keep your lights shining; and you yourselves be like men who wait for their lord, when he will return from the wedding; that when he comes and knocks, they may open to him immediately. And if he shall come in the second watch, or come in the third watch, and find them so, blessed are those servants. And know this: if the owner of the house had known what hour the thief would come, he would have watched, and not have allowed his house to be broken into. Therefore, be ready also; for the Son of Man comes at an hour when you do not think.'

The parables of the virgins awaiting the bridegroom, of the end of the age, and of the last judgment all refer, according to the opinion of interpreters, not merely to the end of the world, but also to the peril in which every man hourly stands.

Death, death, death attends us every second. Our lives are passed in the presence of death. While working individually for your future, you well know that the future will give you nothing but death. And death will destroy all you worked for. Thus, it is clear that life for oneself can never have any meaning. If there is a rational life, it must be some other kind of life; it must be one, the purpose of which does not consist in securing one's own future. To live rationally, we must live so that death cannot destroy our life.

Luke 10:41: 'Martha, Martha, you are careful and troubled about many things. But one thing is necessary.'

All the innumerable affairs that we transact for ourselves will be of no use to us in the future; all such things are but the illusion with which we deceive ourselves. 'But one thing is necessary.'

The state of man from the day of his birth is such that inevitable destruction awaits him, that is, a senseless life and a senseless death, if he does not find what alone is necessary for the true life. Christ reveals to men that which alone gives them the true life. He does not invent it, He does not promise to give it by His divine power; He only shows mankind that, besides the individual life, there must be another life, which is truth, and not deception.

Christ, in his parable of the vine-dresser (Matthew 21:33–42), explains the source of human error, which hides the truth from men, and which makes them consider the shadow of life, their own individual life, as the true one.

Certain men, living in their master's cultivated garden, fancied themselves the owners of that garden; and that error leads to a series of irrational and cruel actions on the part of those men, ending in their banishment, their exclusion from that life in the garden. So likewise do we fancy that the life of each of us is his own, that we have a right to it, and that we can do as we like with it, without being responsible to any one. We cannot, therefore, avoid the same series of senseless and cruel actions and misfortunes, or escape the same exclusion from the life we misuse. As the vine-dressers fancied that the more cruel they were the better they would assure their own prosperity, by killing the servants and the master's son, so do we fancy that the more cruel we are the more independent we shall become.

As it was with the vine-dressers, who, after refusing others the fruits of the garden, were driven out themselves by their master, so is it with men, who fancy that life for self is the true life. Death expels them and others take their place, not as a punishment, but merely because those men did not understand life. As the men in the garden either forgot, or would not admit, that the garden had only been entrusted to their care, that it was already cultivated and fenced around, and somebody had previously been working in it for them, and therefore expected them to work too, for the sake of others; so do men, while living for themselves, forget, or fail to recognize, all that had been done by others before their birth, and all that is done during their lifetime; and that, therefore, something is expected of them too; they choose to forget that all the blessings of life, which they enjoy, were entrusted and are entrusted to them, and must, therefore, either be transferred or given up.

This improved view of life, this μετανοια, is the cornerstone of the doctrine of Christ, as He says at the end of the parable. According to Christ's doctrine, the vine-dressers, who lived in the vineyard that they had not cultivated themselves, should have known and felt that they were deeply indebted to the master; and so should men likewise understand and feel that, from the day of their birth to the day of their death, they owe a heavy debt to those who lived before them, to those who still live, and to those who are to live after them. They should understand that every hour of the life they continue to live that debt grows heavier; and that, therefore, the man who lives for himself, and does not acknowledge the obligation that binds him to life and to the principle of life, deprives himself of life. He should understand that by living thus he destroys his life, while desiring to save it.

The true life is but a continuation of past life, and works for the good of the present life, as well as for that of the future. To be a sharer of that life, man must renounce his own will and fulfill the will of the Father of life, who gave it to the son of man.

John 8:35: 'The servant who does his own will, and not that of his master, does not abide for ever in the house of his master; only the son, who fulfills the will of the father, abides forever,' Christ says, expressing the same idea in another sense.

The will of the Father of life is not the life of the individual man, but of the 'son of man,' that lives in men; and therefore a man keeps his life only when he considers it as a trust given to him by the Father, in order to serve the good of all; and he really lives when he lives not for himself, but for the 'son of man.'

Matthew 25:14–46: A householder gave each of his servants a share of his property and left them, without any instructions. Some of the servants, though they had not received any orders from their master concerning the way in which they were to use their share of the master's property, understood that it was not theirs, but his, and that the property was to grow; they, therefore, worked for the master. And the servants who had worked for the master became shareholders of the master's business, while those who had not worked were deprived of what had been given to them.

The life of the son of man is given to all men, and they are not told why it is given to them. Some understand that life is not their own, but is a trust, and that it must serve the life of the 'son of man.' Others, under the pretext that they do not understand the purpose of life, do not live up to that high aim. Those who do are united to the source of life; and those who do not, are deprived of life. And, from the verses 31 to 46, Christ tells us what is meant by serving the 'son of man,' and in what the reward of that service consists.

The son of man, according to the words of Christ, will say (v. 34) as the king did, 'Come, you blessed of the Father, inherit the kingdom prepared for you, for I was hungry, and you gave me meat; I was thirsty, and you gave me drink; you clothed, visited, and comforted me; for I am the same in you, and in the least of those whom you took pity on, and to whom you have done good. You lived, not for yourselves, but for the 'son of man,' and therefore shall you have eternal life.'

Christ speaks only of that eternal life throughout the gospel. And strange as it may seem to say so of Christ, who Himself rose from the dead, and who promised to raise all men, He never, by a single word, confirmed the belief in individual resurrection or in individual immortality beyond the grave, but He even attached to the raising up of the dead in the kingdom of the Messiah, as taught by the Pharisees, a meaning that excluded the idea of individual resurrection.

The Sadducees disputed the raising up of the dead. The Pharisees acknowledged it, as all true believers among the Jews still do. The raising up of the dead (not the resurrection, as the word has been erroneously translated) will, according to the Jewish belief, be accomplished at the coming of the Messiah, and the establishing of the kingdom of God on earth. And Christ, on meeting with this belief in a temporary, local, and carnal resurrection, rejects it, and sets in its place His doctrine of the restoration to eternal life in God.

When the Sadducees, who said there was no resurrection, and supposed that Christ agreed in opinion with the Pharisees, asked Him, 'Whose wife shall she be, of the seven?' He gives a clear and definite answer to both questions.

He says (Matthew 22:29–32, Mark 12:24–27, Luke 20:34–38), 'You err, not knowing the scripture or the power of God.' And in refutation of the belief of the Pharisees, He says, 'The raising up of the dead is neither carnal nor individual. Those who are raised from the dead become the sons of God and live like angels (the powers of God) in heaven (with God), and there can be no question for them whose wife she will be, because, being one with God, they lose all individuality.' Concerning the raising up of the dead, He continues, in reply to the Sadducees, who acknowledged only an earthly life, and nothing but an earthly carnal life, 'Have you not read what God said to you? The Scripture says that God said to Moses, from the bush, "I am the God of Abraham, the God of Isaac, and the God of Jacob." If God said to Moses that He was the God of Jacob, then Jacob is not dead; for God is not the God of the dead, but of the living. With God all are living. And therefore, if there is a living God, the man who is one with God lives too.'

In reply to the Pharisees, Christ says that the raising from the dead cannot be carnal and individual. In reply to the Sadducees, He says that, besides an individual and temporary life, there is another life in communion with God.

Denying individual and carnal resurrection, Christ asserts that the raising from the dead lies in the transfusion of man's life into God. Christ preaches salvation from individual life, and sets that salvation in the exaltation of the son of man and a life in God. Connecting His doctrine with that of the Hebrews, as far as concerns the coming of the Messiah, He speaks to them of the raising up of the son of man from the dead, thereby meaning, not a personal carnal rising from the dead, but an awakening to life in God. Of individual carnal resurrection He never speaks. The best proof that Christ never preached the resurrection of men from the dead is found in the very two texts quoted by theologians in confirmation of His doctrine of resurrection. These two texts are Matthew 25:31–46 and John 5:28–29. In the first He speaks of the coming, that is, the raising up, the exaltation, of the son of man (we find the same in Matthew 10:23), and the greatness and power of the son of man are likened to those of a king. In the second text, Christ speaks of the raising up of true life here on earth, as expressed in the 24th verse.

It only needs a closer consideration of the meaning of Christ's doctrine of eternal life in God; it only needs to re-establish in our minds the teaching of the Hebrew prophets to enable us to comprehend that if Christ had wished to preach the doctrine of the resurrection of the dead, which, at that time was being embodied in the Talmud, and was a subject of dispute, He would have done so, clearly and definitely; yet, on the contrary, He not only avoided preaching that doctrine, but even refuted it; nor do we find a single passage in the gospel to confirm it. The two above-mentioned texts have a very different meaning.

Strange as the assertion may seem to those who have not studied the gospel, never in a single passage does Christ speak of His own personal resurrection. If, as theologians maintain, the basis of the Christian faith is the resurrection of Christ, the least we could expect would be that Christ, knowing He would rise from the dead, and that upon His rising the chief dogma of the faith would be founded, should at least once have said so, clearly and definitely. Yet He never does; nor do we find any mention made of His resurrection throughout the whole canonical gospel. The doctrine taught is the exaltation of the 'son of man,' or, in other words, of the substance of life in man; and this is to acknowledge one's self to be the son of God. In Himself, Christ personifies man, who acknowledges Himself to be the Son of God. Matthew 16:13–20: He asks the disciples what men say of Him, the son of man. The disciples answer that some think Him to be John, miraculously raised from the dead; some think Him a prophet; some Elijah, come down from heaven. 'And what do you think of me?' He asks. And Peter, thinking of Christ as he himself did, answers, 'You are the Messiah, the son of the living God.' And Christ says, 'Flesh and blood has not revealed it to you, but our Father who is in heaven,' or, 'You have understood, not because you have believed the words of men, but because, knowing yourself to be the son of God, you have understood me.' And having explained to Peter that true faith lies in our knowing ourselves to be the sons of God, Christ says to the other disciples (v. 20) that they should, in future, tell no man that He, Jesus, is the Messiah. And then Christ says that, though He will be put to torture and death, the son of man, knowing Himself to be the son of God, will be raised up and will triumph over all. And yet these words are interpreted as foretelling His resurrection.

John 2:19–22, Matthew 12:40, Luke 11:20, Matthew 16:21, Matthew 16:4, Mark 8:31, Luke 9:22, Matthew 17:23, Mark 9:31, Matthew 20:19, Mark 10:34, Luke 18:33, Matthew 26:32, Mark 14:48. These fourteen texts are all supposed to prove that Christ foretold His resurrection. In three of these texts He speaks of Jonah in the belly of the whale; and in one, of the raising of the temple. In the other ten texts, Christ says that the son of man cannot be destroyed forever; but nowhere do we find one word concerning His resurrection.

Indeed, in the original, the word 'resurrection' does not occur in any one of these texts. Give a man, unacquainted with theological interpretation, but with some knowledge of Greek, these texts to translate, and he will never render their meaning in the way our translators of the gospel have done. There are, in the original, two different words in these texts: the one is ανιϛτημι, the other is εγειρω. One of these words signifies 'to raise.' The other signifies 'to rouse or waken,' or it might be to awaken, to rise. But neither of them can possibly mean 'rise from the dead.' In order to be quite sure that these Greek words, and the Hebrew equivalent 'coum,' cannot signify 'to rise from the dead,' it will suffice to compare the texts in which these words are used. They occur very often, but never in the sense of 'rise from the dead.'

The word 'resuscitate,' 'auferstehen,' 'réssusciter,' does not exist either in the Greek or in the Hebrew languages, any more than did the idea itself, which the word implies. In order to express the idea of resurrection in Greek or in Hebrew, a periphrasis must be made use of — either 'he rose from the dead,' or 'he awoke from the dead.' It is thus in Matthew 14:2, where we read that Herod supposed that John the Baptist had risen from the dead; the expression is, 'woke up from the dead.' We find the same in the gospel according to St. Luke 16:31, in the parable of Lazarus. Christ says that even if a man rose from the dead they would not believe him. We again find, in this text, the words 'risen from the dead.' In the texts where the words 'to rise' or 'to wake up,' are used without the addition of the words 'from the dead,' they never did signify, and never can be supposed to signify, 'resurrection.' When Christ speaks of Himself in the above-mentioned passages, which are considered as proofs that He foretold His resurrection, He never once appends the words, 'from the dead'.

Our idea of resurrection is so far from the Hebrews' ideas of life that we cannot even imagine Christ could have spoken to them of resurrection and of an eternal, individual life common to all men. The idea of a future individual life has not been transmitted to us, either through the teaching of the Hebrews or through the doctrine of Christ. It made its way into the teaching of the Church from a very different source. Strange as it may sound, it must be confessed that a belief in a future individual life is the lowest and grossest conception, based only on a confusion of sleep with death, which is common to all barbarous nations. The teaching of the Hebrews, however, stood immeasurably higher than that conception.

We feel so convinced that this superstition is a very exalted one that we very seriously allege, as a proof of the superiority of our doctrine over all others, the fact that we uphold that superstition, while others, as for instance, the Chinese and the Hindus, do not. This is maintained, not only by theologians, but also by free-thinking learned historians of religion such as Tille, Max Müller, and others. Classifying the various religions, they assert that the religions that keep to that superstition are superior to those that do not. The free-thinker, Schoppenhauer, calls the Hebrew religion the most contemptible (niederträchstigste) of all, because it contains no idea (keine idee) of the immortality of the soul. And, indeed, in the Hebrew religion, neither the meaning nor the word expressive of it exists. Eternal life in the Hebrew language is 'haieoïlom.' The word 'oïlom' signifies, 'endless, immutable.' 'Oïlom' likewise signifies 'world' — cosmos. Life in general, and especially eternal life, haieoïlom is, according to the Hebrews, proper to God alone. God is the God of life — the living God. Man, according to the Hebrew belief, is always mortal. God alone lives forever. In the five books of Moses we find the words 'eternal life' used twice. Once in Deuteronomy 32:39–40, God says, 'See now that I am I, and there is no other God but Me. I kill and I make alive, I wound and I heal, neither is there any who can be delivered from Me. I lift up my hand to heaven and say, I live for ever.' In the book of Genesis 3:22, God says, 'Behold, the man has eaten of the fruit of the tree of knowledge of good and evil, and has become like one of us; and now, he might put forth his hand and take also from the tree of life, and eat, and live for ever.' These are the only two cases in which the words 'eternal life' are used in the Old Testament — excepting one chapter of the apocryphal book of Daniel — and they clearly define the idea the Hebrews had both of life in general and of eternal life. Life itself, according to Jewish belief, is eternal, and it is such in God; man is always mortal — such is his nature.

The Old Testament does not tell us, as our Bible histories do, that God breathed an immortal soul into man, nor that the first man was immortal until he sinned. According to the Book of Genesis (1:26), God created man, as He did all other living creatures, male and female, and commanded them to increase and multiply. God spoke of man just as he spoke of beast. In the second chapter it is said that man learned to 'know good and evil.' But we are told too, that God 'drove man out of Eden, and barred his way to the tree of life.' Thus man did not eat of the fruit of the tree of life, and thus he did not attain the haieoïlom, i.e., eternal life, but remained mortal.

According to Jewish doctrine, man is mortal. Life for him is but a life that continues in the people, from generation to generation. Only the people, according to Jewish doctrine, can live. When God says you shall live and not die, he speaks to the people. The life breathed by God into man is but a mortal life for each individually, but it continues from generation to generation if men fulfill their covenant with God, if they keep the conditions laid down by God.

After expounding the laws, and declaring that these laws were not in heaven, but in their own hearts, Moses says (Deuteronomy 30:15), 'See, I now set before you life and good, death and evil, exhorting you to love God and walk in His ways, and to keep His commandments, that you may live.' And verse 19: 'I call heaven and earth to record against you that I have set before you life and death, blessing and cursing; choose life, that you and your descendants may live, loving God, obeying Him and cleaving to Him; for He is your life and the length of your days.'

The principal difference between our idea of human life and that of the Hebrews is that, according to us, our mortal life — which passes on from generation to generation — is not the true life, but a fallen one, a temporary corrupt life; while, according to the Hebrews this life is the true one, it is the highest blessing given to man, and given to him on the condition that he fulfills the will of God. From our point of view, the transition of that fallen life from generation to generation is the continuation of the curse. From the Hebrew point of view it is the highest blessing man can attain, and he attains it by fulfilling the will of God.

It is on this idea of life that Christ bases his doctrine concerning the true or eternal life, which He opposes to mortal, individual life. 'Search the Scriptures,' Christ says to the Hebrews (John 5:39), 'for in them you think you have eternal life.'

A young man asks Christ (Matthew 19) what he should do to have eternal life. In answer to his question Christ says, 'If you will enter into life' (He does not say life eternal, but 'life'), 'keep the commandments.' He says the same to the lawyers, 'Do this, and you shall live' (Luke 10:28); and again He says 'live' without adding 'eternally.' In both these cases Christ defines what each man should understand by the words 'eternal life.' In using these words He says to the Hebrews what is more than once said in their law, that fulfilling the will of God is eternal life.

Christ contrasts a temporary, personal, individual life with the eternal life, which, according to Deuteronomy, God promised to Israel, with the only difference that, according to the Hebrews, eternal life was to continue only among the chosen people of Israel, and that it was necessary, in order to attain that life, to keep the laws given by God exclusively to Israel; but, according to the doctrine of Christ, eternal life continues in the son of man, and, in order to keep it, it is necessary to fulfill the laws of Christ, which teach what the will of God is for all mankind.

It is not a life beyond the grave that Christ contrasts with individual life, but a life bound up with the present, past, and future of all mankind — the life of the 'son of man.'

Individual life was redeemed from perdition, according to the Hebrews, only by fulfilling the will of God, expressed in the commandments given by God to Moses. It was only thus that life was not destroyed, but was to pass from generation to generation, among the chosen people of God. Individual life is saved from perdition, according to the doctrine of Christ, likewise by fulfilling the will of God, expressed in the commandments of Christ. It is only thus that individual life does not perish, but becomes eternal in the son of man. The only difference between the two doctrines is that, according to Moses, serving God meant the serving Him of but one people, whereas, according to Christ, the serving of God the Father means the serving of God by all mankind. Life could hardly continue through long generations among one people; for the nation itself might disappear off the face of the earth, and its continuation would depend upon the increase or diminution of posterity. But endless life, according to the doctrine of Christ, is sure, for it is transferred into the son of man living up to the will of the Father.

Let us suppose that Christ's words concerning the day of judgment and the end of the world, as well as the words we read in the gospel of St. John, do promise a life beyond the grave for the souls of the dead, yet there can be no doubt that His doctrine of the light of life, of the kingdom of God, has a meaning as intelligible to us as it was to his hearers; i.e., that true life is but the life of the son of man, according to the will of the Father. This can be more easily admitted, as the doctrine concerning true life, according to the will of the Father of Life, includes the idea of immortality and life beyond the grave. It would perhaps be more just to infer that man, after a life passed in following his own will in this world, will not enjoy an eternal individual life of bliss in paradise. That would perhaps be more just, but to think thus, to believe in eternal bliss awaiting me as a reward for the good I have done, and eternal torment as the punishment of my evil deeds, does not lead to a clear comprehension of Christ's doctrine. To think thus is, on the contrary, to do away with the groundwork of Christ's doctrine.

The whole purpose of Christ's doctrine is to teach His disciples that, individual life being but a delusion, they should renounce it and transfer their individual lives into the life of all humanity, into the life of the son of man. The doctrine of the immortality of each soul does not require of us to renounce our lives, but, on the contrary, confirms their individuality forever.

According to the ideas of the Hebrews, the Chinese, and the Hindus, and of all those who do not believe in the dogmas of the fall of man and the redemption, the life we have is life. Man lives, has children, educates them, grows old, and dies. His children grow up and continue his life, which goes on without intermission from generation to generation, existing just as all else in the world exists — stones, metals, plants, beasts, and all else. Life is life, and we must make the most of it. To live for self alone is irrational. And, therefore, since man has first existed on the earth, each one seeks some aim in life beyond his own individual life. He lives for his children, his family, his nation, for humanity, for all that does not die with his individual life.

Now, according to the teaching of our Church, life, the greatest blessing known to us, is only a part of life, the rest of which is kept from us for a time. According to the Church, our life is not the life God wished to give us, not the life God ought to have given to us; but a corrupt, bad, fallen life, only an imperfect specimen of what life should be.

The chief problem of life, according to this thesis, does not consist in leading the mortal life that is given to us as the giver of it whishes us to do; not in our considering it eternal from generation to generation, as the Hebrews do; nor in uniting it to the will of the Father, as Christ taught us to do, but in persuading ourselves that after this life the true life will begin.

Christ says nothing of that imaginary life. The theories of the fall of Adam, of eternal life in paradise, and of the immortal soul breathed by God into Adam, were unknown to Christ, and therefore He does not mention them, nor even allude to them.

Christ speaks of the life that is, and that always will be. We speak of an imaginary life, which never did exist. Then how are we to understand the doctrine of Christ?

Christ could never have supposed so strange an idea among His followers. He supposes all men to understand that individual life must inevitably perish; and He reveals a life that cannot perish. Christ comforts those who are in trouble; but His doctrine can give nothing to those who are convinced that they have more than Christ can give.

Suppose I were to exhort a man to work, assuring him that he would thereby earn food and clothing, and that man were suddenly to discover he was already a millionaire, isn't it obvious that he would not heed my words?

It is thus with the doctrine of Christ. Why should I work, when I can be rich without doing so? What profit shall I have of living up to the commandments of God, when I am convinced that, whether I do or not, I shall live forever, individually?

We are taught that Christ-God, the second person of the Trinity, saved mankind by being incarnate and by taking upon Himself the sin of Adam and of all mankind; that He redeemed man from sin and the wrath of the first person of the Trinity, and that He instituted the Church and the sacraments for our salvation; that we have but to believe this to be saved, and to attain an eternal, individual life beyond the grave. But we cannot deny that Christ likewise saved men by warning them of their inevitable destruction, and still saves them by the same; and that His words — 'I am the way, the life, and the truth' — point out to us the true path of life, instead of the wrong path of individual life that we trod before.

There may be men who doubt the existence of life beyond the grave, and of salvation being based on redemption, but no one can doubt the salvation of all men in general, and of each individually, through their being warned of the inevitable destruction brought on by individual life, and through being shown that the true way to salvation lies in the fusion of their will with the will of the Father. Let any rational being ask himself what are life and death as applied to himself personally. Let him try to attach any other meaning to life and death than that which Christ pointed out.

Every idea of individual life, if it is not based on the renouncing of self for the service of man, of mankind, of the son of man, is an illusion that vanishes at the first touch of reason. I cannot doubt that, though my individual life is perishable, the life of the world according to the will of the Father can never be destroyed; and that a fusion with it alone makes salvation possible for me. But that is so little, compared to the elevated religious faith in a future life! Little, I grant, but it is sure. I lose my way in a snowdrift. A man assures me that he sees lights in the distance; that there is a village nearby. He thinks he sees the lights, and so do I; but it only seems to us that we see them because we desire to see them, for we tried to reach these same lights before, and could not find them. One of us walks on through the snow, and in a short time comes out onto the road and cries, 'Do not go on, the lights you see are only in your imagination; you will lose your way and perish! I stand on firm ground, follow me, this road will lead us out!'

That is but little. While believing in the lights, which glimmered before our dazzled eyes, we saw ourselves in our imaginations already in the village, in a warm hut, in safety and at rest, while here there was only firm ground. Yes; but if we follow the man who spoke first we shall inevitably freeze to death; if we mind the second, we shall reach the good road.

And what shall I do, if I alone have understood the doctrine of Christ and believe in it, among all those who do not understand and will not fulfill it?

What shall I do? Shall I live as all do, or live according to Christ's doctrine? I understand His commandments, and I see that the fulfilling of them will lead me, and all men, to perfect happiness. I understand that it is the will of the Author of all things, the will of Him from whom I have life, that these commandments should be fulfilled.

I understand that, whatever I may do, I shall inevitably perish, as will all those around me, after a senseless life and death, if I do not fulfill the will of the Father; and that the only possibility of salvation lies in fulfilling it.

By acting as others do, I act against the good of all men, I act contrary to the will of the Father of life, and I deprive myself of the only possibility of bettering my hopeless state. By doing what Christ teaches me I shall ensure the good of all men — of those who live at present, and of those who are to live after me. I do what He who gave me life desires me to do. I do what can alone save me.

The circus in Berditche is on fire. All crowd toward the door, crushing each other in their efforts to open the door, which opens inward. A savior comes and says to them, 'Move further from the door, turn back; the closer you all stand to the door, the less hope of safety there is for you. If you turn back you will find an exit, and you will be saved!'

Whether I alone hear the words and believe matters but little; but having heard and believed, can I do otherwise than turn back and call upon the others to follow the voice of him who comes to save them? I shall, perhaps, be smothered, crushed, or killed; but the sole hope of safety is in my going toward the only exit. A savior must be a savior indeed, i.e., he must save. And the salvation of Christ is salvation indeed. He appeared, He spoke, and mankind is now saved.

The circus burned for a whole hour; and it was necessary to make haste, or else all could not have been saved. But the world has been burning for eighteen hundred years; burning from the time Christ said, 'I come to send fire on the earth; and how I languish until it is kindled.' And it will burn until men are saved.

Wasn't man created, and doesn't the fire burn, only that the happiness of man might be saved from it?

I know there is no other door, either for myself or for those who suffer with me in this life. I know that neither those around me nor I can be saved, except by fulfilling the commandments of Christ, which give the highest bliss to all mankind.

I may have more to suffer. I may die earlier, through fulfilling Christ's doctrine. I fear neither suffering nor death. He who does not see how senseless and perishable his individual life is, he who thinks that he will not die, may fear. But, knowing that life for individual happiness alone is foolish to the highest degree, and that the end of that foolish life will be but a foolish death, I cannot fear it. I shall die, as all do, as those who do not fulfill Christ's doctrine do — yet my life and death will have some meaning for myself and for all. My life and death will minister to the salvation and lives of all men; and that is what Christ taught us.

Chapter IX

Were all to fulfill Christ's doctrine, the kingdom of God would be on earth. If I fulfill it, I do what is best for all mankind and myself. I should be helping that kingdom to come.

But where shall I find the faith that will enable me to obey Christ's teaching, to practice it, and never to swerve from it? 'I believe, Lord; help my unbelief.'

The apostles begged Christ to confirm their faith. 'I desire to do good, yet I do evil,' says Paul the apostle.

'It is hard to be saved.' This is what each says and thinks.

A drowning man calls for help. A rope is thrown him. It could save him; but the drowning man cries, 'Confirm my belief that this rope can save me.' 'I believe,' says the man, 'that it can save me; but help my unbelief.'

What does that mean? If a man does not take hold of what alone can save him, doesn't it prove that he is unaware of the danger he is in?

How can a Christian who professes to believe in the divinity of Christ and of His doctrine say that he would believe if he could? God Himself, when on earth, said, 'You are on the eve of eternal torment and fire, of complete, eternal darkness. I bring you salvation; do as I tell you, and you shall be saved.' Can a Christian reject the salvation offered him – remain unmindful of his Savior's words, and say, 'Help my unbelief?'

If a man spoke thus, would it not seem as if he not only refused to believe that destruction awaited him, but was convinced he should not perish?

Some children have leaped overboard into the water. The current, for a time, upholds them before their clothes are entirely soaked through. They swim about, unconscious of danger. A rope is thrown to them from the ship. They are entreated by those on board to take hold of the rope. (We find the same meaning in the parables of the woman who had found a farthing, of the shepherd who found the sheep that was lost, and in the parables of the supper and of the prodigal son.) But the children will not believe; not because they think the rope is an unsafe one, but because they do not believe that they are about to perish. Thoughtless children, like themselves, have told them that they will go on bathing merrily, even when the ship sails away. The children do not believe that the time is near when their clothes will be wet through, their little arms tired out; when they will begin to lose breath, and that then they will choke and drown. They do not believe that, and therefore they do not believe in the rope of salvation.

Men are like the children who have jumped overboard, and are sure they will not perish. Therefore they do not take hold of the rope. They believe in the immortality of the soul and are convinced that they will not perish, and therefore they do not fulfill the doctrine of Christ-God. They do not believe in what is indubitable, only because they believe in what is beyond all possibility of belief.

And they cry, "Confirm our belief that we are not perishing."

But that is impossible. For them to believe they will be saved they must cease to do what brings destruction, and begin to do what will save them; they must take hold of the rope of salvation. But they do not choose to do this; they wish to be assured that they are not perishing, though their companions perish, one after another, before their eyes. And that desire to grow sure of what is not, they call 'faith.' No wonder, then, that they have little faith and that they long for more.

It was only when I understood Christ's doctrine that I saw that what such men call 'faith' is not faith. It is only the false faith that the apostle James opposes in his epistle. The Church did not accept that epistle for a long time; and when it was accepted it underwent several changes. Some words were removed, and others transposed or incorrectly translated. I here give the accepted translation, only correcting what is inexact, according to Tischendorf's text.

James 2:14–26: 'What does it profit, my brethren, if a man supposes that he has faith, and does not have works? Faith cannot save him. If a brother or sister is naked and destitute of daily food, and one of you says to them, "Depart in peace, be warmed and filled," but you do not give them those things that they need; what good is that? Even so faith, if it does not have works, is dead, being alone. Yes, a man may say, "You have faith, and I have works." Show me your faith without your works, and I will show you my faith by my works. You believe that there is one God; you do well. The devils also believe, and tremble. But will you know, O vain man, that faith without works is dead? Wasn't Abraham our father justified by works when he had offered Isaac his son upon the altar? See how faith worked with his deeds, and by his deeds his faith was made perfect? ...You see then how that by works a man is justified, and not by faith alone. ...For as the body without the spirit is dead, so faith without works is dead also.'

The apostle says that the only proof of faith is in the works that proceed from it; and that faith from which no works proceed is but a word, with which we can neither feed any, nor justify ourselves and be saved. And therefore the faith that is not accompanied by works is not faith. It is only a wish to believe; it is only a mistaken assertion that I believe when I do not really believe.

According to this definition, faith must be allied to works, and works make faith perfect, i.e., true.

The Jews said to Christ (Mark 15:32, Matthew 27:42, John 6:30), 'What sign will you give us, that we may see and believe you? What will you do?' The same men said to Him when He was on the cross, 'Let Him descend now from the cross, that we may see and believe.' (Mark 15:32)

Matthew 27:42: 'He saved others, but Himself He cannot save! If He is the King of Israel, let Him now come down from the cross, and we will believe Him.'

In answer to their prayer that He may 'increase their faith,' Christ says that the wish is vain; that they cannot be forced to believe (Luke 22:67). He says, 'If I tell you, you will not believe' (John 10:25–26). 'I told you, and you have not believed. You do not believe because you are not of My sheep, as I said to you.'

The Jews required some outward token to enforce their belief in the doctrine of Christ, just as the Christian followers of the Church do now. And He answers that it cannot be given to them, and explains why it is impossible to do so. He says that they cannot believe because they are not of His sheep, or, they do not follow the path of life that He points out to His flock. He explains (John 5:44) wherein lies the difference between His sheep and those who are not of His flock. He explains the reason why some believe and others do not, and tells them what the basis of faith is. 'How can you believe,' He says, 'when you accept each other's δοξα, teaching, and do not seek the teaching that comes from God alone?'

In order to believe, Christ says we must seek the doctrine that comes from God. 'He who speaks from himself, seeks his own doctrine (δοξαν την ιδιαν); but he who seeks the doctrine of Him who sent Him, the same is true, and no unrighteousness is in Him' (John 7:18).

The doctrine of life, δοξα, is the basis of faith.

All our actions proceed from faith. Faith proceeds from the δοξα of the light in which we consider life. There may be innumerable deeds and numerous beliefs, but there are only two doctrines of life (δοξα). Christ rejects one of them, and acknowledges the other. The one that Christ rejects is that of the existence of individual life, as belonging to man. It is the doctrine that was then, and is still, maintained by the majority of men, and from which proceeds all the various beliefs of men, and all their deeds.

The other doctrine is the one taught by Christ and the prophets: that our individual life has a purpose only when we fulfill the will of God.

If a man has the δοξα that his individuality is of more importance than all else, he will consider his individual happiness as the chief and most desirable object in life; and according as he finds that happiness in the purchase of landed property, in fame, in glory, or in the satisfaction of his lusts, his faith will coincide with his views of life, and all his actions will be guided by it.

If the δοξα of a man is not such, if he understands the true purpose of life to lie in fulfilling the will of God, as Abraham understood it, and as Christ taught it, his actions will coincide with his faith in what he knows to be the will of God.

This is the reason why those who believe in the happiness of an individual life cannot believe in the doctrine of Christ. All their endeavors to do so will be in vain. In order to believe, they must change their views of life. Until they have done so, their actions will coincide with their creed, and not with their desires or their words.

The desire to believe in the doctrine of Christ, both of those who asked Him for some token, and of the believers of the present time, does not coincide with their lives, nor can it ever do so, however hard they may try to fit them together. They may pray to Christ-God, attend the Holy Communion, do good to mankind, build churches, convert others, and yet, with all this, they cannot really work for Christ; because that can proceed only from faith, which is based on a very different doctrine (δοξα) to the one that they profess. They cannot sacrifice the life of their only son, as Abraham did, who did not doubt for a moment that it was his duty to offer up his son as a sacrifice to God, to the God who alone gave importance to his life. And in the same way, Christ and His disciples could not help giving up their lives to others, because in that alone lay the object and blessing of their lives.

It is from men's thus misunderstanding the substance of faith that their strange longing arises. They make themselves believe that it would be better to live up to the doctrine of Christ; and all the while they firmly believe in the individual life, and therefore choose to live contrary to Christ's doctrine.

The foundation of faith is a true comprehension of life, which enables man to distinguish what is important and good in life from what is unimportant and bad. Faith is a correct appreciation of all the manifestations of life. At the present time men, whose faith is grounded on a doctrine of their own, cannot make it agree with the faith that flows out of the doctrine of Christ any more than the disciples could. And we find this misunderstanding more than once clearly and definitely spoken of in the gospel. In the gospel according to St. Matthew 20:20–28, and in that according to Mark 10:35–45, after saying, that the 'rich man cannot enter the kingdom of God,' and after the still more awful saying that 'he who does not leave all, who does not give up his life for Christ's sake, shall not be saved,' Peter asks, 'What, then, shall we have, who have left all and followed You?' In the gospel according to Mark we read that James and John (or, according to Matthew, their mother) ask that 'they should sit, one on His right hand, the other on His left, in His glory.' They beg Him to confirm their faith by the promise of a reward. Christ answers Peter's question by a parable (Matthew 20:1–16); and in answer to James He says, 'You do not know what you ask,' i.e., 'you ask for what cannot be. You do not understand my doctrine. My doctrine is the renunciation of individual life, and you ask for individual honor, and individual reward. You may 'drink of my cup' or live; but to sit on my right hand, or my left, or to be equal to me, cannot be given to you.' And then Christ says that it is only in this world that the powerful of the world think much of the glory and power of individual life, and rejoice in it; but you, who are my disciples, ought to know that the true life does not lie in individual happiness, but in ministering to all, in humbling ourselves before all. Man does not live to be ministered to, but to minister to all, and to give up his individual life as a ransom for all. In answer to His disciples' request, which showed Him how little they understood His doctrine, Christ does not command them to believe, i.e., to change their appreciation of good and evil, which arose from the teaching they had imbibed before Him (He knows that it is impossible); but He explains what the true life is, on which faith is based, and shows that it is a true estimation of good and bad, important and unimportant.

Christ answers Peter's question, 'What reward shall we have for having left all, and following You?' with the parable of the laborers who were hired at different times, and who received the same pay (Matthew 20:1–16). He explains to Peter the error he is in with respect to His doctrine, and that his lack of faith proceeds from his error. Christ says it is only in individual life that reward is important in proportion to the work done. A belief in the necessity of reward being proportionate to the work itself proceeds from the doctrine of individual life. This belief is based on a hypothesis and on rights, which we imagine that we have; but man has no rights and can never have any rights; he is only a debtor for the happiness given to him, and therefore he has no right to expect anything. Even if he gives up his whole life, he cannot give back what he has received, and therefore the master cannot be unjust. If a man declares that he has a right to his own life, and requires compensation from the Author of all — from Him who entrusted him with life — he only shows that he does not understand the true purpose for which life was given to him.

Men, having obtained happiness, require more. These men stood unoccupied and miserable in the market place, and did not live. The master hired them and gave them the greatest good in life: labor. They accepted the master's gracious gift, and then grew dissatisfied. They were dissatisfied because they had no clear consciousness of their state. They came to their work with the false idea that they had a right to their own lives and to their own work, and that, therefore, their work was to be rewarded. They did not understand that work itself was the greatest good given to them, in return for which they were to do good to others, but that they could claim no reward. And men cannot have a just and true faith as long as they possess the same erroneous idea of life as these laborers had.

Christ answers the direct demand of His disciples to confirm, to increase, their faith by the parable of the master and the laborers, and explains still more clearly the groundwork of the faith he taught them.

Luke 17:3–10: The precept given by Christ to forgive our brother not only once, but seventy times seven, fills the disciples with awe at the difficulty that they would experience in putting such a precept into practice, and they say, 'Yes but... to fulfill it we must believe. Increase, and confirm our faith.' As they had asked before, 'What shall we have for it?' so do they again say, just as all who call themselves Christians say, 'I would believe, but I cannot. Strengthen my faith.' They say, 'Make us believe,' just as the disciples did when they asked for a miracle. 'Make us believe in our salvation by miracles and promises of reward.'

The disciples spoke just as we do. It would be well if, while continuing to lead our individual, willful lives, we could be made to believe that by fulfilling God's commandments we should be all the happier. We all ask for what is contrary to the whole spirit of Christ's doctrine, and we are surprised that we can by no means believe. And Christ answers the misunderstanding, which existed then, and still exists, by a parable in which He shows what true faith is. Faith cannot proceed from trust in what He says; faith comes only from a consciousness of our state. Faith is based only on the rational consciousness of what is best for us. He shows that it is impossible to rouse faith in men by promises of rewards and by threats of punishments; that it will be but a very weak trust that will be destroyed at the first temptation; that the faith that moves mountains, the faith that nothing can shake, is based on the consciousness of our inevitable peril, and of the sole salvation possible for us.

Faith needs no promises of reward. It is only necessary to understand that salvation from inevitable destruction lies in a general life for all humanity according to the will of the Master. He who has once understood this will seek no confirmation of his faith, but will be saved without his requiring any exhortation.

When the disciples beg Him to confirm their faith, Christ says, 'When the master comes home with his laborer from the field, he does not tell him to sit down and eat immediately, but first orders him to pen the cattle and to serve him; and, this done, the laborer sits down to his food and eats. The laborer obeys, and does not think himself ill used, neither does he pride himself on his work, nor require thanks or a reward for it. He knows that it must be so, and that he has only done his duty; that is all that is required of him by his service, but just this is, at the same time, for his own good. In like manner, when you have done all you are bound to do, think that you have only done what was given to you to do.' He who understands his duty toward his Master will see that it is only by submitting to his Master's will that he can have life, and can know wherein lies the blessing of his life. And he will have faith — the faith that Christ teaches us. Faith, according to the doctrine of Christ, is based on a rational consciousness of the purpose of life.

The foundation of faith, according to the doctrine of Christ, is light.

John 1:9–12: 'That was the true light, which lights every man who comes into the world. He was in the world, and the world was made by Him, and the world did not know Him. He came to His own, and His own did not receive Him. And as many as received Him and believed in His name, to them He gave power to become the sons of God.' John 3:19–21: 'And this is the judgment, that light has come into the world; and men loved darkness rather than light, because their deeds were evil. For everyone who does evil hates the light, neither does he come to the light, lest his deeds should be seen and disapproved, because they are evil. But he who does truth comes to the light, that his deeds may be made manifest, because they are done through God.'

He who has understood the doctrine of Christ can require no strengthening of his faith. Faith, according to Christ, is based on the light, on the truth. Not once does Christ call upon men to have faith in Him; He calls upon them to have faith in the truth.

John 8:40,46: He says to the Jews, 'You seek to kill Me, a Man who has told you the truth, which I have heard from God. Which of you convicts Me of untruth? And if I tell the truth, why do you not believe Me?' John 18:37: Christ says, 'To this end I was born, and for this cause I came into the world, that I should bear witness to the truth. Everyone who is of the truth hears My voice.'

John 14:6: He says, 'I am the way, the truth, and the life.'

Further on, in the same chapter, Christ says to His disciples, 'The Father shall give you another Comforter, and He may abide with you forever. He is the spirit of truth, who the world does not see and does not know; but you know him, for he dwells in you and shall be in you.'

He says that His whole doctrine is truth, that He Himself is truth.

The doctrine of Christ is the doctrine of truth, and, therefore, faith in Christ is not a trust in anything that refers to Jesus, but a knowledge of the truth. It is impossible to persuade or bribe a man to fulfill it. He who understands the doctrine of Christ will have faith in Him, because His doctrine is truth. He who knows the truth cannot refuse to believe in it. Therefore, if a man feels himself to be sinking, he cannot refuse to take hold of the rope of salvation, and the question, 'What shall we do to believe?' is one that shows a total misunderstanding of Christ's doctrine.

Chapter X

We say that it is hard to live in accordance with Christ's precepts! How can it be otherwise than hard while we conceal our state from ourselves and earnestly try to maintain the trust that our state is not what it really is? Calling that trust 'faith' we exalt it into something sacred, and either by violence, by working upon the feelings, by threats, by flattery, or by deceit we seek to allure others to that false trust. A Christian once said, 'Credo quia absurdum,' and other Christians now enthusiastically repeat the words, thinking a belief in absurdities is the best way to the truth.

A clever and learned man observed to me, a short time ago, in the course of conversation, that the Christian doctrine was of no importance as a doctrine or morality. 'We find the same,' he said, 'in the teachings of the Stoics, the Brahmins, and in the Talmud. The substance of the Christian doctrine is in the theosophical teaching contained in the dogmas.' That means that what is eternal and general to all humanity, what is necessary for life, and what is rational, is not of most value. But what is quite incomprehensible, and therefore unnecessary, but in the name of which millions have been put to death, is the most important point of Christianity!

We have formed an erroneous idea of life, both as concerns ourselves personally and the world in general. We have based it on our own wickedness and on our personal lusts; and we look upon that erroneous idea — united only by outward observances to the doctrine of Christ — as most important and necessary to life. Were it not for that trust in what is but falsehood, which has been upheld by men for ages, the falsity of our view of life, as well as the truth of Christ's doctrine, would have become manifest long ago.

Awful as it may seem to say so, I sometimes think that if the doctrine of Christ, with the Church teaching that has become a part of it, had never existed, those who now call themselves Christians would be nearer than they are now to the doctrine of Christ; i.e., to a rational idea of the true happiness of life. The morality taught by all the prophets would not then have been a closed book for mankind. Men would have had their petty preachers of the truth, and they would have believed them. But now that the whole truth has been revealed, it seems so awful to those whose deeds are evil that they have interpreted it falsely, and men have lost their trust in the truth. In our European world the saying of Christ, that 'He came into the world in order to bear witness of the truth, and that he who is of the truth hears Him,' has long since been answered in the words of Pilate, 'What is the truth?' We have taken in earnest these words of Pilate's, expressive of such sad and deep irony, and we have made them our faith. In our world not only do all live without knowing the truth, and without a desire to know it, but also with the firm conviction that of all idle occupations the idlest is the search after truth.

The doctrine of life that all nations, long before the existence of European society, considered as most important, that doctrine which, as Christ told us, is the only thing necessary, is alone excluded from our lives. This is done by the institution called the Church; and yet even those who themselves belong to that institution have long ceased to believe in it.

The only aperture that lets in the light, toward which the eyes of all who reflect and suffer turn, is concealed. There is but one answer to the questions, 'What am I? What shall I do? Can I not render my life easier by following the commandments of the God who, according to your words, came to save us?' And that answer is, 'Honor and obey the authorities, and believe in the Church.' 'But why is there so much suffering in the world?' cries a despairing voice; 'Why is there so much evil? Can I not refuse to take part in it? Can evil not be mitigated?' The answer is, 'It is impossible. Your wish to lead a good life, and to help others to do so, is but pride and vainglory. The only thing you can do is to save yourself, your soul, for a future life. If you wish to flee from the evils of the world, leave the world.' 'There is a way open to each,' says the teaching of the Church, 'but know that, having chosen it, you have lost all right to return to the world, that you must cease to live, and must voluntarily die a lingering death.' There are only two ways open to us; our teachers tell us that 'we must either believe our spiritual pastors and obey them and those who are in authority over us, and take an active part in the evil they organize, or else leave the world and enter a monastery, deprive ourselves of food and sleep, let our bodies rot on a iron pillar, bend and unbend our bodies in endless genuflections, and do nothing for our fellow-creatures.' Thus, a man must either confess the doctrines of Christ to be impracticable, and live contrary to them, or renounce the life of this world, which is but a type of slow suicide.

Surprising as the erroneous assumption that the doctrine of Christ is sublime but impracticable may seem to him who understands it, the error by which it is maintained, that he who wishes to keep the commandments of Christ, not only in word but in deed, must leave the world, is still more surprising.

The erroneous idea that it is better for a man to leave the world than to submit to its temptations is an old error, known to the ancient Hebrews, but entirely foreign not only to the spirit of Christianity, but even to that of Judaism. It was against that very error that the story Christ loved and so often quoted, of the prophet Jonah, was written. The story contains one idea from beginning to end. The prophet Jonah wishes to be the only just man, and flies from association with the depraved inhabitants of Nineveh. But God shows him that he is a prophet — one whose duty it is to make the truth known to those who have gone astray — and that he must not flee from them, but live among them. Jonah has an aversion to the depraved Ninevites, and once more tries to escape by flight. But God brings him back in the body of a whale, and the will of the Almighty is accomplished; the Ninevites receive the teaching of God, through Jonah, and amend their lives. But Jonah does not rejoice at having been instrumental in accomplishing the will of God; he is angry, jealous of the Ninevites; he wishes to be the only wise and good man. He goes away into the wilderness, bemoans his fate, and reproaches God. And then a gourd grows over Jonah in one night and protects him from the rays of the sun; but on the next night worms eat the gourd. Jonah, in his despair, reproaches God for letting the gourd, so precious to him, wither. Then God says to him, 'You regret the gourd, which you called yours; it grew and perished in one night; and do you think I had no pity for so numerous a people, who were perishing, living like the beasts, unable to distinguish their right hands from their left? Your knowledge of the truth was needed that you might have given to those who did not have it.'

Christ knew this story and often quoted it; we are likewise told in the gospel that Christ Himself, after visiting John the Baptist, who had retired to the wilderness before he began his preaching, was subjected to the same temptation, and was conducted into the wilderness to be tempted by the devil (by delusion). He overcame that delusion and, in the strength of the spirit, came back into Galilee and, from that time, without abhorring those who were depraved, He passed His life among publicans, Pharisees, and sinners, teaching them the truth.

According to the teaching of the Church, Christ, who was God and man, gave us an example of how we were to live. Christ passed His whole life, as we know, in the turmoil of life, with publicans, adulteresses, and the Pharisees in Jerusalem. His two great commandments are love to our fellow-creatures and the preaching of His doctrine to all men. Both commandments require constant communication with the world. Yet the conclusion drawn from Christ's doctrine is that, in order to be saved, we must leave all, cease all communication with our fellow-creatures, and stand on a pillar. Thus it would seem that, in order to follow the example of Christ, we must do just the contrary of what He taught and of what He did Himself.

According to the interpretation given by the Church, Christ's doctrine does not teach either secular men or monks how they are to live in order to make their own lives and the lives of their fellow-creatures better, but teaches the former what they must believe in order to be saved in the next world, in spite of their evil lives, and enjoins the latter to make their lives on earth still harder.

But this is not what Christ teaches us.

Christ preaches truth, and if abstract truth is truth, it will be truth in reality. If life in God is the only true life, blissful in itself, it will be true and blissful here on earth, in all the various circumstances of life. If life here did not confirm the doctrine of Christ, that doctrine would not be true.

Christ does not call men from good to evil, but on the contrary, from evil to good. He pities men, whom He considers as lost sheep perishing without their shepherd, and promises them a shepherd and good pasture. He says that His disciples will be persecuted for His doctrine, that they must suffer, and bear the persecution of the world. But He does not say that if they follow His doctrine they will suffer more severely than if they follow the teaching of the world; on the contrary, He says that those who follow the teaching of the world will be miserable, and those who follow His doctrine will be blessed.

Christ does not teach us that we shall be saved either through faith, or through asceticism, i.e., self-deception, or voluntary torments in this life; but He teaches us a life in which, besides salvation from the ruin of individual life, there will be less suffering and more joy than in individual life, even here on earth.

Revealing His doctrine to men, Christ says that by following His doctrine, even in the midst of those who do not do so, they will be happier than those who do not fulfill His doctrine. Christ says that, even from a worldly point of view, it is a successful plan not to care about the life of this world.

Mark 10:28–31: Then Peter began to say to Him, 'Lo, we have left all, and have followed You.' Matthew 19:27,29–30: 'What shall we have therefore?' And Jesus answered and said, 'Truly I say to you, there is no man who has left house, or brethren, or sisters, or father, or mother, or wife, or children, or lands for My sake and the gospel's, but he shall receive a hundredfold now in this time, houses, and brethren, and sisters, and mothers, and children and lands, with persecutions; and in the world to come eternal life.' (Matthew 19:27; Luke 5:11;18:28)

Christ mentions, it is true, that those who follow Him shall be persecuted by those who do not; but He does not say that the disciples shall lose anything by doing so. On the contrary, He says that His followers shall have more joy in this world than those who are not His.

We cannot doubt that Christ spoke and thought thus. He says it clearly; the spirit of His teaching proves it, as well as the way in which He Himself and His disciples lived. But is it true?

On an abstract examination of the question, whether the state of the followers of Christ or that of those who live for the world will be best, we cannot help seeing that the state of the followers of Christ must be better, because, by doing good to all, they avoid exciting the hatred of men. The follower of Christ will do no harm to any, and will therefore be persecuted by the wicked; but the followers of the world will be persecuted by all, because the law of life, of those who live for the world, is a law of strife, or the persecution of each other. The chances of suffering may be the same for both, with the difference that the followers of Christ will be ready to bear them, while the followers of the world will use all their endeavors to avoid them; the followers of Christ will suffer, but will know that their suffering is necessary for the good of humanity, while the followers of the world will suffer without knowing the reason why they suffer. Reasoning abstractly, the state of the followers of Christ should be more profitable than that of the followers of the world. But is it so?

Let each verify this by calling to mind all the trying moments of his life, all the suffering, both moral and physical, which he has gone through, and still goes through, and let him ask himself in whose name he bore, and still bears, all that misery. Was it for the sake of the world, or for the doctrine of Christ? Let him examine his past life, and he will see that he never once suffered from having followed the doctrine of Christ; he will see that all the unhappiness of his life proceeded from his having, contrary to his own inclinations, followed the teaching of the world.

During my life, which has been an exceptionally happy one, according to the opinion of the world, I can remember so much suffering borne by me for the sake of the world, that it might have sufficed for the life of one of the greatest martyrs of Christianity. All the most trying moments of my life, from the orgies and debauches of my student days, to duels, war, and ill health — all the unnatural and painful conditions of life in which I now live — were and are but martyrdom for the sake of the world.

I speak of my life, which, as I say, has been an exceptionally happy one, according to the opinion of the world. But how many martyrs there are who have suffered, and still suffer, for the teaching of the world, whose sufferings I cannot even picture to myself!

We do not see the difficulty and peril there is in following the teaching of the world, only because we look upon all we bear for its sake as being absolutely necessary.

We have become convinced that all the misfortunes that we create for ourselves are indispensable conditions of life, and we cannot understand that Christ shows us the way to escape suffering and to attain happiness.

In order to examine the question, which life is a happier one, we must cast aside all our mistaken notions, and examine all those around us and ourselves without any preconceived idea.

Pass through a crowd of people, especially those living in a town, and see their wearied, sickly, and anxious faces; then think of your own life, of the lives of those you know; think of all the unnatural deaths, all the suicides that you may have chanced to hear of, and ask yourself what led to all the despair and suffering that drove these men to commit suicide. And you will see that nine-tenths of the suffering there is in this life is borne for the sake of the world; that it is all unnecessary suffering that need not exist; that men are, for the most part, martyrs of the teaching of the world.

A short time ago, on a rainy Sunday in the autumn, I drove in an omnibus through the market place near Souhareva tower, in Moscow. For the space of half a mile the carriage made its way through a compact mass of people. From morning to evening thousands of human beings, the greater part of whom are ragged and hungry, prowl about here in the dirt, abusing, cheating, and hating each other. The same may be seen in all the market places of Moscow. These men will spend their evenings in taverns and public houses, and the night in their corners and dens. Sunday is the best day in the week for them. On Monday, in their infected dens, they will again set to the work that they are heartily sick of.

Reflect what the lives of all these men and women are; think of all they have left, of the hard work to which they have voluntarily condemned themselves; and you will see that they are true martyrs.

These men have left their homes and fields; they have left their fathers, brothers, wives, and children; they have forsaken all, and have come into the town to procure what the teaching of the world forces each to consider as indispensable. And not only these thousands and thousands of miserable beings who have lost all, and now live from hand to mouth on tripe and brandy, but all, I say, from workmen, cabmen, seamstresses, and harlots, to rich merchants, bureaucrats, and their wives, lead the hardest, most unnatural lives, and yet fail to attain what is considered necessary according to the teaching of the world.

Tell me whether you can find among all these men, from the beggar to the rich man, a single man who finds that what he earns is sufficient for all that he considers as indispensably necessary, and you will not find one in a thousand.

Each struggles to get what he does not of himself require, but what is considered requisite by the world, and the want of which, therefore, makes him miserable. No sooner has he attained it, than more and more is required, and so this labor of Sisyphus goes on without intermission, ruining life after life. Take, in an ascending scale, the fortunes of men, from those who spend thirty rubles a year to those who spend fifty thousand, and you will seldom find a man who is not tormented and worn out with his efforts to obtain four hundred if he has but three hundred, five hundred if he has four, and so on without end. There is not one who, having five hundred, would voluntarily exchange with him who has but four hundred. Each strives to lay a still heavier burden on his already heavy-laden life, and gives up his whole soul to the teaching of the world. Today a man has earned an overcoat and galoshes; tomorrow he gets a watch and a chain; then a lodging with a comfortable sofa, carpets in the drawing room, and velvet clothes; then he buys a house, horses, pictures in gilt frames; and then, having overworked himself, he falls ill and dies. Another continues the same career, likewise sacrificing his life to the same Moloch, dying in the same way, without knowing why he does all this. Well, but perhaps, with all this, men are happy.

What are the principal requisites for earthly happiness, those that no one can deny?

The first condition essentially necessary for happiness has always been admitted by all men to be a life in which the link between him and nature is not destroyed – that is, a life in the open air, in the sunshine, in communion with nature, plants and animals. Men have always considered being deprived of this as the greatest misfortune that could befall them. Prisoners feel this privation above all others. And now consider what the life of those who live according to the teaching of the world is. The more successful their worldly career is, the further they are from all that is true happiness. The higher the worldly prosperity they have attained, the less sunshine do they enjoy, the fewer are the fields, woods, and animals they see. Many, indeed almost all, women dwelling in towns live to old age without having seen the rising of the sun more than once or twice in their lives. They have never seen the fields and woods, except through the windows of their coaches or of railway carriages; not only have they never brought up and tended cows, horses, or poultry, but also they have no idea even how animals grow and live. These people see stuffs, stones, and wood worked by human hands, and do not even see them in the light of the sun, but in an artificial light. They hear the noise of machinery, cannons, or musical instruments; they inhale strong scents and tobacco smoke; their enfeebled digestions crave stimulating food that is neither fresh nor savory. Nor are they nearer to nature even when traveling from one place to another. They travel shut up in boxes. Wherever they go, be it into the country or abroad, the same curtains hide the light of the sun from their eyes; footmen, coachmen, and watchmen prevent all communication between them and nature. Wherever they go they are, like prisoners, deprived of this condition that is so necessary for happiness. As prisoners find consolation in a blade of grass that grows in the yard of their prison, or a spider, or a mouse, so do these men and women find consolation, from time to time, in keeping half withered plants on their window sills, or in parrots, lap dogs, or monkeys, the care of which they leave to others.

A second indubitable condition necessary for happiness is labor — congenial, free labor, physical labor, which gives a man a good appetite and sound, invigorating sleep. And, again, the greater the prosperity a man has attained, according to a worldly estimate, the further he is from this second condition, essentially necessary for happiness. All the 'fortunate' of this world, the great dignitaries and rich men, are either as completely deprived of labor as prisoners are, and struggle unsuccessfully against ill health, which is the result of the absence of physical labor, and still more unsuccessfully against the ennui to which they are a prey (I say 'unsuccessfully,' for work is a source of pleasure only when it is necessary), or they have work to do that they hate, as, for instance, our bankers, attorneys, generals, and bureaucrats. I say it is work they hate because I never yet met one among them who liked his work, and who found as much pleasure in it as a stable boy does in clearing away the snow before his master's house. All these so-called fortunate beings have either no work to do or work that they hate; they are, indeed, in much the same position as a galley slave.

A third condition essentially necessary for happiness is family life. And again, the further advanced men are in worldly prosperity, the less accessible that happiness is for them. Most of them are adulterers, and voluntarily renounce all family ties. Even if they are not adulterers, they consider children as a burden rather than a joy, and try by all possible means to make their unions sterile. If they have children, they take no joy in them. They are obliged to confide them to others, for the most part to complete strangers; at first they are left to the care of foreign nurses or governesses, then sent to some government school, and the children grow up as miserable as their parents, and often have but one feeling toward their parents: the wish for their death, that they may inherit their property. These men are not prisoners, but the result is more painful than that entire separation from all family ties to which a prisoner is condemned.

A fourth condition essentially necessary for happiness is a free, friendly communication with all men. And again, the higher the step on which a man stands in the world, the further he is from this condition. The higher your position, the narrower and closer is the circle of men with whom you can have any communication, and the lower in intellectual and moral development are the few persons who form this spellbound circle, out of which there is no escape. The whole world is open to the peasant and his wife. If one million men refuse to have anything to do with him, there are eighty million working men left like himself, with whom, from Archangelsk to Astrachan, he enters immediately into the closest, most brotherly communication, without waiting to be called upon or introduced. There are, for a functionary and his wife, hundreds of men who are their equals; but their superiors do not admit them into their circle, and they are cut off from all the lower classes. There may be ten fashionable families for a rich man of the world and his wife, but they are cut off from all the rest. Bureaucrats and very wealthy men and their families may find about ten friends as important and as rich as themselves. The circle of emperors and kings is still more restricted. Isn't that called solitary confinement, when a prisoner can only have communication with two or three jailers?

The fifth and last condition essentially necessary for happiness is health and a painless death. And again, the higher a man stands on the social scale, the further he is from it. Take, for instance, a moderately rich man and his wife, and a well-to-do countryman and his wife; in spite of hunger and the hard work — which is the peasant's lot through the inhumanity of others, and not through any fault of his own — you will find, if you compare the two, that the lower men stand on the social scale the healthier they are, and the higher they stand the weaker they are in health. Recall to your minds all the rich men and their wives whom you have ever known, and those whom you know at present, and you will see that they almost all suffer from ill health. A healthy man among them — one who does not take medicine continually, or at least periodically every summer — is as great an exception as is a sick man among the working classes. Almost all the 'fortunate beings' are toothless, gray haired, or bald at the age when a working man is still in the full vigor of his manhood. They are almost all sufferers from nervous diseases, dyspepsia or worse, from over-eating, from drunkenness or depravity; and those who do not die young spend half their lives under medical treatment, using frequent injections of morphine, and becoming shriveled cripples, unable to maintain themselves; living on like parasites. Think of what the deaths of these men are: one has shot himself, another's body has rotted from disease, another again has died in his old age from a too frequent use of medicines; one has died in a drunken fit, another of gluttony, etc. All perish, one after the other, for the world's sake. And the crowd crawls after them like martyrs in search of suffering and death.

One life after another is cast under the wheels of their god; the carriage drives on, tearing lives to pieces, and again and again fresh victims fall under its wheels, with groans, wails, and curses.

It is difficult to live as Christ enjoins! Christ says, 'He who will follow Me must leave houses, fields, and brethren, and he shall receive a hundredfold more than houses, fields and brethren in this world, and shall, besides, have life eternal.' And none follow Him. The world says, 'Leave your home and your brothers; leave the country to live in a corrupt town; pass your whole life either as a servant in a bath-house, soaping other people's backs with vapor bath; or as a clerk, counting other people's money; or as an attorney general, spending your life in courts of law, busied with various documents, in order to make the fate of the miserable more miserable still; or as a bureaucrat, hastily signing useless papers all your life; or as a commander-in-chief, killing your brethren. Lead a wicked life, the end of which is always a painful death, and you shall suffer in this life, and not attain eternal life' — and all go the world's way. Christ says, 'Take up your cross, and follow Me,' by which He means, 'Bear the fate allotted you humbly, and submit to Me, your God' — and none do so. But the first lost man, wearing an epaulet, and fit for nothing but murder, who says, 'Take up, not the cross, but your knapsack and your sword, and follow me to suffering and certain death,' is instantly obeyed.

Leaving their parents, their wives and children, they go in their buffoon attire, blindly submissive to some superior whom they hardly know; cold, hungry, worn out by a march above their strength, they follow him like a herd of oxen to the slaughter. But they are not oxen — they are men! They cannot help knowing that they are driven to slaughter, with the unsolvable question, 'Why must I go?' And with despair in their hearts they go on, many dieing off through cold, hunger, and infectious diseases, until those who are left are placed under bullets and cannon balls, and ordered to kill men whom they know nothing about. They kill and are at last killed themselves, and not one of those who kill their fellow-creature knows why he does so. The Turks roast them alive; they flay them; they tear out their bowels. And no sooner does anyone call than others go to the same dreadful suffering and to death. And nobody finds it hard. Neither do they themselves think it hard, nor do their fathers and mothers think so; the latter even advise their children to go. Not only do they think it necessary and unavoidable, but even perfectly right and moral.

We might think the fulfilling of Christ's doctrine difficult if it were really an easy and pleasant thing to live according to the teaching of the world. But it is much more difficult, dangerous, and painful to do so than it is to live up to the doctrine of Christ.

It is said that formerly there were martyrs for Christianity, but these were exceptional cases; we reckon about three hundred and eighty thousand voluntary and involuntary martyrs for Christianity in the course of 1800 years. Now count those that have died for the teaching for the world, and for each martyr for Christianity you will find a thousand martyrs for the world's sake, martyrs whose sufferings were a hundredfold more dreadful. Thirty million have been killed in war during the present century alone.

Those were all martyrs for the world's sake. Had they but rejected the teaching of the world, even without following the doctrine of Christ, they would have escaped suffering and death.

Were a man but to act as he finds best for himself, were he but to refuse to go to war, he would have to dig ditches; but he would not be tortured in Sebastopool or Plevna. Let a man not believe that it is indispensable to wear a watch chain and to have useless drawing rooms, let him but understand that all the foolish things the world teaches him to consider as indispensable are but useless trash, and he will not work beyond his strength; he will not have to endure suffering and constant care; he will not have to labor without purpose or rest; He will not be deprived of communion with nature, or of the work he loves, or of his family or his health, and he will not die a uselessly painful death.

We need not be martyrs for Christ's sake; that is not what He requires of us. But He teaches us to cease making ourselves martyrs for the sake of the false teaching of the world.

The doctrine of Christ has a deep metaphysical purpose; it has a purpose general to all humanity; the doctrine of Christ has the simplest, clearest, most practicable purpose for each of us. We may express this idea in a few words. Christ teaches men not to act foolishly. In this lies the simplest sense of Christ's doctrine, and it is one each has it in his power to understand.

Christ says, 'Never give way to angry feelings, nor consider another as worse than yourself; it is foolish. If you give way to anger, if you abuse others, it will be worse for you.' Christ says, too, 'Do not lust after all women, but take one to you, and live with her; it will be better for you.' He says, likewise, 'Make no promise, lest you be forced to act foolishly and wickedly.' He says, likewise, 'Never return evil for evil, for it will fall back upon you.' Christ says, 'Consider no men as strangers to you because they live in other lands and speak in other tongues than you do. If you consider them as your enemies, they will do the same with respect to you, and it will be worse for you. Do not act thus, and it will be better for you.'

Yes, but as the world is organized it is more difficult to resist it than to live up to its precepts. If a man refuses to become a soldier he will be imprisoned, and possibly shot. If a man does not assure his future by acquiring property for himself and his family, they will all starve. Men say so in order to defend the social organization of the world, but they do not think so themselves. They say so only because they cannot deny the justice of Christ's doctrine, which they pretend to believe in, and they must justify themselves in some way for not fulfilling it.

Christ calls men to the spring that is near them. Men suffer from thirst, eat mud, and drink each other's blood; but their teachers have told them that they will suffer more if they go to the spring toward which Christ calls them, and men believe them rather than Christ, and suffer and die of thirst when they are but a few steps from the spring, and dare not approach it. But if we believed in Christ, if we believed that He came to bring bliss on earth, if we believed that He offers us, who are thirsting, a spring of living water, if we drew near to it, we should see how craftily we are deceived by the Church, and how senseless it is to suffer as we do, when salvation is so near. Accept the doctrine of Christ in all its sublime simplicity, and the grievous deception in which you all live will grow clear to you.

We labor, generation after generation, to secure our lives by violence and the consolidation of property. We think that our happiness depends upon power and property. We are so used to that idea that the doctrine of Christ — which teaches us that the happiness of man does not lie in wealth, that a rich man cannot be happy — seems to us to require some great sacrifice for the sake of future bliss. And yet Christ does not call upon us to make any sacrifice; His doctrine does not tend toward making our present lives worse for us, but better. Christ in His infinite love teaches men to forbear from trying to assure their lives by violence, from caring about riches, just as philanthropists teach men to forbear from quarrelling and drunkenness. Christ says that if men live without resisting evil, and without riches, they will be happier, and He confirms His teaching by His own life. He says that he who lives according to His doctrine must be ready to die at any moment of his life, either of cold or hunger, and cannot call a single hour of his life his own. And so it seems that Christ requires great sacrifices of us; yet it is but a general assertion of the inevitable condition of each man. The follower of Christ must always be ready to suffer and to die. Isn't the follower of the world in the same position? We are so used to the deception we are in that we have come to consider all that we do for the imaginary security of our lives — our armies, fortresses, medicines, property, and money — as indispensable for the welfare of our lives. We forget what happened to him who intended to build barns, in order to provide himself with riches for a long time. He died the same night. All we do for the security of our lives is but what the ostrich does when hiding its head in order not to see itself killed. We do worse, for in order to secure an uncertain life, for an uncertain future, we resolutely ruin our real lives in the actual present.

The deception lies in the false assumption that we can secure the welfare of our lives by a struggle with others. We are so used to this erroneous idea that we do not see all we lose. We lose even our lives. Our lives are swallowed up in the cares of this world, so that no real life is left.

Let us set aside all we have become so used to, and then we shall see that all we do for the imaginary security of our lives is not done to assure our welfare, but to make us forget that our life here is not secure, and that it never can be secure. The French take up arms in the year 1870 to assure their existence, and that leads to the destruction of hundreds and thousands of Frenchmen; and every nation that takes up arms does the same thing with the same result. The rich man thinks his money assures the welfare of his life, and the money attracts a robber who kills him. A man who is overly careful of his health seeks to assure it by taking medicine, and the medicine kills him by slow degrees; and even if it does not kill him, it deprives him of all vigor and makes him like the paralytic who hardly lived during thirty-five years, while waiting for the angel at the pool.

The doctrine of Christ — that life cannot be assured, and that we must be ready for suffering and death every moment of our lives — is incontestably better than the teaching of the world, which says that we must strive to make our lives as comfortable as we can; it is better because, though the impossibility of avoiding death and the uncertainty of life are the same, yet, according to Christ's doctrine, life is not wholly swallowed up in the idle employment of trying to ensure our own comfort, but is free, and can be given up to the only aim natural to it, namely, our own happiness in that of others. The follower of Christ will be poor. Yes, but he will enjoy the blessings given to him by God. We have come to consider the word 'poverty' as expressive of misery, yet it really is happiness. 'He is poor' means that he does not live in a town, but in the country; he does not sit idly at home, but labors in the fields or the woods; he sees the sunshine, the sky, beasts, and birds; he need not take thought what he shall do to excite his appetite, to facilitate his digestion; but he feels hungry three times a day. He does not toss about on his soft pillows thinking how to cure himself of sleeplessness, but sleeps soundly after his work. He sees his children around him, and lives in friendly communion with men. The main point is that he is not obliged to do work that he hates, and he need not fear the future. He will be ill, suffer, and die as others do (and judging by the way the poor suffer and die, his death will be an easier one than that of the rich); but he will indubitably have led a happier life. We must be poor, we must be beggars, wanderers on the face of the earth (πτοχος means 'wanderer'); that is what Christ taught us, and without it we cannot enter the kingdom of God.

'But then we shall starve,' is the answer. Christ has given to us one short saying in reply to this observation, a saying that has been usually interpreted as justifying the idleness of the clergy.

Matthew 10:10; Luke 10:7. 'Take neither money for your journey, nor two coats, nor shoes, nor a walking stick, because he who works is worthy of his meat.

And in the same house remain, eating and drinking such things as they give; for the laborer is worthy of his hire.'

He who works (εξεςτ) signifies literally, 'can and shall have food.' It is a very short saying, but he who understands it as Christ did, will never argue that if a man has no personal property he must die of hunger. In order to understand the saying clearly, we must renounce the idea that the dogma of the redemption has made habitual to us: that the happiness of man lies in idleness. We must re-establish in our minds the idea, natural to all unperverted men, that the necessary condition of happiness for man is labor, and not idleness; that every man must labor, that his life will be as wearisome and as hard without work as it is for an ant, a horse, or any other animal. We must cast aside the barbarous idea that the condition of a man who has an inexhaustible ruble in his pocket — a lucrative post, or some landed property that enables him to live in idleness — is a naturally happy condition. We must re-establish in our minds the idea of labor that all unperverted men have, and to which Christ referred when He said that 'the laborer is worthy of his hire.' Christ never could have thought that men would come to consider labor as a curse, and therefore He could not imagine a man who did not work, or who had no wish to work. It was an understood thing for Him that all His followers labored, and He says a man's labor feeds Him. And if one man profits from the work of another man, he will feed him who works for him; and so he who labors will always have food. He will not be rich; but there can be no doubt of his having food.

The difference is that, according to the teaching of the world, labor is a man's service, for which he considers himself entitled to more or less food in proportion to the work he does; while according to the doctrine of Christ labor is the necessary condition of life, and food is its inevitable consequence. Work is the result of food, and food is the result of work; it is an eternal cycle — one is the effect and the cause of the other. However hard hearted a man may be, he will feed his workman as he feeds his horse, and he will give the workman sufficient food to enable him to work.

'The Son of Man came, not be ministered to, but to minister, and to give His soul as a ransom for many.' According to the doctrine of Christ every man will lead a better life if he understands that his duty is not to get as much work as he can out of others, but to pass his own life in working for them. The man who acts thus, Christ says, is worthy of his hire, and he cannot fail to obtain it. By the words 'Man does not live to be ministered to, but to minister to others', Christ lays the foundation of what is to assure the material existence of man; and by the words 'he who works is worthy of his hire' Christ sets aside the argument, so often used against the possibility of fulfilling His doctrine, that he who does so will perish of hunger and cold. Christ shows that a man does not assure his own food by depriving others of it, but by making himself useful and necessary. The more useful he is, the more assured his existence will be.

In our present social adjustments, those who do not fulfill the law of Christ, but who are forced by poverty to work for their neighbors, do not starve. Then how can we say that those who do fulfill His commandments, who work for their fellow-creatures, will starve? No man can starve while the rich have bread. Millions of men in Russia possessing no property live by their work alone.

A Christian will be as sure of his daily bread among pagans as among Christians. He works for others, consequently he is of use to them, and therefore he will be fed. A dog that is useful is fed and taken care of, then how can we think a human being will not be fed and taken care of?

But if a man is sick, he is of no use; he cannot work; no one will give him food. People say so, but they act in a very different way. The very persons who deny the practicability of Christ's doctrine, in fact fulfill it. They do not even cast a sheep, an ox, or a dog that is ill adrift, neither do they kill an old horse, but give it work proportionate to its strength; they feed their lambs, their sucking pigs, and puppies in expectation of deriving profit from them by and by, and will they not feed a man when he falls ill?

Nine-tenths of the lower classes are fed, as beasts of burden are, by the one-tenth — by the rich and powerful of the earth. And however great the error may be in which this one-tenth lives, and however much they may despise the other nine-tenths, they never deprive the other nine-tenths of the food necessary for their sustenance.

Wherever man has worked, he has received food, as each horse receives its fodder. He is fed even though he works grudgingly, unwillingly, only caring to get his daily labor over as quickly as possible, or longing to earn as much as possible in order to get the upper hand of his master. Even he does not remain without food, and he is happier than the one who lives by the labor of others. And how much happier would the man be who worked in accordance with the doctrine of Christ, whose aim would be to work as much as possible, and to receive as little as possible! How much happier will his position be when there will be several around him, perhaps many such as he who will serve him in his turn.

The doctrine of Christ about work and its fruit is shown in the story of the five and seven thousand men fed with two fish and five loaves. Man will attain the highest happiness possible on earth when each, instead of only caring about his own personal comfort, acts as Christ taught those assembled on the seashore to do.

It was necessary to feed several thousand men. One of the disciples said to Christ that a boy there had a few fish. The disciples had also a few loaves. Christ knew that some of those who had come from a distance had brought food with them and others had not. That many had brought provisions with them is evident from there being twelve basketfuls gathered of what remained, as we read in all the four gospels. (If nobody had had anything except the boy, there would not have been twelve baskets in the field.) Had Christ not done what He did, that is, the 'miracle' of feeding thousands with five loaves, what now takes place in the world would have taken place them. Those who had provisions with them would have eaten all they had and would have over-eaten rather than see that anything should be left. Misers would perhaps have taken the remainder home. Those who had nothing would have remained hungry, looking on with wicked envy at those who ate, and some would very likely have stolen from those who had provisions. Quarrelling and fighting would have ensued, and some would have gone home satisfied, the others hungry and cross; exactly what takes place in our present lives would have happened then.

But Christ knew what He meant to do; He told them all to sit in a circle and enjoined His disciples to offer a part of what they had to those next them, and to tell others to do the same. The result was that when all those who had brought provisions with them followed the example set them by the disciples, and offered a share of their provisions to others, there was enough for all. All were satisfied, and so much remained that twelve baskets were filled.

Christ teaches men to act thus in all the circumstances of life, for this is the law of humanity. Labor is the necessary condition of life; and work is a source of happiness for man. But if a man keeps to himself the fruit of his own or others' work, he prevents its contributing to the general good of mankind. By giving up his work to others he acts for the good of all.

We are accustomed to say, 'If men do not despoil each other they will starve.' Wouldn't it be more correct to say that if men despoil each other there will always be some who will starve, for that is the actual fact.

It does not matter if a man is a follower of Christ or a follower of the world; he is never entirely independent of others. Others have taken care of him, fed him, and still take care of him. But, according to the teaching of the world, man forces others to continue feeding him and his family by threats and violence. According to Christ's doctrine, man is taken care of, brought up and fed by others; and he does not force others to continue feeding him, but tries to serve others in his turn, to do as much good as possible to all his fellow-creatures. Which life is then a truer, more rational, and happier one? Is it a life in accordance with the teaching of the world, or in accordance with Christ's doctrine?

Chapter XI

The doctrine of Christ establishes the kingdom of God on earth. To think that it is difficult to fulfill His doctrine is an error. It is not difficult; indeed, he who has once clearly understood it cannot do otherwise than fulfill it, and the fulfilling of Christ's doctrine does not involve us in suffering; it really saves us from nine-tenths of the suffering that we must bear for the world's sake.

And, when I had understood this, I asked myself why I had never followed Christ's doctrine, which leads to salvation and happiness, but had followed a contrary teaching that had brought me nothing but suffering. There could be but one answer to that question—the truth had been hidden from me.

When Christ's doctrine first grew clear to me, I did not think my having understood it would lead me to renounce the teaching of the Church. It seemed to me only that the Church had not arrived at the conclusions that the doctrine of Christ leads to; but I did not think that the new light, which was revealed to me, and the conclusions that I drew from it, would separate me entirely from the Church. Not once did I try during my researches to discover any error in the teaching of the Church; I intentionally closed my eyes to the views that seemed strange and ambiguous to me, as long as they did not absolutely contradict what I considered to be the basis of the Christian doctrine.

But the further I advanced in the study of the gospel, and the clearer the purpose of Christ's doctrine grew, the more inevitable it became for me to choose between the doctrine of Christ, which was rational, clear, and in harmony with my conscience, and a teaching that was in direct opposition to it and that gave me nothing but the consciousness of my own peril and that of others. I could not help throwing each of the Church theses aside, one after the other. I did it most unwillingly, often struggling with my feelings, longing to soften the discordance between my reason and the teaching of the Church. But when I had ended my work, I saw that however hard I might try to keep something, at least, of Church teaching, nothing really was left for me.

As I was drawing toward the close of my work, it happened that my son, a boy, told me that two of our servants, perfectly uneducated men, who hardly knew how to read, had been disputing about a passage in some book, in which it was affirmed that it is no sin to kill criminals, or to kill men in war. I could not believe such a statement could have been published, and asked to see the book. It was *An Exposition of the Book of Prayer*, third edition (eightieth thousand), Moscow, 1879. I read page 163.

> *Q.* 'What is the sixth commandment?'
> *A.* 'You shall not kill.'
> *Q.* 'What does God forbid by this commandment?'
> *A.* 'He forbids our killing, that is, depriving a man of life.'

Q. 'Is it a sin to punish a criminal by death, according to the law, or to kill our enemies in war?'

A. 'It is no sin to do so. A criminal is put to death in order to put a stop to the evil that he does. Enemies are killed in the war in which we fight for our sovereign and our country.'

These are the only words that explain why this commandment is repealed. I could hardly believe my own eyes.

The disputants asked my opinion upon the subject. I said to the one who maintained that the text was quite right that the interpretation was incorrect. 'Then how is it that incorrect statements are printed?' he asked. I could give him no answer. I kept the book and looked through it. The book contains: (1) prayers, with instructions concerning genuflections, and the way the fingers are to be joined in making the sign of the cross; (2) the interpretation of the Creed; (3) extracts from the fifth chapter of Matthew, without any explanations, in which the sayings contained in the chapter are, for some unknown reason, called the 'beatitudes'; (4) the Ten Commandments, with explanations that annul them; and (5) anthems for feast days.

As I have said, I had not only tried to avoid finding fault with the teaching of the Church, but I had tried to view it in its best light, and had not sought to discover its weak points. Though well acquainted with its academic literature, I was completely ignorant of its books for the use of schools. The enormous circulation of a prayer book, which excited doubt even in ignorant men, struck me.

I could not believe that a prayer book, the contents of which were quite pagan, was the Church teaching, propagated among the people. In order to see if it were really the case, I bought all the books published by the Synod, or that it allowed to be published, in which there were short explanations of the Church Creed, for the use of children and uneducated people, and I read them.

The contents were almost new for me. At the time when I learned the Bible history and the catechism, these books did not exist. There was, at that time, as far as I can remember, neither any explanation of the beatitudes, nor were we told that to kill a fellow-creature is no sin. This was not to be found in the old Russian catechisms of Platon; neither is it to be found in the catechisms of Peter Moguilla, or of Beliakoff. It was an innovation made by Filaret, who likewise wrote a catechism for the military classes. *The Exposition of the Book of Prayer* was taken from that very catechism. The book that serves as the basis is *A Complete Christian Catechism for the use of all Orthodox Christians*, published by order of his Imperial Majesty.

The book is divided into three parts: on faith, hope, and love. The first part contains an analysis of the Nicene Creed. The second, an analysis of the Lord's Prayer, and of eight verses of the fifth chapter of Matthew, which form the introduction to the Sermon on the Mount, and which are, for some unknown reason, termed 'beatitudes.' Both of these sections treat the dogmas of the Church, prayers, and sacraments. The third part treats of the duties of a Christian. We do not find the commandments of Christ expounded in this part, but the Ten Com-

mandments of Moses. These commandments are expounded in a way that seems
to enjoin men to leave them unfulfilled, and to act contrary to them. In reference
to the first commandment, which enjoins us to worship God alone, the catechism
teaches us to worship angels and saints, as well as the Virgin Mary and the three
persons of the godhead. (*The Complete Catechism*, pages 107, 108) In reference
to the second commandment, 'You shall not make for yourself any graven image,'
the catechism teaches us to worship images (p. 108). In reference to the third
commandment, 'You shall not take the name of the Lord your God in vain,' the
catechism tells men it is their duty to take an oath every time the legal authorities
may require it of them (p. 111). In reference to the fourth commandment, 'To
keep holy the Saturday,' the catechism enjoins us to keep Sunday holy as well as
thirteen great holidays and a number of smaller ones, and to fast on Wednesdays
and Fridays (p. 112–115). In reference to the fifth commandment, 'Honor your
father and your mother,' the catechism tells us it is our obligation and duty to
honor our sovereign, our father-land, our spiritual pastors, and all those who are
put in authority over us; and about three pages are taken up with the enumeration of the authorities we are to honor—schoolmasters, civil commanders, judges,
military commanders, masters (sic) for those who serve and whose property they
are (p. 116–119). I cite from the 64th edition of the catechism published in 1880.
Twenty years have gone by since slavery has been abolished, and no one has taken
the trouble to remove the sentence that was added to the commandment, 'Honor
your father and mother,' in order to uphold and justify slavery.

With regard to the sixth commandment, 'You shall not kill,' men are taught
from the very first lines to kill.

> What does the sixth commandment forbid?
>> Murder; or taking away our neighbor's life in any way.
> Is taking a man's life always illegal murder?
>> Murder is not unlawful, when it is our duty to take away a man's life;
>> for instance:
>> When we punish a criminal by death.
>> When we kill the enemies in fighting for our sovereign and our native
>> land.

And further on:

> What other instances can you cite of murder?
>> When a man harbors a murderer or sets him free.

And that is published in hundreds and thousands of copies, and instilled into
the Russians by violence, by threats and fear of punishment, under the pretence
of its being the Christian doctrine. This is taught to the whole Russian nation.
This is taught to innocent children, in speaking of whom Christ said, 'Allow little
children to come to Me, for theirs is the kingdom of God'; to children whom we
must be like, in order to enter the kingdom of God; like them in knowing nothing
of all this; to children, in speaking of whom Christ said, 'Woe to him who tempts

one of these little ones.' And these children are made to learn this; they are told that it is the sacred law of God!

Such things are not proclamations secretly propagated, under fear of being sent to hard work in the mines; but they are proclamations, acting contrary to which leads men to hard work in the mines. While I write, a chill creeps over me at my daring to say what I must say—that we have no right to annihilate the commandments of God, which are written in all His laws and in all our hearts, by adding such words as 'duty,' 'our sovereign,' 'our father-land,' etc., which explain nothing.

Yes, what Christ warned us against has come to pass, for He said (Luke 11:33–36, and Matthew 6:23), 'Take heed that the light that is in you is not darkened. If the light that is in you is darkness, how great is that darkness!'

The light that is in us has indeed become darkness; and that darkness is an awful one.

Christ said, 'Woe to you, scribes and Pharisees; for you shut up the kingdom of God against men. For you neither go in yourselves, nor do you allow others to go in. Woe to you, scribes and Pharisees, hypocrites; for you devour widows' houses, and for a pretence make long prayers; therefore you are still more guilty. Woe to you, scribes and Pharisees, hypocrites, for you search seas and lands to make one proselyte, and when you have done so, you make him worse than he had been before. Woe to you, blind guides!'

'Woe to you, scribes and Pharisees, hypocrites, because you build up the tombs of the prophets, and garnish the sepulchers of the righteous; and you suppose that if you had lived in the days when the prophets were martyred, you would not have joined in shedding their blood. Then you are witnesses against yourselves, that you are no better than those who killed the prophets. Fill up then the measure begun by those like you yourselves. And behold, I will send to you wise prophets and scribes, and some of them you shall kill and crucify, and some of them shall you scourge in your synagogues and drive them from city to city. And may all the righteous blood shed since the days of Abel fall back upon your heads.

'Every blasphemy may be forgiven, but blasphemy against the Holy Ghost shall never be forgiven.'

Isn't it as if this had been written only yesterday against those who now force men to accept their faith, and persecute and destroy all the prophets and just men, who try to bring their deception to light?

And I saw that though the Church calls its teaching a Christian doctrine, it is in truth the very darkness against which Christ strove and enjoined His disciples to strive.

The doctrine of Christ has two parts. First, it bears upon the life of each individual and upon our social lives; or it has an ethical mission. Second, it points out why men ought to live in the way it enjoins and not otherwise; or it has a metaphysical mission. One is the effect and, at the same time, the cause of the other. Man must live thus because such is the purpose of his creation; or the purpose of his creation is such, and therefore he must live thus. These two sides of every doctrine are to be found in all the religions of the world. Such is the religion of Brahma, Confucius, Buddha, and Moses, and such is the religion of Christ. It teaches us how we are to live and explains why we are to live thus. But what befell all these other doctrines has befallen the doctrine of Christ also. Men have turned aside from it, and there are many who try to justify their having done so. Sitting down in Moses' seat, they explain the metaphysical part of the doctrine in a way that makes the ethical requirements of the doctrine no longer obligatory, and they replace them by outward worship, rites, and ceremonies. The same occurs in all religions, but it appears to me that never has the evil influence been so striking as in Christianity. It acted with peculiar force, because the doctrine of Christ is the most sublime of all doctrines; it is the most sublime just because the metaphysical and ethical parts of the doctrine are so indissolubly bound together, and so bear upon each other that it is impossible to separate one from the other without depriving the whole doctrine of its true sense. The doctrine of Christ is ultra-Protestantism, for it rejects not only all the ritualistic observances of Judaism, but also every outward form of worship. This rupture in Christianity could have no other effect than to completely pervert the doctrine and deprive it of all sense. And it did so. The rupture between the doctrine of life and the exposition of how we are to live began with the sermon of Paul, who did not know the ethical teaching expressed in the gospel of Matthew, and who preached a metaphysically cabalistic theory, foreign to Christ. The rupture was definitely accomplished in the time of Constantine, when it was found possible to array the whole pagan course of life in Christian clothing, without any change, and then to call it Christianity. From the time of Constantine, the heathen of heathens, whom the Church has canonized for all his vices and crimes, began 'councils,' and the center of gravity of Christianity was transferred to the metaphysical side of the teaching alone. And this metaphysical teaching, with the rites that form part of it, losing more and more of its fundamental sense, reached its present point. It has become a teaching that explains the mysteries of life in heaven, and gives the most complicated rites for divine worship, but at the same time gives no religious teaching at all concerning life on earth.

All religious creeds, except that of the Christian Church, enjoin, besides the observance of certain rites, good deeds and forbearance from evil ones. Judaism requires circumcision, the keeping of the Sabbath, the bestowing of alms, the keeping of the year of jubilee, and many other things. Islam requires circumcision, daily prayers five times a day, the tenth part of a man's riches to be given to the poor, the adoration of the tomb of the prophet, and so on. We find the same in all other religions. Be the duties good or bad, they are deeds. Pseudo-Christianity alone exacts nothing of its followers. There is nothing that is obligatory to a Christian, if we exclude fast-days and prayers, which the Church itself does not consider as obligatory; there is nothing that he must refrain from. All that is necessary for a pseudo-Christian is never to neglect the sacraments. But the believer does not administer the sacraments to himself; others administer them to him. No obligation lies on the pseudo-Christian; the Church does all that is necessary for him: he is baptized and anointed, the sacraments of Holy Communion and Extreme Unction are administered to him, his confession is taken for granted if he is unable to make it orally, prayers are said for him, and he is saved. From the time of Constantine the Church never required any deeds of its members; it never even enjoined a man to refrain from anything. The Christian Church acknowledged and consecrated all that had existed in the pagan world. It acknowledged and consecrated divorce, slavery, courts of law, and all the powers that had existed before, such as war and persecution, and only required evil to be renounced in word at baptism. The Church acknowledged the doctrine of Christ in word, but denied it in deed.

Instead of pointing out to the world what life ought to be, the Church expounded the metaphysical part of Christ's doctrine in a way that required no duties, and did not hinder people from living on as they had lived before. The Church, having once given way to the world, followed it ever after. The world organized its existence in direct opposition to the doctrine of Christ, and the Church invented metaphors according to which it appeared that men who really lived contrary to the law of Christ lived in accordance with it. And the world began to lead a life that rapidly grew worse than that of the pagans, and the Church began to justify this way of living and to affirm that it was strictly in accordance with the doctrine of Christ.

But a time came when the light of the true doctrine, which lies in the gospel, penetrated among the people in spite of the Church, which had tried to conceal the doctrine by forbidding the translation of the Bible; the time came when this light penetrated among the people through so-called sectarians, and even through free-thinkers, and then the falsity of the Church teaching grew evident to all, and men began to change their former lives and live up to that doctrine of Christ that had reached them independently of the Church.

Thus men annihilated slavery, which had been justified by the Church; annihilated religious executions, which had been sanctioned by the Church; annihilated the power of sovereigns and popes, which had been consecrated by the Church; and now the turn of property and kingdoms has come. The Church never rose in defense of anything, and cannot do so, because the annihilation of these false principles of life is based on the Christian doctrine that the Church has preached and still preaches.

The doctrine of life has emancipated itself from the Church, and has established itself independently of it. The Church retains the right to interpret Christ's doctrine; but what interpretation can it give? The metaphysical explanation of the doctrine has weight only when it explains what life is, or ought to be. But no such teaching is left to the Church. It could only speak of the life that it had organized of old, which is now no more. If any of the old interpretations remain, as, for instance, when the catechism tells us that we must kill when it is our duty to do so, nobody believes them; and nothing is left to the Church but its temples, images, brocades, and words.

The Church has carried the light of the Christian doctrine of life through eighteen centuries; and while trying to conceal it in its raiment it has been burnt itself in this light. The world, with its social adjustments consecrated by the Church, has now thrown the Church aside in the name of the same Christian truths that the Church unwillingly carried along with it, and the world now lives without it. The Church is done with, and it is impossible to conceal the fact. All those who really live, and do not drearily vegetate, in our European world have left the Church.

All Churches, whether Catholic, Orthodox, or Protestant, are like sentinels keeping guard over a captive, while the captive has escaped and even walks about among the sentinels. All that now forms true 'life' in the world, Socialism, Communism, theories of political economy, utilitarianism, liberty and equality, all the moral opinions of men, all that governs the world and that the Church considers to be inimical to it, is a part of the very doctrine the same Church unwittingly brought in together with the doctrine of Christ that it tried to conceal.

The life of the world in our time follows its own course, independently of the teaching of the Church. That teaching has remained so far behind that men of the world hearken no more to the voices of the teachers; and, indeed, there is nothing worth listening to, because the Church only gives explanations that the world has already grown tired of – explanations of an organization that is rapidly decaying.

Certain men set out in a boat, while a man at the helm steered. He was a skilful pilot, and the boat glided rapidly on; but a time came when a less skilful helmsman took his place. Finding the latter incapable of steering well, those in the boat first ridiculed him and then drove him away.

That would not have mattered much if the men had not forgotten, in their anger against the useless helmsman, that without one they would not know in what direction they were going. So it was with our Christian world. The Church does not stand at the helm any more; we row rapidly on, and all the progress of knowledge on which our nineteenth century prides itself is only the result of our floating without a helmsman. We do not know where we are going. We go on leading our present lives absolutely without knowing why we do so. And yet it is as unreasonable to live without knowing why we do so as it is to set off in a boat without knowing to where we are bound.

If men did nothing themselves, but were placed in the position they occupy by some outward power, then they might answer the question, 'Why are you in such a position?' by saying that they did not know why. But men make their own positions for themselves, for each other, and especially for their children, and they must therefore be able to answer when asked why they assemble into armies, to cripple and to kill each other; why they waste the immense strength of millions in erecting useless and pernicious cities; why they organize their petty courts of law, and send men whom they call criminals out of France to Cayenne, out of Russia to Siberia, and out of England to Australia, while knowing that it is senseless to act thus. When they are asked why they leave the fields and woods they love to work in factories and sweatshops that they hate; why they bring up their children to lead the same lives though they disapprove of them; they ought to be able to give some reason for their conduct. Even if all this were pleasant, men should be able to give their reasons; but when it is the hardest possible work, when men groan over it, how can they go on acting in this way without trying to find adequate reasons. Men never have lived without trying to solve these questions; men cannot live without making the attempt.

The Jew lived as he lived – he made war, he executed men, he built temples, he organized his life thus and not otherwise—because it was enjoined him by the Law, which, according to his conviction, came from God Himself. It is thus likewise with the Hindus and the Chinese, it was thus with the Romans and the

Muslims, it was thus with the Christians a hundred years ago, and it is thus now with the ignorant crowd. The unthoughtful Christian now solves these questions in this way: soldiery, war, courts of law, and executions exist according to the commandments of God, transmitted to us by the Church. The Church teaches that the world, as we know it, is a lost world. All the evil that fills it exists only by the will of God as a punishment for the sins of men, and therefore we must submit to it. We can only save our souls by faith, by the sacraments, by prayer, and by submission to the will of God. The Church teaches us that each must submit to the sovereign, who is the anointed of God, and to those who are in authority over us; that each must defend his own property by violence, make war, and execute or be executed according to the will of the authorities placed over him by God. It does not matter if this explanation good or bad, it formerly explained all the various phases of life to the believing Christian, and man did not renounce his own reason while living according to the law that he acknowledged as divine. But now the time has come when only the most ignorant believe in this, and even their number decreases with every day and every hour of the day. There is no possibility of stopping this progression. All eagerly follow those who are in front, and all will soon reach the point where the foremost now stand. But the foremost are standing upon the brink of an abyss. The position of the foremost is an awful one. They point out the path to those who are to follow them, and are themselves completely ignorant both of what they are doing and of the things that impel them to act as they do. There is not one man among them who could now answer the direct question, "Why do you lead the life that you lead?' 'Why do you do what you do?' I have addressed such questions to hundreds of men, and have never received a direct reply. Instead of a plain answer to the question, I always received an answer to some question that I had not asked. Whenever I asked a Catholic, Protestant, or Orthodox believer why he lived as he did—so contrary to the doctrine of Christ, which he professed—instead of a direct answer, each would begin to talk of the lamentable want of faith of the present generation, of the wicked men who propagate irreligion, and of what awaited the Church in future. But the answer why the man did not do what his creed enjoined was never given to me. Instead of answering about himself he would speak of the general state of mankind, and of the Church, as if his own life was of no importance whatever, and as if he were engrossed by the idea of saving all mankind, and especially the institution called 'the Church.'

A philosopher, whether an idealist, a spiritualist, a pessimist, or a positivist, would answer the question of why he did not live according to his philosophical teaching by talking of the progress of mankind and of the historical law of that progress, thanks to which mankind was rapidly advancing toward perfect happiness. But he would never give a direct answer to the question, why he himself, in his own life, did not fulfill what he considered rational. The philosopher, like the believer, seems to be taken up with observing the general laws of all humanity rather than with the ordering of his own individual life.

If you ask an average man, a representative of the great majority of the civilized men who are half believers, half unbelievers, and who are all, without a single exception, dissatisfied with their own lives and with our social adjustments, and who always foresee approaching ruin – such an average man, on being asked why he leads a life that he himself finds fault with, and why he does nothing to improve it, never gives you a direct answer and never speaks of himself, but turns the conversation to some general question about justice, trade, the state, or civilization. If he is a policeman or an attorney he will say, 'And how are things to go on if, in order to better my own life, I take no part in the affairs of the country? How will trade progress?' If he is a merchant he will say, 'What progress will civilization make, if I do not cooperate in its advancement?' Each speaks as if the problem of his life did not lie in attaining the happiness toward which he strives, but in serving the state, commerce, or civilization. The average man answers exactly as the believer and philosopher do. He answers a personal question by a general one; and the reason why the believer, the philosopher, and the average man retort by a general question is that not one of them has any true notion of life. And each of them really feels ashamed of his ignorance.

It is only in our Christian world that, instead of the doctrine of life, the explanation of what our life ought to be—which is religion—there is only the explanation of why life must be such as it was of old; and the name of religion is given to a teaching that nobody needs. Nor is that all; science has acknowledged this same fortuitous, defective position of society as the law of all mankind. Learned men, such as Tillet, Spenser, and others, argue very seriously about 'religion,' understanding by the word the metaphysical teaching of the 'origin of all,' without suspecting that, instead of speaking of religion as a whole, they speak of only a part of it.

The result of all this is that, in our century, we see wise and learned men who are 'naively' convinced that they are devoid of all religion, only because they do not acknowledge the correctness of those metaphysical explanations that were, in some past time, given as explanations of life. The idea never occurs to them that they must live in some way or other, that they do live in some way or other, and that it is exactly the principle on which their lives are based that is their religion. These men imagine that they have very elevated convictions and no faith. But, whatever they may say, they have faith if they accomplish any rational work, because rational work is always the result of faith.

We may live according to the teaching of the world; we may lead an animal life without acknowledging anything higher and more obligatory than the decrees of the existing authorities. But he who lives thus cannot be said to live rationally. Before saying that we live rationally we must answer the question, 'Which doctrine of life do we consider as a rational one?' Miserable beings that we are, we have no such doctrine; we have even lost all consciousness of the necessity for gaining any rational doctrine of life.

Ask the men of our day, whether they are believers or unbelievers, what doctrine they follow. They will be obliged to confess that they follow only the laws written by the officials of the Second Section, or by the Legislative Assembly, and put in practice by the police. This is the only teaching that our European world acknowledges. They know that this teaching does not come either from heaven or from the prophets, neither was it taught by the sages. They blame the regulations of these officials and of the legislative assemblies but submit to its executors, who are the police, and obey the most barbarous exactions without a murmur. The legislative assemblies have decreed, and officials have written, that each young man must be ready to submit to insult, death, and murder; and all the fathers and mothers who have grown-up sons obey that law.

But all notions of there being a law that is indubitably rational and that each feels in his inmost soul to be obligatory are so lost in our world that the existence of a law among the Hebrews, which defined the whole order of life, for them, a law that was rendered obligatory by the moral feeling of each, is considered as existing exclusively among the Hebrews. It is regarded as a peculiarity of the Hebrew nation that they obeyed what they considered in their inmost souls to be the indubitable truth, received directly from God, and they knew it to be such because it was in unison with their conscience. The position of an educated man, a Christian, is considered to be a normal and natural one when he obeys what he knows was only written by despised men and is enforced by policemen, that is, when he obeys what he feels to be unjust and contrary to his conscience.

It was in vain that I looked in our civilized world for some moral principles of life that should be clearly expressed. There are none. There is even no consciousness of such principles being necessary. There is even a firm conviction that moral principles are unnecessary; and that religion only consists in words about a future life, about God, about certain rites that, as some say, are necessary for salvation, while others consider them as totally unnecessary, and say that life goes on independently of all rules—that all that is necessary is to obey passively.

The main points of faith are the doctrine of life and the explanation of what life is and ought to be. Of these the first is considered as unimportant and as having nothing to do with faith, while the second is only an explanation of a life that was, in some past time, together with some conjectures about the historical progress of life, and this is considered as the most important and serious point. In all that really enters into the life of man—for instance, how he is to live, is he to commit murder or not, is he to condemn his fellow-creatures or not, in what way he is to bring up his children—men submit without a murmur to the rule of others who know no more than they do themselves why they themselves live as they do, and why they insist upon others living the same way.

And men consider such a life as rational, and are not ashamed of it. This state of things would be awful, were it universal. Fortunately, there are men in our days, the best men of our time, who, dissatisfied with such a creed, have a creed of their own concerning the life that we ought to lead.

These men are considered as pernicious and dangerous unbelievers; and yet they are the only believers. They are believers in the doctrine of Christ, or at least in a part of it.

These men often do not know the whole doctrine of Christ. They do not properly understand it, and indeed they often reject the chief basis of the Christian faith, which is non-resistance of evil; but their faith in what life ought to be is derived from the doctrine of Christ. However these men may be persecuted and slandered, they are the only men who do not passively submit to all that they are ordered to do, and therefore they are the only men who do not vegetate, but lead a rational life, and they are the only true believers.

The link between the world and the Church grew weaker and weaker, according as its teaching flowed more and more into the world.

And now the last link, which bound us to the Church, is breaking, and an independent process of life is beginning.

The teaching of the Church, with its dogmas, councils, and hierarchy, is unquestionably bound up with the doctrine of Christ.

Our European world, outwardly so self-confident, bold, and decided, and yet in the depth of its consciousness so terrified and confused, is undergoing what a new-born babe does; it tosses about, turning from side to side crying, and not knowing what it is to do. It feels that the source of its former nourishment has dried up, but does not yet know where to look for a new one.

It is thus with our European world. See what a complicated, seemingly rational, energetic life there is in our European world. Art, science, trade, and social activity—all are full of life. But all this only lives because its mother has recently fed it. The Church brought the rational doctrine of Christ into the world. It has done its business, and now has withered away. All the organs of the world are full of life, but the source of their former nourishment is stopped, and they have not found a new one. They seek it everywhere.

The world now has to comprehend that the former unconscious process of nourishment has outlived its time, and that a new, conscious process of nourishment is necessary.

This new process consists in admitting those truths of the Christian doctrine that had formerly flowed into the world through the medium of the Church, and that are the sources of life. Men must again lift up the light that was hidden from them, and they must place it high before themselves and others and consciously live in that light.

The doctrine of Christ as a religion that defines life, and gives an explanation of human life, stands now as it did 1800 years ago before the world. But before, the world had the interpretations of the Church, which, while hiding the doctrine from their eyes, seemed to suffice for its life; but now the time has come when the Church has served its time and the world has no one to explain to it the problem of its new life, and feeling its helplessness, must accept the doctrine of Christ.

Christ teaches us, first of all, to believe in the light while the light is in us. Christ teaches men to place this light of reason above all else, to live up to it, and not to do what they themselves acknowledge to be irrational. If you consider it irrational to kill Turks or Germans, do not do so; if you consider it irrational to force poor creatures to work hard, in order that you may wear fine hats or have fine drawing rooms, do not do so; if you find it an irrational proceeding to shut up those who have been depraved by idleness in a prison, in this way to condemn them to the worst possible company and to complete idleness, then do not do so; if you think it irrational to live in an infected town when you can live in the fresh fields, do not do so; if you consider it irrational to make your children study the dead languages more than they do anything else, then do not do so.

The doctrine of Christ is 'light.' The light shines. It is impossible not to accept the light when it shines. It is impossible to struggle against it; it is impossible to refuse to accept it. It is impossible to refuse the doctrine of Christ because it encompasses all the errors in which men live, and, like the ether, which those who study the philosophy of nature speak of, it penetrates all. The doctrine of Christ is essential for each, whatever position he may be in. Christ's doctrine must be accepted by men, not because it is impossible to deny the metaphysical explanation of life that it gives (we may deny all we choose), but because it alone gives us rules of life, without which mankind cannot live, if, at least, they wish to live as rational beings.

The power of Christ's doctrine does not lie in the explanations it gives of the sense of life, but in the doctrine of life that flows out of it. The metaphysical teaching of Christ is not new. It is a teaching that is written in the hearts of men and that all the truly wise men of the world preached. But the power of Christ's doctrine lies in the practical application of this metaphysical teaching to life.

The metaphysical foundation of the teaching of the ancient Hebrews and of that of Christ is the same: 'love to God and love to our neighbor.' But the application of this doctrine to life, according to Moses and according to the law of Christ, is very different. According to the Law of Moses it was necessary to fulfill 613 commandments, including some most senseless and cruel ones, all based upon the authority of the scriptures. According to the law of Christ the teaching that flows out of the same metaphysical basis is expressed in five rational commandments, which carry their own meaning and their own justification along with them, and which embrace the life of all mankind.

The doctrine of Christ would not be rejected either by Jews, Buddhists, Muslims, or others, even if they doubted the truth of their own creed; still less can it be rejected by our Christian world, which has no other moral law.

The doctrine of Christ does not disagree with men in respect to their view of life, but, including it, gives them what is wanting in it, what is indispensable. It points out to them a path that is not a new one, but one familiar to them from their childhood.

You are a believer, whatever creed you may profess. You believe in the creation of the world, in the Trinity, in the fall and the redemption of man, in the sacraments, in the efficacy of prayer, or in the Church. Christ's doctrine does not tell you that your creed is wrong; it only gives it what is wanting. While you keep to your present creed you feel that the life of the world and your own life are full of evil, and you see no way of escape from this evil. The doctrine of Christ (obligatory to you, being the teaching of your God), gives you simple rules that will deliver you and others from that evil. Believe in resurrection from the dead, believe in paradise, in hell, in the pope, in the Church, pray as your creed enjoins you to do, keep the fasts, sing psalms, and all this does not prevent you from fulfilling what Christ tells you to do in order to attain true happiness, namely, avoid anger, do not commit adultery, do not swear, do not defend yourself by violence, never make war.

It may, perhaps, happen that you will not always fulfill all this. You will yield to temptation and transgress one of these laws, just as you violate the rules of the civil law or the laws of good breeding. You will, perhaps, in a moment of impulse, swerve from the rules laid down by Christ. But in your calmer moments do not act as you do now, do not organize your life in a way that renders it difficult to avoid anger and adultery, to abstain from swearing and using violence or making war; but organize it in a way that should make all these things difficult to do. You must admit the duty of acting thus, for these are the commandments of God.

You are, perhaps, an unbeliever or a philosopher. You say that all goes on in the world according to a law that you have discovered. The doctrine of Christ fully acknowledges the law that you have discovered. But, independent of this law, which will bring good to mankind after thousands of years, is your own individual life. Now you have no rules at all for your own individual life, except those written by men whom you despise, and enforced by the police. The doctrine of Christ gives you rules that decidedly agree with your law, for your law of altruism is nothing but a bad periphrasis for the doctrine of Christ.

Or you are neither a believer nor an unbeliever, you have no time to seek the purpose of life, and you have no definite creed; it is enough for you that you act as all others do. Then Christ's doctrine says in effect to you, you are unable to verify the truth of the doctrine that is preached to you – you find it easier to follow the example of those around you; but, however humble you may be in mind, you have a judge in your heart who sometimes makes you feel that you have acted rightly, and at other times shows you that you are wrong. However modest your lot may be, you cannot help sometimes asking yourself, 'Ought I to act as all around me do, or according to my own feeling?' And no sooner does the question arise in your mind than the precepts of Christ are found to answer both your reason and your conscience. If you are more a believer than an unbeliever, you act according to the will of God by following the precepts of Christ; if you are more a free-thinker than a believer, by obeying Christ's precepts you follow the most rational laws that ever existed in the world, as you will see yourself, because the precepts of Christ bear their own justification in themselves.

Christ says (John 12:31), 'Now is the judgment of this world; now shall the prince of this world be cast out.'

He says likewise (John 16:33), 'These things I have spoken to you that in Me you might have peace. In the world you shall have tribulation; but be of good cheer, I have overcome the world.'

And it is in this way that the world, or the evil that is in the world, is overcome.

If a world of evil still exists, it exists only as something that is dead. It lives only by inertia; there is no force of life in it. It does not exist for him who believes in the commandments of Christ. It is conquered by the rational consciousness of the son of man.

'For whatever is born of God overcomes the world. The victory that overcomes the world is your faith' (1 John 5:4).

The faith that overcomes the world is faith in the teaching of Christ.

Chapter XII

I believe in the doctrine of Christ, and the articles of my belief are as follows.

I believe that true happiness will only be possible when all men begin to follow Christ's doctrine.

I believe that the fulfillment of this doctrine is easy, possible, and conducive to happiness.

I believe that, even if it is left unfulfilled by all around me, if I have to stand alone among men, I cannot do otherwise than to follow it in order to save my own life from inevitable destruction.

I believe that, while I followed the teaching of the world, my life was a life of suffering, and that it is only by living according to the doctrine of Christ that I can attain the happiness that the Father of life destined me to enjoy in this world.

'The law is given through Moses; but happiness and truth are given through Jesus Christ' (John 1:17). The doctrine of Christ is happiness and truth. When I did not know the truth I did not know true happiness. Thinking that evil was happiness, I fell into evil, and I doubted my right to long for happiness. Now, I have understood and believed that the happiness for which I long is the will of the Father, and is the lawful basis of my life. Christ says to me, 'Live for your happiness and for that of others, but do not believe in the snares — temptations (σκανδαλος) — that attract you by a semblance of happiness, while they, in reality, deprive you of it and entice you into evil. Your happiness is in your unity with all men. Do not deprive yourself of the happiness given to you.'

Christ has revealed to me that love toward all men is not only a duty that we must all strive after, but that in it lies true happiness — a happiness as natural to men as it is to children, as He says; and it is innate in all men until it is destroyed by deceit, error, and temptation.

Christ has not only revealed this to me, but has enumerated in His commandments all the temptations that draw me away from the state of unity, love, and happiness natural to man, and entice me into the snares of wickedness. The commandments of Christ show me how to escape the temptations that led me away from true happiness.

Happiness was given to me, and I have destroyed it. Christ's commandments reveal the snares that have destroyed my happiness, and therefore I cannot help endeavoring to avoid them. My creed is in this, and in this alone.

Christ has shown me that the first snare is enmity — anger. I believe this, and can, therefore, no longer harbor a feeling of enmity against any man. I can no longer pride myself upon my anger as I used to do, nor justify it to myself by thinking myself great and clever, and others insignificant and foolish. As soon as I remember that I am giving way to anger I can no longer refuse to acknowledge myself in the wrong, nor can I help seeking to be reconciled to those who are at enmity with me.

Nor is that all. If I know that my anger is unnatural and wicked, I likewise know the snare that led me into it. The snare was my standing aloof from others, acknowledging only a few as my equals, and all the rest of the world as insignificant (racas) or foolish and ignorant (you fool!). I see now that these habits of holding myself aloof from others and considering them as fools (racas) were the chief causes of my enmity toward men. On recalling my past life to mind, I now see that I never once harbored a feeling of enmity toward those whom I considered my superiors, and that I never intentionally wounded their feelings; that, on the contrary, the most trifling circumstances sufficed to excite my anger against a man whom I considered my inferior, and the more I considered myself above him the easier I found it to outrage him. But I know now that he who humbles himself before others and who works for others is the only one who stands above the rest. I understand now that what is highly esteemed by men is abomination in the sight of God, why woe is foretold to the rich and famous, and why beggars and those who are humble are the blessed. My understanding of this has changed my view of all that is good and noble or bad and base in life. All that had formerly seemed good and noble in my eyes — such things as honor, glory, education, riches, all the refinements of life, elegant furniture, good food, fine clothes, etc. — have grown worthless to me. All that had seemed bad and base — such things as obscurity, poverty, uncouth manners, simplicity of furniture, of food, of clothes, etc. — have grown good and noble in my eyes. If, therefore, I now inadvertently give myself up to anger and wound another's feelings, I dare not, after a moment's serious reflection, yield to the temptation that deprives me of true happiness, union, and love, any more than a man can set a snare for himself in which he was once caught. I can no longer try to rise above other men and to separate myself from them, nor can I allow either rank or title for others or myself, except the title of 'man'. I can no longer seek fame or glory, nor can I help trying to get rid of my riches, which separate me from my fellow-creatures. I cannot help seeking in my way of life, in its surroundings, in my food, my clothes, and my manners to draw nearer to the majority of men, and to avoid all that separates me from them.

Christ has shown me that the second snare that destroys my happiness is 'lasciviousness,' 'sensuality.' Knowing this, I can no longer acknowledge such passions to be natural, and I cannot justify them to myself. No sooner do I feel that I am giving way to my passions than I know myself to be in an unhealthy, unnatural state of mind, and try by all possible means to escape this evil.

And, knowing the sin, I know, too, the snares that led me into it, and I can no longer yield to it. I know now that the chief cause of temptation lies in the separation of men and women from those to whom they were once united. I know now that the forsaking of those to whom men and women have been once united is the 'divorce' that Christ forbids, for it brings depravity into the world. On recalling my past life, I see clearly that it was not only the unnatural education I had received that had led me into lasciviousness, by both physically and morally exciting my passions and justifying them by all the refinements of wit, but likewise my having forsaken the woman with whom I had first been united. I understood the full meaning of Christ's words, and saw that God had created man and woman in order that they might live in couples, and that what God had joined together should never be put asunder. I now see clearly that monogamy is the natural law of mankind and must never be broken. I understand the words that 'he who divorces his wife,' that is, the woman to whom he was first united, 'forces her to commit adultery,' and brings new evil into the world. My belief in this has changed my former estimate of what is good and noble or bad and base in life. The things that I had formerly prized — a refined, elegant life and the passionate and poetic love extolled by all poets and artists — has become wicked and hideous in my eyes. A hard working, poor, simple life, which masters human passions, alone seems desirable.

It is not our human institution of marriage that makes really lawful the union of man and woman. I consider as sacred and obligatory that union alone which, once and forever, binds a man to the first woman he loves.

I can no longer give way to idleness and an easy life, which always tends to excite inordinate desires, nor can I find pleasure in novel reading, poetry, music, or balls, which I had hitherto regarded, not only as innocent, but even as refined occupations. I cannot forsake my wife, for I now know that my doing so is a snare for others, for her, and for myself; neither can I cooperate in the separation of any husband and wife, whether their union has been associated with church rites or not. Every union between a man and woman I consider to be sacred and binding to the end of their days.

Christ has revealed to me that the third snare that destroys my happiness is the 'taking of an oath.' I believe this, and I dare not take any oath. Nor dare I allege, for my justification, that my doing so cannot harm anyone, that all do so, that the State requires it of me, and that my refusing to do so will do no good either to others or myself. I know that this is an evil for all men and me, and I cannot do it.

I know, besides, wherein the temptation lay, which enticed me into this evil, and I dare not yield to it any more. I know that the snare lies in our sanctioning deception. Men swear to submit to the commands of other men, whereas man must submit to God alone. The most awful evils in the world, by the consequences they entail, such as war, imprisonment, executions, and torture, only exist through this snare, by which all responsibility is taken off those who do evil. I now understand the meaning of the words, 'All that is more than a simple affirmation or negation, yes or no, is evil.' Every promise is evil. Having understood this, I now see that the taking of an oath is against my own good, as well as the good of others; and the knowledge that it is so has altered my estimate of what is good and noble or bad and base. All that had seemed most good and noble to me before — obligatory allegiance to the government, the extortion of oaths from men, all the deeds conscience condemns that are mostly the result of a man's having taken an oath — seem bad and base to me now. Therefore, I can no longer set aside the commandment of Christ, which says, 'Swear not at all.' I cannot now swear an oath, nor can I insist upon others dong so, nor can I encourage men to consider taking an oath as necessary or even harmless.

Christ has revealed to me that the fourth snare is 'resisting evil by violence.' I know that my doing so leads others and me into evil, and cannot therefore justify myself by saying that it is necessary for the protection of others, of my property, or of myself. No sooner do I remember this than I cannot help abstaining from violence of every kind.

And I know, likewise, what the snare is. It is the erroneous idea that my welfare can be secured by defending my property and myself against others. I now know that the greater part of the evil men suffer from arises from this. Instead of working for others, each tries to work as little as possible, and forcibly makes others work for him. And on recalling to mind all the evil done by others and myself, I see that it proceeded, for the most part, from our considering it possible to secure and better our conditions by violence. I now understand the meaning of the words, 'man is born, not to be ministered to, but to minister to others.' I now understand the saying, 'the laborer is worthy of his hire.' I now believe that my happiness, and that of all men, will only be attained when each labors for others and not for himself, when none refuses to labor for him who is in need of help. My belief in this has altered my estimate of good and evil. All that I had formerly prized — such things as riches, property, honor, and self-dignity — have grown worthless in my eyes; and all I had formerly despised — such things as hard work, poverty, humility, the renunciation of property, and the renunciation of one's rights — have grown good and noble in my eyes. If I now feel tempted to defend others or myself, the property of others or my own, by violence, I can no longer give way to temptation. I dare not amass riches for myself. I dare not use violence of any kind against my fellow-creatures, except, perhaps, against a child in order to save it from present harm; nor can I now take part in any act of authority, the purpose of which is to protect men's property by violence. I can neither be a judge, nor take part in judging and condemning.

Christ has revealed to me that the fifth snare is 'the distinction we make between our own and foreign nations.' If, therefore, a feeling of enmity arises in my heart against a foreigner, I cannot help acknowledging, after a few moments' serious reflection, that the feeling is a wicked one; I can no longer justify this feeling to myself by acknowledging the superiority of my own nation over others, or by the cruelty or barbarity of any other nation. I cannot help trying to be kinder and more friendly toward a foreigner than toward my own countrymen, rather than otherwise.

And knowing that the distinction I formerly made between my own and other nations is evil, I see the snare that led me into this evil, and can no longer consciously let myself be drawn into it. It is the erroneous idea that my welfare is linked only with that of my native land, and not with that of all mankind. But I now know that my unity with other men cannot be destroyed by frontiers, barriers, the disposal of kingdoms, or by my belonging to some particular nation. I now know that men are equal everywhere — that all are 'brethren.' On recalling to mind all the evil that I did myself and that I suffered from others in consequence of the enmity that so often exists between different nations, it is clear to me that the cause was the gross imposition called 'patriotism'. I can remember perfectly well that the feeling of enmity toward other nations, the assumption that a difference existed between them and myself, was not a feeling natural to me, but was grafted upon me by the senseless education given to me. But I now understand the meaning of the words, 'Love your enemies, do good to them.' You are all the children of one Father, therefore be like the Father; that is, make no distinction between men, treat all as brethren. I now see clearly that I can only attain happiness by being in unity with all my fellow-creatures. I believe in this. And this belief has completely altered my former estimate of what is good and noble or bad and base. All that I formerly prized as something worthy of respect — love for our native land, pride in our country, and our administration in military exploits — now seems not only pitiful but also hideous to me. Cosmopolitanism, which I had formerly despised, now seems a noble thing to me. I can no longer take any part in quarrels between various nations, either in speech or by writing; neither can I take part in any of the various administrations based on the difference of nationality, either in custom-houses, in collecting taxes, in preparing ammunition or fire-arms, or in military service; still less can I take part in war against other nations. And having understood what is conducive to happiness, I can no longer do what deprives me of it.

I believe that I must live thus. I believe that it is only by living thus that I can find a rational purpose in life. I believe that my rational life is the light given to me in order that it should shine before men, not in my words, but in my good deeds, that men may glorify their Father (Matthew 5:6). I believe that my life and my knowledge of the truth are the treasure that has been entrusted to me; that they are a fire that cannot be quenched. I believe that I am a Ninevite in relation to other Jonahs, from whom I have learned the truth, but that I am also Jonah in relation to other Ninevites, to whom it is my duty to reveal the truth. I believe that the only true purpose of my life is 'to live up to the light that is in me,' not to conceal it, but to set it high before men, that all should see it; and this belief gives me new strength to fulfill the doctrine of Christ, and destroys all the obstacles that had formerly stood in my way.

All that had undermined my belief in the truth of Christ's doctrine and had made it seem impracticable; all that had set me against it, such as having to endure privation, suffering, and death at the hands of those who do not know His doctrine, is just what now confirms its truth in my eyes and attracts me toward it.

Christ has said, 'When you lift up the son of man, all will be drawn up,' and I felt myself irresistibly drawn to Him. He said, likewise, 'The truth will set you free,' and I felt completely free.

I had previously thought that enemies would come to make war or wicked men would assault me, and if I did not defend myself they would despoil me and all my family; they would abuse us, torture and kill me and mine; and this seemed horrible to me. But all that troubled me before has now turned to joy, and confirmed the truth. I know that my enemies, the so-called wicked men of the world — robbers, etc. — are men, and are the 'sons of men'; that they, like me, bear love for goodness and hatred of evil innate in them; that they live, as I do, on the eve of death, and, like me, can only be saved by fulfilling the doctrine of Christ. If the truth is unknown to them, and they do evil, my knowing the truth makes it my duty to reveal it to those who do not know it. I cannot do so otherwise than by refusing to take any part in evil, and by confessing the truth by my deeds.

You say if enemies, such as Germans, Turks, or savages, come to attack you, and if you do not make war, they will kill you all. This is an error. If there were a society of Christians who did no evil to anybody, and who gave the surplus of their labor to others, no enemies, either Germans, Turks, or savages, would torture or kill them. They would take what these Christians (for whom there would exist no difference between Germans, Turks, or savages) would give up to them. If a Christian is called upon to take part in war, that is the moment for him to testify the truth to those who do not know it. Nor can he testify it in any other way than in deed, by refusing to go to war and doing good to all, whether they are enemies or not.

But if the family of a Christian is assaulted, not by foreign enemies, but by wicked men in his own country, if he does not defend himself, he and his family will be robbed, tortured, and killed. This is an error, again. If all the members of a family were Christians, and gave up their lives to the service of others, not one man would despoil them or kill them. Mikluha Mackli settled among a most brutal tribe of savages and was not murdered by them; they learned to love him, and submitted to him, because he did not require anything of them, but did as much good to them as he could.

If a Christian has to live amidst relations and friends who are not Christians in the full sense of the word, who defend themselves and their property by violence, and who call upon him to take part in their violence, then is the time for him to fulfill the duty for which life was given to him. The knowledge of the truth is only given to a Christian in order that he should make it known to others, and especially to those he is more closely connected with, and to whom he is bound by ties of relationship or friendship; and the Christian can testify to the truth in no other way than by avoiding the errors into which others have fallen, and refusing to take part either in the violence of the aggressors or of those who resist them, by giving all up to others, and by showing that his only desire is to fulfill the will of God and that he fears nothing as much as acting against it.

But the country cannot allow a member to evade fulfilling the duties incumbent on every citizen. The administration of the country requires each man to take his oath of allegiance, to take part in judging and condemning; each man is obliged to enter the military service, and if he refuses he will be exposed to punishment, exile, imprisonment, and even death. And here again the Christian is called upon to fulfill his duty toward God. The Christian knows that all these things are required of him by men who do not know the truth, and therefore he who does know it must testify it to those who do not. The violence, imprisonment, perhaps even death, to which the Christian will then be exposed in consequence of his refusal, will enable him to testify to the truth, not in words, but in deeds. Every act of violence, pillage, execution, and war is the result, not of the irrational force of nature, but of man's ignorance of the truth. And therefore, the greater the evil these men do, the further they are from the truth, the more desperate is their state, and the more necessary it is that they should be taught the truth. And a

Christian can only transmit the knowledge of the truth to others by keeping away from the error they are in, and by returning good for evil. The whole duty of a Christian, the whole purpose of his life, which cannot be destroyed by death, lies in this.

Men linked together by deception form, we might say, a compact body. In the compactness of this body lies all the evil of the world.

Revolutions are only efforts to break this compact body by violence; but its component parts will last until an inward power is communicated to them that can force them asunder.

The chain that fetters them is 'falsehood,' 'deception.' The power that sets each link of this human chain free is 'truth.' The truth is transmitted to men by deeds.

Deeds, which bring the light to each man's heart, can alone destroy the chain and remove one man after another out of the compact mass fettered by falsehood.

And this has gone on for eighteen hundred years.

The work began when the commandments of Christ were first placed before the world, and it will not end until all is fulfilled as Christ says (Matthew 5:18).

The Church, whose members tried to unite men by persuading them that it was necessary for salvation to blindly believe that the truth was in her, is no more. But the Church, whose followers are not united by promises of reward, but by good deeds, lives, and will live forever. That Church does not consist of men who cry 'Lord, Lord,' and live in sin, but of men who hear His words and follow His commandments.

Those who belong to that Church know that their lives will be blessed if they do not break the unity of the 'Son of Man,' and that their happiness can only be destroyed by their leaving the commandments of Christ unfulfilled. And therefore they follow them, and teach others to do the same.

It does not matter if these men are few in number or many. They are that Church which shall not be overcome, and which all men will join, sooner or later.

'Fear not, little flock, for it is your Father's good pleasure to give you the kingdom.'

Practice and Precepts of Jesus
by *J.C. Kumarappa*

Editor's Forward

Much of Christian thought and many of our writings are written from a position of privilege and relative safety. These writings come from bishops, professors, pastors, nobility, or others who are relatively secure in their positions and writing under the shelter of a relatively stable state. People in this position have the freedom to consider the more esoteric corners of systematic theology at their convenience.

J.C. Kumarappa was in an entirely different situation. He was one of the soldiers in Gandhi's nonviolent campaign to banish England. He struggled to establish an independent India where all people are treated with dignity. Kumarappa was known as "Gandhi's economist", and was motivated by his own devout Christianity to serve with Gandhi. His account of Christianity is born out of an erudite and educated mind, as well as a practioner's soul and experience.

Like many of the greatest Christian writings, Kumarappa's *Practices and Precepts of Jesus* is written from behind the bars of a prison. Kumarappa explicitly credits Tolstoy's *What I Believe*, and he describes here his own pragmatic, gritty reading of Tolstoy's high ideals. Kumarappa's *Practices and Precepts of Jesus* is theology written by someone in the midst of a political revolution fraught with racism and oft-violent religious tension. It is also written by someone with an unwavering faith in the the message of Jesus and the power of the new kingdom to bring peace. If anyone doubts the practicality of the message of Jesus, then let them be reassured by Kumarappa's life and his witness.

Publication History

This book was originally composed in English. It was transcribed into this anthology by the editor from a booklet published by the Navajivan Publishing House, Amedabad, India, ©1945. There had been a total of a mere 8,000 copies of this vital and enlightening text published and distributed by Navajivan as of 2009.

TO
MY MOTHER

"She stretcheth out her hand to the poor;
yea she reacheth forth her hands to the need,"
"And let her own works praise her at the gates."
(Proverbs 31:20,31)

A Word
by Mahatma Gandhi

Having carefully gone through these chapters, I can recommend their perusal to every believer in God, be he a Christian or a follower of any other religion.

The booket presents Professor J.C. Kumarappa's views on Christian teaching in a nutshell. It is a revolutionary view of Jesus as a man of God. It is none the less revealing and interesting. The interpretation of the Lord's Prayer is novel and refreshing as are many other interpretations.

If all believe as Professor Kumarappa does, there will be no religious feuds and rivalries between sects and sects and other religions. Anyway, this reading of the Bible must bring solace to the Christians of India. If they will read the Bible as Professor Kumarappa does, they need not be apologetic of their forefathers or their ancient faith. What is bad and superstitious in the old they are able to throw off by means of the liberal teaching presented in the following pages but it helps one to see that there is much of the old which is imperishable and worthy of being treasured.

Indeed, Professor Kumarappa has a message beyond the confines of India. He speaks with confidence born of a living faith in the belief that the West, though nominally Christian, has not known the true Jesus of the Gospels.

As I was going through these pages, I was reminded of the late Advocate F.A. Laughton of Durban. I was then no student of Roman Dutch Law nor the case of the four States of South Africa. In difficulty, therefore, I used to go to Mr. Laughton for help. But, after I had done with my work he would proudly bring forth from his drawer a green cover book with his father's annotations from the Bible. It was Edwin Arnold's *Song Celestial*, and had Mr. Laughton's father's parallel passages from the Bible showing that there was much in common between the New Testament and the Gita. I was then a novice trying to find out Truth in all its aspects without then knowing that I was so doing. Professor Kumarappa's interpretation with copious quotations form the Bible reminded me of what I used to believe even as early as 1894–95. I can, therefore, speak from experience of the truth of the intrepretation of the Gospels, given in the following pages by Professor Kumarappa.

Sevagram,

M.K. Gandhi
21-3-1945

Preface

This booklet has no pretensions to being the product of a philosopher or a scholar in Christian theology. All the drilling in Christian literature I can lay claim to came in my childhood at my mother's knee and then the Sunday School and daily family prayers.

My mother was not a learned woman in the sense of possessing a university education. She came of devout Christian stock of South India. She had read widely for her generation, especially in Tamil. She spent her life of comparative simplicity in the practice of the tenets of Jesus. Her piety, her sympathy for and love of her neighbors she expressed by her attempt, however humble it may have been, to help those in distress. Her life and actions made an impression on my child mind much greater than many volumes of theology could have done. Her ways of inculcating religion were simple and unique.

As a child I was fond of pets. My mother encouraged me to breed poultry, turkeys, guinea fowls, etc. When she went to the market at the beginning of the month to get her monthly stores she would take me with her to buy chicken feed. During the month I would sell the eggs and keep accounts and at the end of the month she would interest me in finding out what profit had been made. This profit had to be made over to her for being disbursed on simple charities—like the support of an orphan child at some school. Even when I was grown up and working as a Public Auditor, on the first of the month I had to send her my "tithes" out of my income. This "tithe" did not mean a mathematical one tethn but was a liberal tax calculated by the needs of her chairty budget! Once when I was spending a summer holiday with her at Kodaikanal in the early twenties, on a Sunday at church the announcement was made that China was visited by a terrible famine. That day, the noon dinner was a perfect feast. We could not assign any reason for its provocation. When we inquired, mother smilingly replied, "I shall eplain later." We enjoyed our nap. Then at tea time, mother called us together and told us of this famine in China and constrasted it with the sumptuous meal we ourselves had enjoyed and invited us to help in feeding the distressed in China. She brought out a subscription list with amounts set against our several names according to her conception of our respective ability to pay down the sum immediately. She had put me down for fifty rupees and took it too! Besides such personal contributions she made us go round and collect from our friends also. She used the lever of her mother-love to goad us on. This was the home training.

As regards outside influence, in the church organization and its services I found great deviation from the teachings of Jesus. When I came to the discerning age of 16 years, at my confirmation service, in spite of all the catechism and theory we were taught, I was frankly perplexed at the "Communion service". A Bishop of the Church of England will freely partake "Communion" with his chauffeur at the "Lord's Table" but will abhor doing so with a Scotch Presbyterian Doctor of

Divinity and perhaps a Chancellor of a university. While on the other hand, his Lordship, the Bishop, will be pleased to invite socially the Presbyterian Divine to his home to dinner but will not dream of sitting at the same festive board with his driver![1]

Again, as a student in England during the World War I, when I attended war services at St. Paul's Cathedral or at Westminster Abbey, however imposing the service may have been, I failed to reconcile the worship of a Universal Father and the Prince of Peace with tribal appeals to destroy the enemy. Nor could I understand the use of the pulpit by Bishops and other clergy for recruiting. The blood bespattered banners of many a battle and the tombs of noted generals in these places of worship seemed a desecration. These and similar contradictions between Jesus and the churches shook my faith in the "Christianity" of the churches.

The life of the "Christians", both Indian and Western, did little to assuage it. Indian Christians imitated the Westerners even in their mode and standard of living. While they proposed to follow the Master who had not where to lay His head, all the cross they carried was a gold one on their watch chains! I was often told it was not feasible to put the teachings of Jesus literally into practice in this 20th century. This reduced all formal religion to a farce as far as I was concerned. The term "Christian" denoted only a community with certain habits and standards of life—largely westernized and divorced from the national culture of our land, priding itself on its close association with Western culture and civilization.

Up to this time I had little contact with Hindus or Muslims and knew nothing at all of their religions beliefs. (Even to this day, I must confess, I know little of these.) Then a strange set of circumstances brought me in touch with Gandhiji.[2] When I was requested by him to carry out an economic survey in Gujarat some of my best "Christian" friends discourged me from helping a "heathen". However, as the life of "Christians" was not particularly elevating, I did not share their repulsion for the "heathen". When I got acquainted with Gandhiji's programme of work, much on lines familiarized to me in my childhood, my eyes were opened to the practicability of the teachings of Jesus, even in this century, in our life on earth.

As the word "Christian" itself had lost all association with the life and example set by Jesus I have advisedly styled in this pamphlet all those who follow precepts such as the ones Jesus taught "Followers of Jesus", be they Hindus, Muslims, Buddhists, or, perchance, even "Christians", irrespective of their own religious affiliations.

Thus, it will be seen, that the sole authority I hold for the views expressed in this booklet is provided by the life and teaching of Jesus as recorded in the four Gospels. I have not even drawn on the Acts or the writings of the Apostles as I feel that for the practical purposes of today we should depend more on the guidance of the Spirit of Truth to supplement the teachings of Jesus than on the records of the application of the teachings of Jesus than on the records of the application of the

---

[1] [In addition to the obvious classist critique, remember also that Kumarappa is writing from within a South Indian context, and that chauffeur is streotypically Indian, whereas the Bishop is streotypically British.—ed.]   [2] ["Gandhiji" is an honorific version of the name "Gandhi".—ed.]

tenets of Jesus to conditions prevailing in Eastern Asia and Southern Europe two thousand years ago, however inspiring they may prove as corroborating evidence.

Besides all my other handicaps, as this was written in June 1944, in Jabalpur Central Jail, where I spent over fifteen months of my incarceration, I had no means of access to any books other than (1) the Authorized Version of the Bible, (2) the Modern Reader's Bible by R.G. Moulton, (3) the New Testament, translated by James Moffatt, and (4) the New Testament, translation by E.J. Goodspeed. Ordinarily I have quoted the Authorized Version excepting where its translation was defective; in such cases, I have indicated the other sources.

With all this background, I offer these thoughts in the hope that some wandering soul, similarly placed, may draw some help from them.

I am sure the reader will share my gratitude to Gandhiji for the heartening word of testimony drawn from his own rich experience.

J.C. Kumarappa
27-3-1945
Maganwadi,
Wardha, C.P.

Preface to the Reprint

That a reprint should have been called for within six months of the publication shows that this book has had much better reception than was expected. Even orthodox Christians have welcomed it. This presumably indicates that people are thinking about their brand of Christianity which had not brought satisfaction to their souls under the stress and strails and trials and tribulation visisted upon the world in the past few years.

Most of the reviews have been appreciative, just a few have been critical. To this latter group I wish to emphasized the fact that no final revelation is possible as long as man is finite. Each individual has to accept the guidance of the Spirit of Truth. There are likely to be differences in the intrepretation of passages. What satisfies one may not satisfy another. This does not necessarily indicate that the intrepretations or the lessons drawn are wrong. It only reveals that each person has his own approach to the Infinite. Hence no attempt need be made to answer any of the criticisms offered as this book does not claim to present the one and only possible interpretation of the teachings of Jesus.

A sister from Tamilnad, who hwas translated this book into the provincial toungue, points out that the Tamil translation, compared with the original Greek revised and published in 1936 by the Madras Branch of the B. and F. Bible Society, renders the Precept "You are not to resist an injury"[1] as "Resist not with evil". This makes the meaning crystal lear. It contemplates resistance but not with evil weapons or means. My thanks are due to the sister for the valuable assistance she ahs given.

I am grateful to Rev. J.F. Edwards of Poona for his painstaking revision of this booklet and setting right many clerical errors. The text of this book has undergone no material change.

J.C. Kumarappa
17-1-1946
Maganwadi,
Wardha, C.P.

---

[1] Matthew 5:39

Canons of Intrepretation

When shorn of all jewish theological phraseology and subjective literary gloss, the four gospels—Matthew, Mark, Luke, and John—form some of the most human documents setting forth the life and teachings of a Master who taught, not as a professional, but as one having authority and as one who understood all men and needed not that they should testify to Him of human nature for He knew what was in man's heart. Though heaven and earth may pass away the message of such a personality will endure for ever.

For a complete understanding of the teachings of Jesus, naturally one has to turn mainly to these four narratives. In so doing, however, as already suggested, we have to allow for the limitations of expression and language.

The English gospels are translations from the original Greek, although Jesus Himself did not use that tongue. These books were written decades after the happening of events recorded therein. Further, in the coruse of transmission down to us interpolations by the manuscript makers, often repugnant to the spirit of Jesus, have crept into the texts. If we are not aiming at a literal rendering of the teachings of the Master, and if we prayerfully seek to listen to His voice, nothing of these physical handicaps can stand in our way.

Personality is more eloquent than words and Jesus Himself did not intended to confine His eternal message to the words that might have passed His lips. He promised us that the spirit of Truth will lead us into all truth, as His disciples were not then ready to receive His whole message. Hence, to us words are not to be final but it is the guidance of the Spirit that should matter. Signs and miracles are not essential to bear witness to truth.

While interpreting His words we shall also grasp their significance better if the oriental setting and background are kept in mind. Unfortunately, the interpretations handed down to us through the Churches are so mixed up with their own secular history in the West that we are often led into accepting the externals at the cost of the substance.

Frequently has the spirit been made of none effect through the weather-beaten traditions of the Church. We have to shake ourselves free of these if we would see Jesus.

It is a common practice among oriental teachers and devotees to identify themselves with the Godhead. This is never understood to signify an exclusive claim to divinity. The fourth gospel depicts Jesus in this mode throughout. He Himself confers a divine sonship on all those who believe in His name.[1]

In this setting the word "believe" does not connote the expression of a pious opinion nor does it signify simple credence about a state of affairs. Belief is fundamental to the very being of a person. True belief will manifest itself in

---

[1] John 1:12

action. Jesus says, "He who believes in Me will do the very deeds I do and even greater." Does our belief show itself in such a holy life or does it only result in a vain repetition of the Athanasian creed?

Again, what does "Name" signfy? In this connection it stands for the principles of the person denoted. When persons shout "Gandhijiki Jai", they do not pray merely for victory or success to the 105 lbs. of mortal flesh and blood, but for the cause Gandhiji espouses, e.g. Non-violence and Truth. Therefore, we can only be said to believe in the name of Jesus when we consecrate our very being to the ideals He stands for.

The interpretation of Jesus submitted in the following pages, therefore, is an attempt to present His teachings in the light of His personality. In so doing, if at any place it appears to transcend the written word, the above lines are humbly offered in explanation.

Chapter 1

The Law and the Prophets

To appreciate fully the significance of the advent and teachings of Jesus we have to keep in mind the background against which He was working.

Jesus was born a Jew, was dedicated to God as the firstborn and brought up strictly according to the rites then known amongst the Jews as "the Law of the Lord".

The Jews were a proud nation, though then they were writhing under the political domination of the Romans. They considered themselves a people chosen by God to fulfil His purposes and as one especially favoured by Him for over two thousand years, since the days of Abraham. They looked down upon all other nations as Gentiles and considered them all as their natural enemies who were to be destroyed and to whom no courtesy or obligations were due. This approach naturally bred in them a self-centred and self-righteous attitude, narrow in outlook and patriarchal in conception.

The Lord God Almighty. Their conception of the Deity was that of a tribal god, who ordained nature itself for their benefit, who was the Lord of Hosts to subdue their enemies, who was a jealous God visiting the iniquities of the fathers upon the children unto the third and fourth generation and showing mercy unto thousands of them that love Him. Therefore, they worshipped Him in fear and trembling and refrained even from pronouncing His name—Jehovah.

The Law. The rule of life was made known to them through Moses who laid down in minute detail the observances to be followed under every conceivable circumstance of life. This was the law the least breach of which was to be visisted with severe punishment also prescribed by law.

Sin. The Jewish conception of sin was the transgression of their law "written and engraven on stones".[1]

The Prophets. Such a rigid dispensation of this kind called for an intermediate priesthood, who, in course of time, exploited their impregnable status by laying down various ways and means of thwarting the wrath of God by sacrifices and peace offerings. This in its turn led to the formation of a complicated code of rules and regulations—the tradition of the elders—and to the rising into power of a vested interest, a close community of lawyers, to intrepret these rules. Anyone who obeyed these rules literally took pride in his self-righteousness and despised all others as "publicans and sinners". The spirit was ultimately lost in the letter.

Under such a hierarchy, life became oppressive and burdensome and people were living in constant fear of the priesthood. They served God to escape punishment and to secure personal reward. People tended to become more and more

---

[1] See also Romans 5:13 and 1 John 3:4.

materialistic with strong worldly attachment which even to this day, in common opinion, characterizes the Jew. Even the glory of the Messiah was reduced to the conception of a worldly kingship. Life was governed by external forms and fear of consequences. The relationship between man and man became purely legalistic governed by the principle of "an eye for an eye".

This was the state of affairs when the precursor of Jesus, John the Baptist, appeared on the scene preaching, "Ye generation of vipers, who hath warned you to flee from the wrath to come? Bring forth therefore fruits worthy of repentance." And he was to be the last of the prophets before the regime of grace and truth was ushered in by Jesus the Christ.

Chapter 2

"For This Cause Came I into the World"

1. Jesus came to fulfil the law and the prophets.[1]

The Jews had mistaken the means for the end and thereby converted the camp of this world into a permanent abode, forgetting that "here we have no continuing city". Instead of developing along the divine plans laid out in the law and the prophets, they got stuck in the mud and Jesus appeared among them to pull them out of the rut and set their feet on the firm highway to realizing their unity with God and thus to complete the work begun by the law and the prophets and bring it to full fruition. This task Jesus conceived to be His Messianic mission.

God the Father. To begin with He had to get them out of their smug feeling of righteousness and self-complacency in following the letter of the law. He came to call the sinners to repentance.[2] To do this He had to smash through their narrow fossilized ideas of a tribal god with a limited range of love and extend it to cover the universal conception of an all-loving Father of mankind who is "Your Father and my Father, your God and my God". Thus the old terrible Lord God Almighty blooms through the revelation of Jesus into "Our Father in Heaven".

Worship. With the advent of this conception, the highly ritualistic ceremonial worship becomes out of place, and with it falls the bulwark of priesthood as now the direct relationship between God and man of a filial nature calls for no mediator. "In that day ye shall ask Me nothing. ...Whatsoever ye shall ask the Father in My name He will give it to you...and I say not until you, that I will pray the Father for you; for the Father Himself loveth you."[3] And we are to worship God, not with sacrifices and burnt offerings, but in spirit and in truth.[4]

Service. Up to the time of John the Baptist, the carrying out of the law depended on an external discipline based on violence.[5] Jesus substitutes for this the control of life by the inner spiritual discipline of a developed personality and the method of self-suffering in all relationship between man and man.

At that time the rule of the letter of the law was in such ascendency that man himself was regarded as secondary, and judging from the practice then obtaining, as existing for the purpose of carrying out the law. Repeatedly Jesus battled against these ceremonial observances which had become so wooden that all humanitarian and spiritual considerations were lost sight of. Again and again, He was accused of curing the sick on sabbath days and they even sought to kill

---

[1] Matthew 5:17 [2] Matthew 9:13 [3] John 16:23,26,27 [4] John 4:23 [5] Matthew 11:12

131

Him for this because it was considered He was defying and disobeying the law as they interpreted it.[1] Jesus asserted the supremacy of man over administration and organization[2] and mate it clear that it is not the act that constitutes sin by the spirit behind it and that the observance of external ceremonials was of little avail when the heart was impure.[3]

Apart from ceremonials, even in life, mere adherence to the letter of the law was not sufficient if the spirit underlying the commandments was absent. When the rich young ruler came to Jesus and asked what further he should do to be saved as he had already kept all the commandments from his youth up, Jesus, knowing that he had kept to the letter of the law but that the spirit of greed and covetousness was within him still, directed him to go and sell all he had and give to the poor. This touched the rich young man on the sore spot and it recorded that because he had great possessions he turned away sorrowful.[4] Under the law such a man would have been justified—held to have led a meritorious life—but under the new dispensation he was found wanting.

When Jesus was questioned by a lawyer as to which were the great commandments in law He replied, "Thou shalt love the Lord thy God with all thy heart, and with all thy soul and with all thy mind. This is the first and great commandment and the second is like unto it. Thou shalt love thy neighbor as thyself." On these two commandments hang all the law and the prophets.[5] Then we are told in the parable of the Good Samaritan[6] that our neighbour is one who stands in need of our help irrespective of race, creed or caste. here Jesus cuts across the Jewish racial superiority complex. We are enjoyed to worship God in love and service to our fellow men. Unless our goodness excels that of the scribes and Pharisees we shall never enter into the Realm of Heaven.[7]

2. Jesus came to bear witness unto the Truth.[8]

He Himself is the Truth and the Life[9]—the Prime Cause and Regulator of the universe as stated in the first four verses of the fourth gospel.[10]

"In the beginning the Word existed. The Word was with God and the Word was divine."

"It was He that was with God in the beginning. Everything came into existence through Him, and apart from Him nothing came to be. It was by Him that life came into existence, and that life was the light of mankind." To know the only true God is eternal life[11] and the knowledge of the truth will make us free[12]—free from the slavery of sin. Moses, representing the law, was the accuser.[13] Under the law men acted in a certain way, not because it was right and proper to do so but, because it was so enjoined by the law and any deviation from that course would be visited by severe punishment. Man had lost all freedom of thought and action. Robot-like he had to follow blindly the path laid out for him from the cradle to

---

[1] See Matthew 12:14, Luke 13:14;14:3, and John 9:16.   [2] Mark 2:27   [3] Matthew 15:18,19   [4] Matthew 19:16–22   [5] Matthew 22:37–40 [The odd placement of the closing quotation marks is in the original text.—ed.]   [6] Luke 10:30–35   [7] Matthew 5:20, Moffatt.   [8] John 18:37   [9] John 14:6   [10] Goodspeed's translation   [11] John 17:3   [12] John 8:32   [13] John 5:45

the grave. But now when the Spirit of Truth comes into our lives and takes the helm there will no longer be any necessity to follow the-rule-of-thumb method of the law. We shall have to act according to our light and the guidance of the inner voice. We shall not be subject to an external code of laws based on force but to a sensitive conscience which will be the arbiter of an internal discipline. The law carries with it the sense of slavery to sin[1] and engenders fear and hate, while the life of the Spirit works through love. A man will not steal, not because he fears the policeman and the punishment that will be meted out to him by the law, but simply because his own conscience tells him that it is wrong to benefit through another's loss. Once we get the Spirit of Truth we shall not require tomes to direct us on the right methods to pursue nor shall we need to be told by others as to what course we should take. The Spirit of Truth Himself will guide us into all truth and teach us all things,[2] things that even Jesus had not explained to us.[3]

Unthinking obedience to external law is irksome and by no means ennobling, while the following of one's own light or conscience, even if it be through the valley of the shadow of death, is satisfying and elevating. Jesus, therefore, calls all those that labour and are heavy laden with the burden of the life under the law—"the ministrations of death"—to come to Him and find rest unto their souls for His yoke is easy and the burden light for those who accept the revelation of the Father and the gift of His Spirit and enter into "the ministration of the Spirit" ushered in through Him.

Thus does Jesus save from sin those who come to Him by delivering them from death under the reign of law and encompassing them with His love and grace.[4]

3. Jesus came that every one who believeth on Him may have eternal life,[5] and become perfectly unified in the Godhead.

Jesus in prayer says, "Let them all (those who believe on Him) be one. Just as You, Father, are in union with Me and I am with You, let them be in union with Us. ...I have given them the glory that You gave Me, so that they may be one just as We are. I in union with them and You with Me, so that they may be perfectly unified and the world may recognize that You sent Me and that You love them just as You loved Me."[6] Eternal life is not something which we cannot enjoy while on this earth and a state that is to be awarded only in the hereafter. It is to be possessed here and now. "I tell you, whoever believes already possesses eternal life."[7] "I tell you, whoever listens to My message and believes Him who has sent Me possesses eternal life, and will not come to judgement, but has already passed out of death into life."[8] While still encased in this mortal body, the soul, by its union with the Father attains immortality. *Belief* in Him does not consist in the vain repetition of a creed. Jesus says, "He who believes in Me will do the very deeds I do and even greater."[9] This then is the criterion by which it shall be known whether the professed belief is sound or not. What are these deeds that

---

[1] John 8:34, Goodspeed   [2] John 14:26   [3] John 16:12–13   [4] See Romans 6:14;7:6;8:2 and Galatians 5:18.   [5] John 6:38,40   [6] John 6:21–23, Goodspeed   [7] John 6:47, Goodspeed   [8] John 5:24, Goodspeed   [9] John 19:12

Jesus did by which we shall know the genuine article? When John the Baptist sent his disciples to know if He was the one that should come, Jesus asked them to go and tell John the things Jesus was doing: "The blind receive their sight, and the lame walk, the lepers are cleansed, and the deaf hear, the dead are raised up and the poor have the gospel preached to them."[1] Only when the belief is translated into such action can the true believers look forward to hearing the Father say: "I was a hungered, and ye gave Me meat; I was thirsty, and ye gave Me drink; I was a stranger, and ye took Me in; naked and ye clothed Me; I was sick and ye visisted Me; I was in prison and ye came unto Me....Inasmuch as ye have done it unto one of the least of these ye have done it unto me."[2] Thus, instead of a ceremonial worship of God in fear and trembling devoid of deeds, our devotion will have to manifest itself in a life consecrated to the living service of those in need. In such service, our physical life and natural instincts will be sublimated and we shall find true happiness in spending our talents in the relief of the distress of those around us, in a life consecrated by truth.

4. Jesus came that we might have life and that we might have it more abundantly.[3]

When we thus lead a life dedicated to the service of others in need, our life becomes fuller and richer. From the animal plane, where the circle of our natural family consists of a few brothers and sisters, life reaches up into the spiritual plane where our family love encompasses the millions the world over.

The material world will sink into insignificance. A man's life will not consist in the abundance of things he possesses;[4] and whosoever will try to make the best of his life of three score years and ten for his own comfort and enjoyment will miss the real life, and whosoever will discard such selfishness and lead a life that brings light and relief into the life of others around him will gain eternal life. [5] [6] "For what is a man profited, if he shall gain the whole world, and lose his own soul? Or what shlal a man give in exchange for his soul?"[7]

Under the old dispensation, rewards were promised for good deeds done. But Jesus wants us to do our duty, not for any personal gain it may bring us, but just because it is our duty.[8] He says, "When you have done all your are bidden, say, we are but servants, we have only done our duty."[9] In the parable of the labourers in the vineyard[10] Jesus teaches us that neither ought we to expect commensurate rewards for our work. In the parable of the talents[11] He exhorts everyone to do his utmost according to the ability vouchsafed to him by God. In so doing, whether our contribution be much or little, we shall be fully discharging our obligations. Jesus Himself finds satisfaction in the fact that that which was to be done had been

---

[1] Matthew 11:5   [2] Matthew 25:35,36,40   [3] John 10:10   [4] Luke 12:15   [5] Matthew 16:25
[6] *[This claim comes from a person with a degree in business administration from Syracuse and a degree in economics from Columbia, who moved back to India and dedicated himself to the uplift of impoverished rural villages and the freedom of the Indian people. Spoken from that background, it is arguably one of the most moving claims I have ever read.—ed.]*   [7] Matthew 16:26   [8] See Matthew 5:45–46.   [9] Luke 17:10, Moffatt.   [10] Matthew 20:1–16   [11] Matthew 25:14–30

accomplished. "My food is to do the will of Him who sent me, and to accomplish His work."[1] He urges us to be perfect even as our heavenly Father is perfect.[2]

The foregoing paragraphs have shown us that the advent of Jesus was to reveal the Fatherhood of God and the consequent universal brotherhood of man and thereby to confer on man the dignity of a spiritual being. He taught us to base all our relationships on love and service and He freed us from the fear of those who can only destroy the body. His life exemplified the fact that the moment we surrender ourselves unreservedly to God's will and bring the flesh under the subjection of the spirit we can become free from the bondage of legalistic relationship and can acquire the right to override man-made rules and regulations where such orders are repugnant to the Spirit of Truth. We are not to seek after results but only to strive to do the will of the Father and carry out our duties without reference to any rewards. He broke through the chrysalis of the law and the prophets and took wing into the free atmosphere of Grace and Truth.

---

[1] John 4:34, Mofffatt   [2] Matthew 5:48

Chapter 3

"But I Say unto You"

In the last chapter, we considered the prupose of the advent of Jesus. In the following paragraphs we shall study some of the precepts that He enunciated while reorientating the law of Moses. Jesus lays his whole emphasis on the spirit, thought and motive behind a deed rather than on the act itself. According to His standards a man may be guilty of sin even where the act, considered a sin in law, may be wanting. His attempt is to control the source of sin in our hearts rather than be satisfied merely with the physical prevention of the deed.

The reply Jesus gave to the rich young ruler indicates to us that Jesus considered the following to be the principal commandsments of Moses:[1]

1. Thou shalt do no murder.

2. Thou shalt not commit adultery.

3. Thou shalt not steal.

4. Thou shalt not bear false witness.

5. Honour thy father and thy mother.

6. Thou shalt love thy neighbour as thyself.

Jesus takes up these commandments and projects them into the spiritual plane and provides us with His own version of these in the "sermon on the mount".[2] In this chapter, our reflections will centre round the five new commandments laid down by Jesus in striking contrast to the Mosaic Law.

1. Whosoever is angry with his brother
shall be in danger of the judgment.[3]

Anger is placed on a level with murder. Murder is the result and anger the cause, hence Jesus reaches out to the root of the evil and places it in the same category as the antisocial act itself. Judged by this standard which of us is not a murderer and a multiple murderer at that?

This code was thought to be rather too drastic and so a considerate scribe, about the 5th century, interpolated the words "without cause" after the word "brother", thus rendering it of no effect. Which of us is so mad as to be angry without a cause? Generally, are we not always in the right? If Britain goes to war

---

[1] Matthew 19:18,19   [2] Matthew 5:17–48   [3] Matthew 5:22

with Germany on the defensive, Germany declares she also goes to the same war with Britain on the defensive! If individuals cannot even be angry how can a nation war against another and carry out large scale bloodshed, and obtain the blessing of the High Priests of the churches on this organized murder? Hence this phrase was found most useful by the Church Militant to annex the support of the State. Thus these practical men of the world chose to gag Jesus. Modern wars also cannot be waged without the people being whipped up into a rage by a false propaganda giving "reasons" why war has been forced on the people. By the interpolation of these three words into the text, Jesus' authority also can be invoked for the large scale murders, which our modern wars are, with plausible reasons. What a brain wave to have modified Jesus' standard to the point of futility by the insertion of a few simple words! This convenient phrase I understand, is not to be found in Luther's translation, or Tischendorf's, or in any of the best of manuscripts. It is also omitted by such modern translators as Dr. R.G. Moulton and Dr. Goodspeed among others. In any case, it is most repugnant to the spirit of the Master.

Jesus would have us abandon the legalistic attitude and banish all hatred and any feeling of contempt from our very innermost thoughts. This is His sublimation of the Mosaic Law "Thou shalt do no murder" and we find its active counterpart in His injunction to love our enemies, bless them that curse us and do good to them that hate us.

2. Whosoever looketh on a woman
to lust after her hath committed adultery
with her already in his heart.[1]

Here we have in a nutshell Jesus' attitude towards the primary instinct of sex and other questions of sex relationships arising out of it. The body and its requirement are to be subject to the needs of the spirit. The body represents the animal in us. If we aspire to arise above the level of brute beasts and to become the sons of God we have to be born again, not of blood, nor of the will of the flesh, but of the spirit of God.[2] Sex is of the will of the flesh and is of nature.

In nature the male and the female come together for breeding purposes only. But the will of the flesh had made man prostitute this natural function for his own pleasure even when no progeny is desired. In doing so, man falls below the level of even the brute beasts. This view, of course, precludes all birth control by the us of contraceptives, for no man should approach a woman for the satisfaction of his lust, be she his wife or otherwise. Marriage, as a legal tie, will not modify the standard. A married man and a woman may come together, not for the satisfaction of their lust but only for the definite purpose of bearing children. Only such relationships can be that of a true Brahmachari. Hence, even a married man who looks on his wife to lust fater her commits adultery with his own wife in his heart. The sin contemplated here is not of the legalistic type—breaking a social rule—but of the spirit as being a departure from God's plan. Thus it is that the principle laid down

---

[1] Matthew 5:28   [2] John 1:12,13

here by Jesus, since it is above the reach of man-made laws, no mere marriage licence can ever convert what is lust into anything nobler. Even the physical act is not necessary to constitute the sin, for the thought itself transgresses God's law in that contemplates the use of the body, not in the service of God, but for one's own pleasure. This body and all its functions have been entrusted to us by God to be used to fulfil His purposes. Satisfying one's own lust is not amongst His purposes.

As a corollary to this standard of Jesus, we should expect Him to countenance marriage between a man and a woman only where true love exists and not for lust. In such marriage there can be no room for divorce. Jesus says, "What therefore God hath joined together let not man put asunder."[1] Divorce is after all a legal device with which a spiritual relationship can have nothing to do. If, however, the binding factor love is absent, the registrar's certificate by itself does not constitute marriage; since a marriage, where no love is, stands dissolved already, divorce or no divorce.

Countermanding Moses' provision in law for divorce, He says, "whosoever put away his wife,[2] besides the sin of dissoluteness, causeth her to commit adultery."

In this Jesus is charging the husband with licentiousness on his own part and also as being the cause of his wife's sin, of adultery, if she marries again.

The disciples of Jesus found this teaching so hard that they remarked, "If the case of the man be so with his wife, it is not good to marry."[3]

Divorce, even because of fornication, is certainly repugnant to the ideals of one who taught us to forgive at all times and always, and who said to the woman taken in adultery, "Neither do I condemn thee: go and sin no more."[4]

Divorce is purely a matter for the legal relationship and was introduced by Moses as a concession to human frailty and Jesus said this was not so from the beginning, i.e. from the inception of the institution of marriage.[5]

3. Let your communications be Yea, Yea; and Nay, Nay;
for whatsoever is more than these is of the evil one.[6]

Under the Jewish hierarchy bearing false witness had become a menace. Jesus is here attacking this evil practice and restoring to man his dignity and integrity. Our speech, to bear the impress of truth, has to maintain the face value, neither being reinforced by oaths nor being discounted by mental reservations. We should say what we mean and mean what we say. When we attempt to embellish our speech any further we are in danger of transgressing the limits of truth. As the Persian proverb has it:

---

[1] Matthew 19:6   [2] Here we may note in passing that Count Leo Tolstoy points out in his book, *What I Believe*, that there is an error in the rendering of the Greek for the phrase "besides the sin of dissoluteness". This is an attempt by a man-governed order to wrench the law in his favour and make divorce possible. While far from excusing the man, Jesus places on him a double responsibility, for his own licentiousness and that of his wife's marriage a second time. Luke, who is noted as a historian for his veracity and accuracy, omits this phrase altogether, so does Mark in his version. (See Luke 16:18 and Mark 10:11–12.)   [3] Matthew 19:10   [4] John 8:11   [5] Matthew 19:8   [6] Matthew 5:37

"Tell no man all thou knowest,
For he who tells all he knows,
Often tells more than he knows."

4. You are not to resist an injury.[1,2]

This is in striking contrast to the ruthless, deterrent punishment provided under the Mosaic Law which says, "If a man cause a blemish in his neighbour, so shall it be done to him again. And thine eye shall not pity; but life shall go for life, eye for eye, tooth for tooth, hand for hand, foot for foot. And those which remain shall hear and fear and shall henceforth commit no more such evil among you."[3] To this Jesus answers, "Resist not an injury."

It doe snot mean that we are passively to let all social wrongs and evils go unchecked. Jesus' sayings would be meaningless unless backed by His own example. His life was nothing if it was not a continuous pitched battle raged against the evils of the regime of scribes and Pharisees. This injunction and violence can have no place in His scheme. This commandment may be freely rendered into, "Do not hurt your neighbour even under the gravest provocation." We are to meet violence, not with violence, but with self-suffering, in a compromising and generous spirit. We are not to stand on our own personal rights nor claim our dues. We are to meet the opponent with perfect goodwill unflurried by any injury done to us.

If a woman's honour is endangered the old rendering of this passage into "resist not evil" may be construed into meaning that she should meekly submit to be violated; or if one nation holds or attempts to hold another in subjection, the subject nation should not assert itself to obtain or retain its freedom. Such inference will be wholly against the spirit of Jesus. The woman will resist to the best of her ability even unto death to maintain her God-entrusted honour unsullied but there should be no intention on her part to hurt her assailant or to punish him or wreak vengeance on him. Similarly, a nation too ought to resist, non-violently, an intrusion on its God-ordained privilege of liberty. While a violent struggle will aim at injuring and, if possible, destroying its opponent, a non-violent campaign will be directed towards preventing the opponent from doing a wrong.

It may not be out of place at this stage to note what the modern prophet of nonviolence and truth—Gandhiji—has to say to guide non-violent resisters. Here are a few rules drafted by him:

"It is no part of the duty of those who are attacked to render any assistance to the attacker. It is their duty to offer complete non-co-operation."

"We may not bend the knee to the aggressor nor obey any of his orders."

---

[1] Matthew 5:39.   [2] Note: The translation in the Authorized Version "see that ye resist not evil" as well as Dr. R.G. Moulton's "Resist not him that is evil" do not bring out the meaning in the context. Hence I have used Dr. Moffatt's rendering which is very similar to Dr. Goodspeed's.
[3] See Leviticus 24:18,20; Deuteronomy 19:20,21.

"We may not look to him for any favours, nor fall to his bribes. But we may not bear him any malice nor wish him ill.'

"If he wishes to take possession of our fields, we will refuse to give them up even if we have to die in the effort to resist him."

"If he is attacked by disease or is dying of thirst and seeks our aid, we may not refuse it."

As regards the modern strategy of a "Scorched Earth Policy" Gandhiji remarks:

"I see neither bravery nor sacrifice in destroying life or property for offence or defence. I would far rather leave, if I must, my crops and homestead for the enemy to use than destroy them for the sake of preventing their use by him. There is no reason, sacrifice and even bravery in so leaving my homestead and crops, if I do so, not out of fear but because I refuse to regard any one as my enemy—that is, from a humanitarian motive. There is no bravery in my poisoning the well or filling it so that my brother, who is at war with me, may not use the water. Let us assume that I am fighting him in the orthodox manner. Nor is there sacrifice in it, for it does not purify me; an sacrifice, as its root meaning implies, presupposes purity. Such destruction may be likened to cutting one's nose to spite one's face. I do claim that there are bravery and sacrifice in my leaving the wells, crops, and homestead intact; bravery in that I deliberately run the risk of the enemy feeding himself at my expense and pursuing me, and sacrifice in that the sentiment of leaving something for the enemy purifies and ennobles me."

This quotation from Gandhiji naturally leads us on to the next commandment of Jesus.

5. Love your enemies.[1]

The Jews regarded all members of their race as neighbours and all others as Gentiles and natural enemies of Jehovah, their God. Hence the Jewish commandment, "Love thy neighbour and hate thine enemy." There was also the commandment, "Honour thy father and thy mother." Jesus extends such limited loyalties to cover all human beings.

When our life is sublimated by the spirit of Truth, and our love encompasses the whole world, then humanity, as the creation of the Father in Heaven, constitutes our family circle. Black or white, brown, yellow or red, all are our brethren and we can have no enmity within this family. All personal relationships should be based on love though we may hate certain evil deeds, systems and organizations and fight against these and try to exterminate them. As regards individuals we have to do good to them that hate us, and pray for those that despitefully use us and persecute us.

These high ideals and precepts could have been brushed aside as impractible had not Jesus Himself set us an example by His life as to how to practise these. He healed the ear of Malchus, the servant of the High Priest, when he came to arrest Him. When He was spat upon and smitten He did not resist the injury. On the Cross He prayed for the forgiveness of those who crucified Him.

---

[1] Matthew 5:44

When our life is guided by such high ideals as stars, is it possible for us to find fault with our neighbour? We shall feel too humiliated at our own shortcomings to sit in judgment over others. The beam in our eyes will shut our vision from noticing the mote in our neighbour's eye. Like the publican, we shall not dare even to raise our eyes to heaven but shall beat our breasts and say, "God be merciful to me, a sinner."[1]

These precepts, however lofty they may be, do not determine once and for all the shores of the spiritual ocean. Those who hold that Jesus gave the final and a complete revelation and that there is no further scope for further developments, do Him a grave injustice, unknowingly though it may be. Great masters are limited by the capacity of their pupils. Such masters can only lay down broad principles along the lines of which further experiments may be made to explore deeper into truth. The function of the master is not merely to bequeath a store of knowledge to his pupils but to instill in them a thirst for truth and inspiration, and drill them in proper methods of research. Thenceforward the pupils should go full speed ahead on their own steam. Does the quantitative knowledge in physics stop where Newton left it? Do our modern physicists sit and watch apples fall? Has not Einstein opened up newer fields? The great contributation of the late Acharya P.C. Ray was not so much in his own researches, great as they may have been, but rather in the creation of a band of able scientists to carry on his tradition. No less can Jesus' claim be. At the time of His advent the Jews were a narrow-minded race obesessed with a racial superiority—like that of the Nazis over the Jews—and they inherited a most violent tradition. Even the few disciples He had were mostly a group of fisherfolk, for the most part practically unlettered. Within His ministry of hardly three years to have taught them what He did was one of His greatest miracles, and the ideals and principles He set forth were in themselves revolutionary. Is it to be wondered then that He found that His disciples could not take in and digest all He had to say and that He had to leave them witha rpomise that when they got the Spirit of Truth more things would be revealed to them? His revelation was therefore, partial, being naturally limited by the capacity of His disciples.[2] How then can we claim finality for His revelation?

If Jesus' promise is to find fulfilment, those who profess to follow Him ought to find new facets of truth opened to them as they advance on the route indicated by their Master. Unfortunately, man is so constitute that if he does not progress he does not merely stagnate but deteriorates. To justify the trust and responsibility reposed in him, man has to make use of his talents. That is the condition of all advance. In the parable of the talents the servant who buried his talent in the earth hoping to preserve it is condemned.[3] The Churches which claim finality for Jesus' revelation are in this position. The tragedy of it all is the Churches usurped the place of the Spirit and Truth and professed authority to lay down the way of life for all. Anything new from any other source was considered heretic and was suppressed with all the violence human ingenuity could devise. The results have been a terrible backsliding from the standards of Jesus. As proof, behold the battlefields of Europe.

---

[1] Luke 28:13 [2] See John 16:12,13. [3] Matthew 25:24,30

The two mighty and doughty champions of the Church—the Britain of Wesley and the Germany of Luther—are locked in the most deadly, violent, and bloody struggle in the history of mankind. What place is left for the precepts of Jesus—not to be angry and not to resist an injury, not to mention "Love your enemies"? This is the achievement of the Church two thousand years after the Prince of Peace! We were then taught to regard the whole world as one family of our common Father in heaven. Today, Nazi Germany has more racial arrogance than the Jews of old.

This retrogression is due to regarding Jesus' revelation as final. The road to progress was blocked. The Churches had usurped the place of the Spirit of Truth but had fallen far short of the great responsibility undertaken by them by claiming to be the sole arbiter and interpreter of the Master. Jesus taught us to have direct relationship with God,[1] and finally attain eternal life by union with the Father.[2] But the Churches have interposed themselves between man and God with such incompetence followed by such dire results as we witness on the battlefields of Europe. Even noble science has been pressed into the service of Moloch and prostituted into inventing diabolical weapons of destruction. God endowed us with talents to serve and glorify Him. Are the battlefields of Europe a glory to God? Where is goodwill among men to be found? Revenge, avarice, and hatred have the day. What are the Churches doing to undo the mischief brought about by their failure? They are holding up their holy hands on either side of the fighting lines, praying to the Father of mankind to help them to devise more and more deadly ways and means of destroying His children on the opposite side. May God open our eyes to realize the degredation and blasphemy of the situation and retrieve the position before it is too late. Sodom and Gomorrah are as candle smoke before the sulphurous fumes belching forth from London and Berlin. If Jesus, who wept over Jerusalem, were amongst us in flesh and blood, would not He, who said, "Whosoever shall break one of these least commandments and shall teach man so, he shall be called the least in the kingdom of heaven; but whosoever shall do and teach them, the same shall be called great in the kingdom of heaven.",[3] also lament with a bleeding heart, "O Europe, O Europe, ye that suppress meek and mild nations and live on their lifeblood, ye that controvert and distort My teachings and thereby exploit the ignorant, how often would I have gathered thy children together, even as a hen gathereth her chickens under her wings, and ye would not! Behold, your countries are left unto you desolate."

Jesus was no static force. His was a dynamic personality. Growth is its essence. We may be legitimately asked how then can we supplement or extend the application of the precepts laid down by Jesus? We shall consider such new spheres in a later chapter. Here we shall be content to cite but one instance. Jesus extended the Jewish love for their own nation and made it to apply to the whole world of human beings. Buddha had extended his love to cover not merely human beings but all sentient creatures, and following him the Jains even extended it to all things having life including even roots. Surely the Spirit of Jesus can take in such applications. But flesh-eating, even at the risk of offending our neighbours—

---

[1] Matthew 6:6, John 16:26,27   [2] John 6:21–23, Goodspeed   [3] Matthew 5:19

Muslims by pork and Hindus by beef—is still the hall-mark of Christendom! Do we not come under Jesus' condemnation of having a milestone[1] hanged about our neck and being cast into the sea? Is not life more than meat? We are enjoined to let our light so shine before men that they may see our good works and glorify our Father in heaven.

---

[1] *[sic.—ed.]*

Chapter 4

"After This Manner Pray Ye"

Prayer forms or provides the binding factor between God and man. It is the medium by which man establishes union with God. Therefore, one who wishes to do the will of the Father has always to pray. Indeed such a person's life itself should be one continuous prayer—prayer in thought, word, and deed to escape all those things Jesus warned us against when He said, "Take heed to yourselves, lest at any time your hearts be overcharged with surfeiting, and drunkenness and cares of this life, and so that day come upon you unawares. Watch ye therefore, and pray always."[1] Through prayer it is that man remains in communion with God and derives his strength. It is the conductor connecting the live wire charged with electrical energy that drives the powerful engine and the railway train or the street tram car; these remain but mases of dead metal until the connection is established.

Unfortunately, the English word "prayer" does not connote all this but carries a strong sense of request or begging and so supplication for our wants has largely coloured the forms of prayers offered in churches. True prayer should have mediation as the base and full and free communion with God as the means of obtaining the needed power from on High. Such supplication as there may be will be for the better fulfilment of His purposes focussing sharply our intense desire for service.

The method of praying that Jesus taught His disciples is a perfect model which we ought to follow closely. As in many other respects the churches have stuck to the letter and have missed the spirit of what has been misnamed "The Lord's Prayer". This lays down merely the general outlines on which prayer has to be made, and it forms more or less a beautifully put together concise table of contents. In effect, it is a gnome of the whole of the philosophy of Jesus. It is as absurd and puerile to repeat these words as being a complete prayer in itself as it would be to enumerate the names of the books of the Bible beginning from Genesis through Malachi and Matthew right down to Revelation and then be satisfied as though you had gone through all the contents of those books from cover to cover. The High Churches have even gone to the limit of setting these lines to music and chanting them by the Preist giving the lead, intoning loudly, "Our Father" and then the congregation following and keeping time with the organ! All this in spite of instruction laid down by Jesus just before this formula was enunciated directing us:

1. Not to pray so as to be seen of men.

2. But in a private chamber with the doors shut.

3. Not to use vain repetitions.

---

[1] Luke 21:34,36

4. Not to beg for personal needs, "for your Father knoweth what things ye have
    need of before ye ask Him."

"The Lord's Prayer"[1] consists of seven stages or chapters and we shall study
them in their order. The first is devoted to the contemplation of the Infinite
as Creator and Sustainer; the second to His ways and to eternal principles and
Truth; the third is concerned with personal self-surrender to God's will, which is
followed by a meditation on the consquences of a consecrated life as manifested in
deeds; and the last three supplications are for strength, purity, and steadfastness
of purpose, respectively. Each stage is pregnant with meaning and is capable of
bbeing developed into volumes of philosophy which is much beyond our scope.
We shall content ourselves with a simple indication of the possibilities.

1. Our Father which art in heaven.

This opening thesis is one of the great purposes of Jesus' mission on earth which
we considered in the second chapter. If He came to earth to reveal the Fatherhood
of God the Creator, He came also to establish the consequent brotherhood of
mankind and mould the human race into one family, though drawing the members
from different "folds",[2] building up a single fold under one Shepherd, the Sustainer.
Contemplation on this field throws up many challenging questions to our generation. If there be but one Father, is not humanity in the position of a joint
family wherein there should be equality among all the brothers and sisters com-
posing it and who should live in complete amity? Does it behove us to carry on
fatricidal wars for any reason, economic or otherwise? Should not all the members
pool their resources for the common good? Under the existing state of affairs is
it not tantamount to blasphemy to address God as "Father"?
Let us consider the circumstances under which we shall be entitled to this filial
relationship.us Himself has laid down most of these conditions, of which naturally
the foremost is an all-embracing love.
(a) "Love your enemies, bless them that curse you and do good to them that
hate you...that ey may be the children of your Father which is in heaven. For He
maketh His sun to rise on the evil and on the good and sendeth rain on the just
and on the unjust."[3]
And here is the charter of our rights:
(b) "As many as received Him, to them gave He the right to become sons of
God, even to them that believe on His name."[4]
We have already noticed in the 3rd section of the 2nd chapter what implications
"belief" carries. What connotation the word "name" bears in this connection will
be seen in the next thesis of this "prayer".
Then follows the duty to be performed:
(c) "Whosoever shall do the will of My Father which is in heaven, the same is
my brother, and sister, and mother."[5]

---

[1] Matthew 6:9–13   [2] John 10:16   [3] Matthew 5:44,45   [4] John 1:12   [5] Matthew 12:50

As we have seen previously, God's will is that we should rise from the animal plane to the realm of the Spirit and be unified in Him, doing the works that Jesus did and even greater.

By such means we shall attain the characteristic that should declare the quality of our sonship as visualized in the following:

(d) "Be ye therefore perfect, even as your Father which is in heaven is perfect."[1]

"Be ye therefore merciful, as your Father also is merciful."[2]

And then, at last we achieve the final goal or destination of all children of God when we attain immortality in the Infinite.

(e) "That they all may be as one; as Thou, Father, art in Me, and I in Thee, that they also may be one in Us."[3]

If we acclaim the prime cause of creation as our "Father" what should our relationship to our other fellow-creatures commonly called the lower orders—animals, birds, etc.—which also owe their existence to the same Father? Will not devouring these constitute fatricide and a kind of cannibalism?

2. Hallowed be Thy name.

God is Love, God is Truth. May we hold in reverence the eternal principles and practice. These bring to our mind His name as manifested in the life of Jesus and all its signifies[4]—such as teachings, preaching, and doctrines.[5] We have considered some of His precepts in Chapter III. Holding these "sacred" does not mean locking them up in a golden ark enshrined in a noble church or other edifice, much less repeating the words in season and out of season, but taking them to heart and consecrating our lives for the fulfilment of these in our deeds.

"Herein is My Father glorified, that ye bear much fruit."[6]

"That they may see your good works and glorify your Father which is in heaven."[7]

Is our life a credit to Jesus? Do those around us thank God for our presence amongst them?

3. The kingdom come.

What sort of a kingdom is this? Where is it to be? And what are its chief features?

The then prevalent Jewish idea was that when the Messiah came he would reign on earth as a temporal monarch, holding sway over all other kings of the earth. Jesus refers to this conception in His talks with the Jews[8] but states that His kingdom is not of this world[9] and promises to give His followers a kingdom of His conception[10] and points out that the kingdom of God is located neither here

---

[1] Matthew 5:48   [2] Luke 6:36   [3] John 17:21   [4] John 17:6   [5] Acts 5:28,42   [6] John 15:8
[7] Matthew 5:16   [8] Matthew 8:11,12;21:13   [9] John 18:36   [10] Luke 12:32;22:59

nor there but that it is "within you"[1] and He urges them to work with a singleness of purpose towards bringing it about.[2]

Jesus shows up the fundamental differences between this kingdom and the earthly ones:

(a) The ordinary attribute of royalty is power to lord it over others, but the kingdom of God is known by the spirit of service that pervades it.[3] Jesus Himself came ot to be ministered unto but to minister and to give His life as a ransom for many.[4]

(b) Earthly royalty is nothing without wealth and splendour. Jesus warns us that life consisteth not in the abundance of the things which one possesseth.[5] He directs those that seek the kingdom of God to sell all they possess and distribute it to those who need and thus transfer their worldly wealth into heavenly treasure, for where the treasure is there will the heart be also.[6] The foxes have holes and the birds of the air have nests but the King in this kingdom hath not where to lay His head.[7]

(c) What attraction will there be in a life in a royal place that has no pomp and pride! Jesus would ahve us practice humility as a characteristic of His kingdom.[8] He, the Master, sets the example by washing His disciples' feet.[9]

When we pray "Thy kingdom come" are we ready to open wide the doors of our hearts to let such a King to dominate in His kingdom within us and reign over a life of service characterized by simplicity and humility? Are we prepared to dedicate all our talents and faculties loyally for the fulfillment of His purposes and spend and be spent in carrying out His will?

4. Thy will be done on
earth as it is in heaven.

Liek the previous section this too means submission to Go'd swill on the part of the one who prays. The previous one is for a personal surrender, while this craves to have such a consecrated life transformed acatively into deeds. Jesus' life declares to us God's will. We should love our fellow-men and such love should manifest itself in the service of the needy.[10] God has no other agents on earth but ourselves to carry out His will, so if we intensely desire that His will be done on earth as it is in heaven, it is up to us to fall in line with God's ways and execute them. In heaven, there is no departure from His will, but on earth, man's selfishness and perversity interefere with the even progress planned by God and form a destructive deviation from the eternal law and order. This is sin. We can help to eradicate these evils by surrendering ourselves wholly to His will by a discipline from within us guided by the Spirit of Truth.

---

[1] Luke 17:21   [2] Matthew 6:33   [3] Luke 22:25–27   [4] Matthew 22:28   [5] Luke 12:15   [6] Luke 12:33,34   [7] Matthew 8:20   [8] Matthew 23:11,12; Mark 9:34,35   [9] John 13:14   [10] Matthew 25:35,36

When God's will is done on earth there can be no injustice: social, economic, or political. Wherever there is such injustice, our place and function are indicated. We have to lose our bodies to gain our souls. Where God's will prevails can there be:

1. Social inequalities, high and low, prince and peasant, colour and race?

2. Economic differences of rich and poor, the exploiter and the exploited, owner, labour, and slave? Famines, pestilence, and oppression?

3. Traffic in goods harmful to the body such as narcotics and strong drink?

4. One nation lording it over another—imperialism?

5. Nations warring against nations?

What are we doing to abolish these? If our desire, that God's will should be done on earth, is intense and is not mereley a pious wish expressed in vain words, we cannot rest until all these departures from His will are put right. To this end we should be prepared to offer ourselves as complete living sacrifices on these altars. Under such circumstances it is not possible to create watertight compartments within which "religion has no jurisdiction", nor can there be reserved portfolios for chuches, hospitals, schools, and asylums. No religion is worth our allegiance if it does not comprehend all life and the whole of it, from the cradle to the grave.

Where God's will is the sole objective there can be no such separate organization as religion having its being within well demarcated boundary lines. God pervades the universe and all that is within it. So does His will. Hence our efforts to bring God's will on earth has, of necessity, to be equally expansive as its field of activity.

Jesus' very existence was to do with the will of him that sent Him and to finish His work.[1] Should not we also be such ambassadors of God? Then alone can God's will be done on earth as it is in heaven.

> At the gates of Heaven,
> There will be no question
> As to thy race, wealth or birth.
> But just "what hadst thou done on
> earth?" (Arabian saying)

5. Give us today our bread for the morrow.[2]

Before we proceed to contemplate this supplication there are one or two explanations to be made in regard to the words used in the Authorized Version "Guve us this day our daily bread". Immediately before formulating this "Prayer" Jesus

---

[1] John 4:34   [2] Moffatt

instructed His disciples not to burden their prayers with unnecessary words, "for your Father knoweth what things ye have need of, before ye ask Him"; and again a little later after pointing out the futility of seeking to satisfy bodily needs, He says "therefore take no thought saying, what shall we eat? or what shall we drink? or wherewith shall we be clothed? (For after all these things do the Gentiles seek.) For your heavenly Father knoweth that ye have need of all these things. But seek ye first the kingdom of God and His righteousness; and all these things shall be added unto you. Take therefore no thought for the morrow; for the morrow shall take thought for the things of itself."[1] In the light of these teachings it would be absurd for Him to teach his disciples to pray for their bodily needs. These words are obviously a mistranslation. Dr. Moffatt renders this, "Give us today our bread for the morrow." Here again the word "morrow" would be better substituted by "the coming day". With the Jews, "the coming day" was used to signify the day of the Lord,[2] i.e. the life to come; and hence, by contrast "this day" would mean "this life". Then with these changes the sentence would read, "Give us in this life the bread of the life to come."

Once more, with the context, the word "bread" cannot signify food for this mortal shell we live in. Jesus Himself quotes, "Man does not live by bread alone but by every word that proceedeth out of the mouth of God." This word then referes to "the word that proceedeth out of the mouth of God"—the bread of life in the same sense in which Jesus says, "My Father giveth you the true bread from heaven. For the bread of God is He that cometh down from heaven and giveth life unto the world."[3] Hence a liberal translation would read, "May we realize in this life the ideals and conceptions we associate with the life to come", meaning we crave for the spiritual strength needed to sustain us in leading the life abundant we obtain through Jesus.

Jesus, in explaining His mission to His unsophisticated disciples, often uses words applicable to this mortal body and its functions to signify things of the spirit. Thus, He says, "I am that bread of life." "This is the bread that cometh down from heaven, that a man may eat thereof, and not die. I am the living bread which came down from heaven If any man eat of this bread, he shall live for ever; and the bread that I will give is My flesh, which I will give for the life of the world." "For my flesh is meat indeed, and My blood is drink indeed."[4] He told the Samaritan woman, "whoever drinketh of this water shall thirst again; but whosoever drinketh of the water that I shall give him shall never thirst; but the water that I shall give him shall be in him a well of water springing up into everlasting life."[5] Then again He states, "I am the bread of life; he that cometh to Me shall never hunger; and he that believeth on Me shall never thirst."[6] After this he goes on to explain what He means, "He that eateth My flesh, and drinketh My blood, dwelleth in Me, and I in him. As the living Father hath sent me, and I live by the Father; so he that eateth Me, even he shall live by Me. This is that bread which came down from heaven: ... he that eateth of this bread shall live for ever."[7] Jesus repeated this idea at "the last supper" also. The food we take, when fully digested, gets assimilated through the blood into our system

---

[1] Matthew 6:31–34   [2] See Jeremiah 23:5;31:31, etc.   [3] John 6:32,33   [4] John 6:48,50,51,55
[5] John 4:13,14   [6] John 6:35   [7] John 6:56–58

and thenceforward becomes part of the body, indistinguishable and inseparable from it. So also when we perceive fully Jesus' teachings and His precepts and have assimilated the ideals—the bread of life—set forth by Him, we shall be so spiritually developed as to follow Him completely surrendering ourselves to God's will. We shall thus ultimately lose our separate identity and become merged in the Father.[1]

This teaching of Jesus of a complete union with the Father is being caricatured still by the churches in their "Communion Service" where, in literal accordance with Jesus' words, bread and wine are being distributed; and, indeed, in some of the orthodox churches they actually go to the full extent of professing under their "doctrine of transubstantiation" that the eucharistic elements of bread and wine, after being blessed by the priest, are transformed into the real body and blood of the Christ. What a perversion of the original figure of speech, and what a gruesome and almost cannibalistic rite to be performed in the name of Love and Truth! The spiritual significance of accepting Jesus' standards and His Spirit of Truth and leading such a selfless life as to be eventually unified with God is totally lost sight of.

Jesus spent a period of preparation in the wilderness, fasting and praying, before starting on His minstry and it is recorded that angels ministered unto Him[2] and after that He returned in the power of the Spirit to start his work.[3] This was a special time when He lived on such nourishment from on High and became united with the Father. He states, "blessed are they which do hunger and thirst after righteousness for they shall be filled."[4]

Is our seeking of the kingdom of God and His righteousness eager enough to secure for us the blessing of being filled with the Spirit of Truth and being given strength for our work? Are we leading a life so completely merged with God and His plan and work that our pysical existence is of little avail to us? Do we so fully identify ourselves with the Father?

6. Forgive us our debts, as we
ourselves have forgiven our debtors.

This section deals with an intense and honest searching of our own innermost self to see how and where we have fallen short of the moral standards set by Jesus. By such constant examination and vigilance we have to direct our steps towards perfection under the ever helpful Spirit of Truth.

When we measure ourselves against these new standards of Jesus, as we have already seen, our sense of personal sin will be so intense that we shall have no heart to sit in judgment over others. If we have been angry with someone, thus being ourselves guilty of murder, how can we condemn a simple brother who has taken the life of another in a fit of rage? If we, in our innermost hearts harbour covetous feelings against the property, wealth, or status of another, and thus are guilty of stealing, how can we point the finger of scorn at one who has picked another's

---

[1] See John 17:21,23,26   [2] Matthew 4:11   [3] Luke 4:14   [4] Matthew 5:6

pocket to appease his hunger? The cleaerer our spiritual vision, the greater is
the need for a contrite heart. When we realize our greater short-comings in view
of our superior development and standards, we shall see that we have no right
to be angry or vindictive. We shall have to humble ourselves before God and be
forgiving. This should not slacken our course to suit ourselves. Jesus Himself set
us an example by praying for the forgiveness of those who spitefully used Him and
crucified Him.

7. Lead us not into temptation
but deliver us from evil.

In the previous section, we looked back on our life to take stock of our past
deeds and to know where we have been found wanting; and in this section, conscious of our failings and weaknesses, we have to guard ourselves about the future.
There is need for us to mount the watchtower and survey the path that lies ahead
of us. Jesus warns us ever to watch and pray as the danger of stumbling is always
present. Life is made up of small decisions from moment to moment. Unless our
vigil is constant the animal nature within us will lead us astray on the downward
path. "The spirit indeed is willing but the flesh is weak." At each step we need to
have our eyes on the lodestar. Jesus is our light. He says, "He that followeth Me
shall not walk in darkness, but shall have the light of life."[1] "But he that walketh
in darkness knoweth not whither he goeth."[2]

In the following chapter, we shall study in some detail the great temptations
that confront us in this life.

---

[1] John 8:12   [2] John 12:35

Chapter 5

"Get Thee Behind Me, Satan"

Man is endowed with a free will. The course he wishes to take in accordance with the exercise of his free will to gratify the wants of the animal part of his make-up may deviate from the line laid down by his Creator for the well-being of his spiritual side. This conflict between following the dictates of his will and obeying or submitting to God's higher purposes constitutes the temptations of life. We can be delivered from temptations only when our free will has been trained and dsicplined into perfect alignment with the will of the Father.

The three recorded temptations[1] came to Jesus after His period of preparation in the wilderness and when He was about to start on His public work. Such temptations were not peculiar to Jesus but confront each one of us when we are faced with the coice of methods we should take in the little parts we may have to play in this stage of life's drama. Every boy and girl, and man and woman has, therefore, to study carefully how Jesus Himself met His own life problems.

1. That stones be made bread.

fter the fast of forty days when Jesus was famished for nourishment, the tempter came to him and said, "If Thou be the Son of God, command that these stones be made bread." Jesus replied, "Man shall not live by bread alone, but by every word that proceedeth out of the mouth of God."[2]

The rounded brown stones in riverbeds and ravines are suggestive of fermented home-baked bread. Hence, Jesus again uses this simile when he asks, "If a child wants bread will any father give it a stone?"[3] When looked at superificially, such stones present the semblance of that which satisfies a great physical need, but on closer examination it would be realized that the outward apperance is deceptive and a pure illusion as these stones are perfectly useless to sustain real life—life that matters.

Many a young person, when he chooses a career, is tempted to follow a courrse of action which appears to be satisfying because of its material value as a means of earning money.[4] Is our life to be content with mere material wellbeing? Are we to exploit the reosurces of the earth for our own personal material wealth? A merchant carrying on business on a profit motive regardless of any other consideration, a medical man running his dispenary for the income it brings him, a scientist working on his researches for the successful patents he is able to sell to manufacturers, a lawyer arguing his cases for the fees he can command, a preacher

---

[1] Matthew 4:1–11   [2] Matthew 4:2–4   [3] Matthew 7:9   [4] *[Key examples of this point include Kumarappa's business degree and Gandhi's aspirations into being a barrister.—ed.]*

or a preist or a teacher pursuing his avocation for the pay that will meet his living expenses, an engineer or a Government servant working for the salary he is given irrespective of any ideals, all these in their several walks of life are converting stones into bread every day of their lives. They are utilizing the God-given faculties to obtain things that do not satisfy. Such persons, living on the animal plane, content with the supply of primary bodily needs of ther own and with physical comforts and luxuries, not looking beyond the horiztion on their domestic circles, succumb to this temptation. Their material wants are satisfied. They would have a good home, a car, a radio, a club, and a congenial circle of friends similarly circumstanced. This then is their world and the end of their being. Their daily prayer is:

God bless me and my wife,
My son, John, and his wife,
Us four,
And no more.

Such an existence is narrow, self-centred and is based on the gratification of the animal senses—the aim in life being the abundance of the things one can possess. Jesus speaks of such people in the parable of the rich fool,[1] who pulls down his inadequate barns and builds larger ones, stores all his rich harvest of grains and fruits and says to himself, "Soul, thou hast much goods laid up for many years; take thine ease, eat, drink, and be merry." But God says to him, "Thou fool, this night thy soul shall be required of thee; then whose shall those things be, which thou hast provided?" Such are they that lay up treasure for themselves but are not rich toward God. We have to realize that this earthly life is but a camp—fleeting and transient—we cannot establish a home here. Even Peter was tempted by the temporary ecstasy of the moment into wishing that the passing experience be made more permanent while on the mount of transfiguration.[2]

Do we put our trust in worldly things? We are told, "Man shall not live by bread alone." Is the satisfaction that wealth brings everything that matters in life? Should we live and die like well-provided pet dogs?

This is the temptation that confronted Jesus also. Should He convert His divine powers to meet His pressing personal need of the moment—hunger, and use them for Himself? He scornfully turns away from such a course and finds His food and satisfaction in doing the will of God and finishing His work.[3] Shall our choice fall differently? Shall we serve mammon and sell our birth right for a mess of pottage and just live to eat, drink, and be merry? Shall we labour for that which perisheth but not for that which endureth to everlasting life?[4] Shall we reject the bread of life that cometh down from heaven for the rounded stones of the ravines? Shall we not rather provide ourselves with bags that wax not old, a treasure in the heavens that faileth not, where no thief approacheth, neither moth corrupteth?[5] May God grant us strength to make our aim the kingdom of God and His righteousness and then all these things will be added unto us.

2. To jump from the pinnacle and yet be unhurt.

---

[1] Luke 12:16–21   [2] Matthew 17:4   [3] John 4:34   [4] John 4:27   [5] Luke 13:33

"Then the devil taketh Him up into the holy city and setteth Him on a pinnacle of the temple, and saith unto Him, 'If Thou be the Son of God, cast Thyself down;' for it is written, He shall give His angels charge concerning Thee; and in their hands they shall bear Thee up, lest at any time Thou dash thy foot against a stone."

This second temptation is one of a slightly higher order. The first one ended with physical satisfaction on the animal plane. This one deals with a mental gratification of being able to exercise with considerable skill certain of the faculties we are endowed with. A Ford may gloat over the excellent performance of a car he has manufactured, a physician may be proud of the cures he effects, a scientist may be pleased with his discoveries into the mysteries of nature, a lawyer may boast of his forensic skill which enables him to get his guilty client scotfree, a preacher may be happy over his oratory, an engineer may exult over his ability to harness nature and her formidable forces, and the Government servant may feel gratified with his efficiency.

These are all good in their places but they do not reach far enough. They do rise above the animal plane of the former temptation to the human plane of satisfaction derived from the proper and full use of our faculties. We may work, not for filthy lucre, but for name and fame. Yet we shall fall short of the goal God has set for us.

What then shall we do with our lives? If we do not want to cash in our faculties for worldly gains, neither are we to exchange them from the pleasure of work well done and mental satisfaction?

Jesus gave the answer to this eternal question, that turns up before every one, to the rich young ruler, who felt he had led a spotless life from his youth up, following every detailed requirement of the Mosaic law, when He said to him, "One thing thou lackest, go thy way, sell whatsoever thou hast, and give to the poor, and thou shalt have treasure in heaven; and come, take up the cross, and follow Me."[1] Jesus took in at a glance the self-complacency of the young man and knew that his life had been a stagnant pool which had not reached out to succour those around him. He, therefore, suggested to him expanding his life so as to encompass within the range of his ambit those in need. We have to devote all the talents vouchsafed to us, not merely to the achievement of success, but, to the service of those in need without the expectation of any return to ourselves. Jesus directs us to give our inmost life as charity.[2] Nothing short of consecrating our whole life will meet His demand. We can neither hold anything back for ourselves nor even take credit for whatever we may be able to accomplish. When we have done everything He bids us do, we are to feel that we have been but unworthy servants who have only carried out their mere duty.[3] Can we resist our vainglorious nature? Are our actions motivated by what others think of us and the desire to gain respect in the eyes of this world? Science, art, emotional pleasures, etc., are not to be our goal in themselves. We are not to regard man and his faculties as an isolated end but as parts of an eternal dispensation of God in which no mutations can take place. Let us then render unto God the things that are God's.

---

[1] Mark 10:21   [2] Luke 11:41   [3] Luke 17:10

3. The glory of the Kingdoms of the earth.

The devil shows Jesus all the kingdoms of the world and the glory of them and says to Him, "All these things will I give thee, if Thou wilt fall down and worship me." Jesus answers, "Get thee hence, Satan; for it is written, 'Thou shalt worship the Lord thy God, and Him only shalt thou serve.'"

At the threshold of His ministry, Jesus was, naturally contemplating His method of operation. The Jews of his time were eagerly seeking for the signs of their Messianic kingdom. In the previous temptation He considered the way open to Him of placating the Jewish desire by performing miraculous signs and thus drawing them to Himself. he rejected that course of action. Then comes up this alternative of establishing a temporal sway over his people, banishing and displacing the domination of the Romans. Neither does this means of approach to the fulfilment of His mission appeal to Him. He decided to serve God and Him only.

The former two temptations concern man as an individual. But he soon outgrows that stage and realizes that he is one of a group. In the first, he seeks to live within his skin, as any animal does. In the second, his ambit is widened to the extent of his mind and his faculties. In this third, the whole human family is brought within his range. Now, man is seized with the ambition of holding others in his power and controlling and shaping their lives as he deems fit. Here we are faced with our social consciousness leading us into temptation.

Such power over others may be obtained by pure brute force, by financial intrigues or by political strategy. Alexander wanted to conquer the world. Japan wants to overrun and 'develop' China, Mussolini was obsessed with the idea of "civilizing" Abyssinia. New York penetrates the Latin American Republics with loans and securities. Hitler holds Germany in the hollow of his hand by the Nazi social organization. We may not all aspire to such world-wide powers. We may but play to the gallery for popular applause, or we may aim at controlling a school committee, or the parish council, or dominating the village panchayat or the District Board or even swaing the provincial legislatures. Whatever it be, what is the motive that should provide the urge? Personal aggrandizement or selfless service? God alone knows our innermost hearts. Let us not pretend to be what we are not. This is a most subtle temptation. Even Jesus' disciples, James and John fell into this temptation when they sought to sit on the right and left of Jesus in His glory.[1] The danger is great. WE may not seek material advancement nor even personal gratification but just the glow of the adoration of our neighbours and the exercise of patronage. Whatever the motive be, in each case we shall have our reward, such as we seek, but no more.

But the choice of Jesus was to worship God and serve Him alone regardless of whatever by-product such service might bring in its trail. We may be, as it rarely happens, crowned with unsought for glory, with even wealth and satisfaction added to it, but it may also land us, and in most cases it does, in a conflict with powers that be. Doing his duty cost John the Baptist his head. Jesus had not

---

[1] Mark 10:37

where to lay His head, and He was hounded out and hunted by the scribes and Pharisees and, finally, He gave His life on the Cross.

Jesus makes no promise to us of a cushy time if we decide to follow Him. On the contrary, He offers His Cross. He adds, "Yea, the time cometh, that whosoever killeth you will think that he doeth God service."[1] "Blessed are ye when men shall revile you, and persecute you, and shall say all manner of evil against you falsely for My sake. Rejoice, and be exceedingly glad; for great is your reward in heaven."[2]

Shall we shoulder the Cross and follow Him and be glad over the crown of thorns that awaits us and rejoice that we have been counted worthy to suffer for the cause? If we surrender ourselves to Him He will grant us the strength to banish Satan from our lives.

In the chapter following, we shall survey the strait gate and the narrow way open to the few who will thus follow Jesus.

---

[1] John 16:2   [2] Matthew 5:11,12

Chapter 6

"Behold, I Send You Forth"

It was never Jesus' ambition to found new religion. He said He was sent but to the lost sheep of Israel.[1] That is, He considered His duty to be that of a reformer who would purge Judaism of its malpractices and its excrescences and bring it back on to the lines God had laid out for it; not even to strengthen its numbers by conversion. He denounced, in no uncertain terms, the eagerness of the scribes and Pharisees who encompassed land and sea to make one proselyte.[2] His instruction to His disciples also was definitely "not to go in the way of the Gentiles nor enter into any city of the Samaritans" but to confine their work to Israel.[3]

To fulfil the task He set before Himself, He reletlessly fought all restrictive provisions that cramp man's free growth and full development into a son of God ultimately merging into the Father. He concedes that religion is good only in so far as it is a help to man to attain his goal.

He requires helpers who will sanctify and dedicate themselves to this cause and continue the work He has started. He is fully aware that a large number of persons will not be able to follow Him through the straight gate into the narrow way, because of hardships, but who will prefer the broad way to destruction paved with pleasures.[4] The call may come to many, but the chosen will be a few only.[5] He himself left behind only eleven disciples of an inner circle, and sent out seventy of a wider range during His lifetime. Therefore, it will be futile to expect whole nations to be "Christian" until the millennium comes. The churches have attempted to "convert" every one to join their own special brand of "religion" with the result that they have had to let down the barriers to widen the narrow path indicated and trodden by Jesus. This building of a broad highway has gone to such limits as to grant dispensations to compromise or to throw overboard principles Jesus held to as fundamental. This same process has watered down the teachings of Jesus to suit the needs of the majority.

In this chapter, we shall restrict ourselves to the ideals Jesus held up to those few who were willing to leave all, take up the Cross and follow Him.

Terms of Service. A palace equipped comfortably, with sumptuous appointments and many servants, together with a princely allowance is not what Jesus offers His workers. His conditions have been very definitely laid down: "Provide neither gold, nor silver, nor brass in your purses, nor scrip for your journey, neither two coats, neither shoes, nor yet staves: for the workman is worthy of his food. And into whatsoever city or town ye shall enter, enquire who in it is worthy; and there abide till ye go hence."[6] In effect, the insignia of His worker is not a golden Cross elaborately embroidered on an ermined robe, but the simple beggar's bowl. They are not to accept entertainment as guests from house to house but

---

[1] Matthew 15:24   [2] Matthew 23:15   [3] Matthew 10:5   [4] Matthew 7:13   [5] Matthew 20:16;22:14   [6] Matthew 10:9–11

are to eat whatever is set before them.[1] Hospitality, given or received, is good but it absorbs attention which may be better devoted to more elevating occupations. While chiding Martha for worrying about entertaining her guests, Jesus commends her sister, Mary, who left the house work and sat at His feet listening to His discourse, as having chosen the good part that will not be taken away from her.[2]

A high standard of living may not be an evil in itself but its allurements are dangerous. Even a stalwart like Peter was led into denying his Master by seeking, on a cold night, warmth and comfort round a fireside in the palace of the High Priest.[3] There is danger lurking in currying favour with the powers that be and being entertained by them. We are warned against the deceitfulness of riches making us unfruitful.[4] The material losses that may be involved in following Jesus may act as a drag and may even result in the rejection of Jesus as happened in the country of the Gergesenes where He was asked to depart out of their coasts because of the loss of their swine.[5]

Status. When we contemplate the immensity of the universe and the perfect rhythm with which it works out God's will, what is man? He is less than dust. In eternity, where there is no time, what is man's span of three score years and ten? He is but as the flower of the field. Throughout this time and space and beyond, God's plan unfolds itself irrespective of our merits or demerits. We are where we are and what we are, and not by virtue of what we have done, but, through God's grace, as Jesus explains in the parable of the labourers in the vineyard.[6] In this setting there is no room for conceit or pride.

The workers are to be humble and not even allow themselves to be addressed as "Guru" (rabbi) or "Master";[7] naturally it follows that none can be called "Father" nor styled "Reverend", "Right Reverend" or "Most Reverend" or "His Grace" or "His Holiness", etc. He Himself set an example by washing the feet of His disciples,[8] and He told them not to aspire to the order of precedence followed in royal courts but that whosoever wishes to be the chiefest should be the servant of all,[9] as He Himself came not to be ministered unto but to serve and spend His life in helping others. Therefore, the workers can secure at best an equal status with Jesus as sons of God,[10] and merge their identity in Him.[11] There is a general misconception that Jesus claimed a divinity peculiar to Himself. He explains the grounds of His claim based on his performing "the works of my Father".[12] So that anyone else who does the will of the Father will also be a "son of God".

Even popularity for service rendered may not be enjoyed as a compensation. "Because ye are not of the world, but I have chosen you out of the world, therefore the world hateth you... If they have persecuted Me, they will also persecute yyou."[13] This hatred, of course, will be without cause.

It may so happen that the service rendered may be such as to evoke strong public appreciation. Even such may detract from proceeding on the set course with a singleness of purpose and so caution is necessary. After Jesus fed the five

---

[1] Luke 10:7–8   [2] Luke 10:42   [3] John 18:18   [4] Matthew 13:22; Luke 21:34   [5] Matthew 8:34   [6] Matthew 20:1–16   [7] Matthew 23:8,10   [8] John 13:14,15   [9] Mark 10:44   [10] John 1:12   [11] John 14:20   [12] John 10:33–38   [13] John 15:19–20

thousand, the masses of the people were so moved emotionally that they sought to make Him king by force. But when He sensed the situation, He withdrew into the solitude which the mountain fastness offered.[1]

Nevertheless, Jesus did accept loving devotion as in the case of Mary, when she anointed His feet with costly ointment. This was not for His gratification but to allow one who had been through a great deal of tribulation to give vent to her pent up feelings. It was for her good that He accepted the homage.[2] Again, on His triumphal ride into Jerusalem, when the multitudes demonstrated their enthusiasm by shouting "Hosanna in the highest" the Pharisees, who were jealous of His popularity, suggested His rebuking the people for such tumultuous behaviour. But He refused to do so as He recognized the human value of such demonstrations of appreciation and affection in advancing the cause.[3]

Detachment. The workers are to place their duty above even family ties. Those who place father or mother, son or daughter higher than their duty are not worthy to follow Him.[4] When one of His disciples asked for permission first to fulfil his duties to his father and then return to follow Him, He would not consider such a proposition.[5] From this it cannot be inferred that we should shake off all family responsibilities. Jesus Himself set an example of filial duty when he provided for His mother while He was dying on the Cross by entrusting her to the care of the disciple whom He loved.[6]

Are we willing to enter such a strait gate and shoulder such a heavy Cross? The one reward will be union with the Father ultimately, with the inheritance of eternal life.[7]

The Acid Test. Whether we are followers of Jesus or not is not a matter that can be decided by a certificate of entry in the parish baptismal register. Jesus has prescribed certain definite tests by which His followers may be recognized. He says, "Not everyone that saith unto Me, Lord, Lord, shall enter into the kingdom of heaven; but he that doeth the will of My Father which is in heaven,"[8] and again "By this shall all men know that ye are My disciples, if ye have love one to another."[9] When there is this love and an allegiance to truth such shall hear the voice of Jesus.[10] He adds, "Ye have not chosen Me, but I have chosen you and ordained you, that ye should go and bring forth fruit."[11] "Herein is My Father glorified, that ye bear much fruit; so shall ye be My disciples."[12] True love is bound to lead to action. Need a mother be coerced into attending on the child she bore? Will not even a starving mother give the last morsel to her child without expecting a return? Similarly, our love has to be translated into deeds and the quality of our self-denial will declare the intensity of the love. "If ye salute your brethren only, what do ye more than others?" "If ye salute your brethren only, what do ye more than others?" "If ye love them which love you, what reward have ye?"[13] Our service has to be disinterested to exceed the contractual relations of give and take of the general run of worldly people. Such deeds are the fruits of love. "Wherefore, by the fruits ye shall know them."[14]

---

[1] John 6:15 [2] Luke 7:47,48 [3] Luke 19:39,40 [4] Matthew 10:37 [5] Matthew 8:21,22 [6] John 19:26,27 [7] Matthew 19:29 [8] Matthew 7:21 [9] John 13:35 [10] John 8:31 [11] John 15:16 [12] John 15:8 [13] Matthew 5:47,46 [14] Matthew 7:20

Function. Jesus conceived His function here below to be "not to do Mine own will, but the will of Him that sent Me."[1]   And how He went about doing that will of the Father is indicated in the credentials He presents to John the Baptist when the latter enquires who Jesus was. "The blind receive their sight, the lame walk, the lepers are cleansed and the deaf hear, the dead are raised up and the poor have the gospel preached to them;"[2]   and He charges His disciples also to "heal the sick, cleanse the lepers, raise the dead and cast out devils."[3]   In the parable of the last judgment, God commends those who come to inherit the kingdom of heaven, and states their claims as being based on their service to the needy. "For I was an hungered, and ye gave Me food; I was thirsty, and ye gave Me drink; I was a stranger, and ye took Me in; naked and ye clothed Me; I was sick, and ye visited Me; I was in prison and ye came unto Me." "Inasmuch as ye have done it unto one of the last of these My brethren, ye have done it unto Me."[4]   From these it is clear that the love of the Father has to be transformed into loving service to our neighbours. Jesus says His followers are to be "the salt of the earth" and "the light of the world". Salt and light are nothing in themselves aprt from their quality through which alone others are aware of them and are benefited thereby. If there be no such benefit derived from these, then their existence is useless. Similarly, if the followers of Jesus do not make their presence felt by the service they render to others they are as good as dust and ashes. Service, then, is the function of all who profess to follow Jesus.

Methodology. How should this function in life be performed? Here again, Jesus sets us His gentle example. Of Him it was said "He shall not strive, nor cry; neither shall any man hear His voice in the streets. A bruised reed shall He not break, and a smoking flax shall He not quench."[5]   until He makes religion victorious. His was no church militant attempting to spread the gospel with inquisiton, torch and sword. He worked like the leaven that leavens the whole mass, without any hurly-burly silently by its very nature. His followers are not to sit in judgment over others' actions[6] but to shed their light by good work and devoted service,[7] so that others may follow in their train. They are to season others by their own inherent qualities as salt seasons food and preserves perishable articles.[8]

Though Jesus' ideals were high and uncompromising He expects performance according to the best capacity of each individual. "For unto whomsoever much is given, of him shall be much required."[9]   Hence, those who are talented have great responsibility laid on them. On the other hand, Jesus commends the poor widow who put into the temple treasury her coppers. He considers that she contributed more than all the rest, for "she of her want did cast in all that she had, even all her living,"[10] while the others were giving out of their surplus wealth.

Jesus leads gently those that are weak. In speaking to the people in general, He does not lecture over their heads, but pick words and incidents familiar to them in their everyday life and infuses by means of such simple parables profound

---

[1] John 6:38   [2] Matthew 11:5   [3] Matthew 10:8   [4] Matthew 25:35,36,40   [5] Matthew 12:19,20
[6] Matthew 7:1   [7] Matthew 5:16   [8] Matthew 5:13   [9] Luke 12:48   [10] Mark 12:44

ideas, for though they seem to look, yet they do not see and though they listen, yet they do not understand.[1]

Such then should be the approach and methods used by those who would follow Jesus. They have to set an example by their life and actions and infuse the love of the Father into the lives of those amongst whom their lot is cast.

The Field of Work. Thus the love of God has to be demonstrated by a devoted life spent in service of those in need. We ought to heal the sick and teach the unlettered. But, this is not all. As the life of man grows and society assumes more complicated aspects, the sphere of usefulness and service widens. Today, great departments of life are crying out for selfless workers. Children of light are not to be confined to the parish compounds. Every walk of life needs their light and every department needs to be toned up by them right through the great sweep of the social, political and economic world. Let us study in broad outline, a few spheres where such influence can be effectively used and then content ourselves with a few detailed instances presenting opportunites of service. Naturally, we restrict ourselves to conditions prevailing in our country.

As we have noticed, Jesus' mission is to shift the emphasis from the external control of life under the Law to self-discipline imposed by the Spirit within us. Such living will naturally and ultimately lead to complete control of our desires and not to indulgence of them. Hence, the present economy of the West based on the cultivation and the gratification of wants is diametrically opposed to the teachings of Jesus.

The charge of Jesus to the rich young ruler, "sell whatsoever thou hast and give to the poor," is not only applicable to the rich in material wealth but to every one who possesses something that others lack. That ruler happened to be rich in a special way. Silver and gold we may have none, but, such as we have, we are directed to use in the service of those in need of that special possession of our as good stewards of the manifold grace of God. One may be rich in physical health and strength, in the rare gift of common sense, in possessing social influence, in sagacity, in having natural organizing powers, in inherent commercial ability and industrial foresight, in the enviable capacity to impart knowledge, in learning, in administatrive skill, in some applied art—music, painting, sculpture, oratory, or in some professional training—Medicine, Law, etc., in the methods of research and investigation, in technical knowledge relating to agriculture, forestry, geology, pisciculture, etc. Whatever it be, we have to surrender it all without expecting a return.

In so serving, the worker will neither rust out nor wear out, because such service is twice blessed—like a spring in a well which becomes clearer for the greater quantity of water that is drawn out. This selfless service blesses both him who gives and him who takes. By the discipline he imposes on himself, he who serves develops his own personality till he becomes perfect as the heavenly Father is perfect. He who is served, not only gets his needs met but he too becomes the better for it. If he be an artisan, who was guided by turning out better work as directed, also develops his faculties, the sense of accuracy, art, method, fine finish, responsibility. A great musician cannot be produced without

---

[1] Matthew 13:13

the discipline of years spent in practice, repteating many times the same lessons on his instrument. During that period he develops his nervous system, synchronizes touch and ears, etc. Such is the case in all work. All these contribute to man's growth and the expansion of his faculties. There is no such item as drudgery in individual work awhich needs to be eliminated. Without work man deteriorates. It is through work that man expresses his personality. It is most unforutnate that work has come to be looked upon as a curse from God. The unemployed know by experience that there was never a greater blessing for man than steady work.

Men with sagacity, commonsense and organizing powers, who are wise as serpents and harlmess as doves, can devote their special gifts to promoting social harmony, to organizing the villagers to co-operate among themselves, to settle disputes between them, to arranging for the smooth working of the economic activity of the village and, generally, to looking after their welfare.

The appalling illiteracy in our country is a challenge to all those who have had the benefit of a liberal education. Similarly, the lot of millions of social outcasts is a call to those who have their hearts attuned to the cry of distress.

is there a better way to serve God for a scientist than to devote all his talents and powers of research in perfecting the methods of production of indigent artisans and thus helping to banish poverty? Jesus charges Peter to "feed the lambs" as an outcome of the love he professes towards Jesus.[1] Where is a more effective way of feeding the people than placing them on their feet, and making them capable of helping themselves? Free gifts of grain are but a crude form of charity, perhaps affording momentary relief, but anything to be lasting needs a life of sacrifice.

The only material return such workers "who are worthy of their food" may expect is to have their minimum requirements of food, clothing, and shelter on the basis obtaining amongst those for whom they work. Freely we have received, freely must we give without hoping for any gain.

Those gifted with specialized knowledge can help with medical relief, aid in agricultural and industrial production, storage, marketing, etc. To a certain extent, self-seeking Mahajans had performed these latter functions on the economic production side until modern capitalism attracted them elsewhere by greater profits, leaving the whole range of cottage and village industries and agriculture as orphans under the present system. Here is an urgent call for hundreds of thousands of trained public workers in all our villages scattered throughout the length and breadth of our land.

On the consumption side, the best help that can be rendered is to limit one's purchases to the articles produced by the indigent artisans and to adjust one's consumption accordingly, thus providing them with a ready market. It may be that to a certain extent, especially in the early stages, such production may fall short of our requirements in finish and appearance, and better and cheaper articles may be available from abroad and from centralized large scale capitalist concerns. Of course, we must do our best to perfect the methods of village production, but we need not wait till that is done in order to patronize village products. Such difference in price and quality that we have to put up with is part of the cross we may have to bear. But can such privations be properly termed a "cross"? A

---

[1] John 21:15–17

child may present its mother with a handkerchief hemstitched by its own little fingers, with a few stitches badly made or missing. Will the mother look upon such an article as a "cross"? Would she not rather look upon the labour of love behind it and the effort made and cherish the gift for these reasons? That mother does not measure with material commercial scales, but she covers the whole with a heart of love. Should not this also be the approach of those who are devotees of the God who is love? Every one, rich or poor, can take part in this programme of discriminating consumption as there is hardly anyone who is not a purchaser of some article—food stuffs, baskets, pots, pans and other utensils, tools and simple implements, clothes, leather goods, household requirements such as mats, charpoys, lamps, etc. can all be of local production by artisans who are our poor neighbours. Jesus says, "Give ye them to eat." This mode of limiting our consumption to such articles is one of the most effective ways of removing the distress of the poor and letting them have what they need.

Those with administrative capacity may enter Government service on the same basis of remuneration as village workers, on a subsistence level of salaries and devote themselves to ameliorating the conditions of life in villages, by the performance of governmental functions cosnscientiously in the sole interest of the governed and not for securing ambitious careers, or for personal advancement or princely emoluments. A great many departments—forestry, irrigation, power production, communications, etc.—need a long range view for their satisfactory planning and execution. These can best be attended to by selfless workers who can well afford to take a detached view of affairs. At present, at every such point, we have exploiters and self-seekers working for their own selfish personal gains to the detriment of the cause of the poor. Hence, there presents itself a most appropriate sphere of activity for every one who would compete to be the greatest servant of all in India. We should all fight oppression of the poor and injustice to the weak, unceasingly with all our health, strength and spirit, not fearing those who are able to kill the body but are helpless against the soul.

A system of living based on self-discipline and self-control is the rock-bottom on which political democracy can be built. Jesus brought us the seeds of genuine democracy, which, alas, in the West have fallen among the thorns of the philosophy of multiplication of wants and have been choked by them.

In our country, with the growth of the conception of true democracy, the sphere of activity of the worker is coeval and coextensive with the whole of human life. The people's representatives must lose their own selves, merging themselves completely in the needs of their constituents. Who can do this better than workers who have forsaken the world and its allurements in the service of their motherland? Ultimately, this can be carried into the international field where, today, greed, avarice, and ruthless competition hold undisputed sway, pluging the world periodically into rivers of blood. If men who have consecrated their lives on the altar of service can be found to handle these thorny problems in an atmosphere clear of hatred and suspicion, in the spirit of truth and love, there shall then be inaugurated the reign of peace and love in the place of the present one of hatred and turmoil.

Peace that passeth all understanding cannot be ushered in as long as "following" Jesus is confined to the narrow limits ascribed today to "religion". We have to break down these restrictive barriers. Life, in all its bearings, has to be a continual prayer. Worship of God is not to be confined to Sundays or to be limited to this mountain or that cathedral, to this church or that chapel, or temple or mosque, but is to be open to all activities in every walk of life from the cradle to the grave, and to all mankind. Whosoever opposes such a widening of the field comes of the evil one and cries out demanding "Release unto us Barabbas and crucify Jesus".

Heal the Sick. Jesus' conception of His Messianic mission was to call sinners to repentance and to save that which was lost.[1] He offers salvation from sin and so becomes the Saviour of the world. "Those that are whole need not a physician." He said to those whom He healed, "Go and sin no more", thus establishing the connection of sin with disease. Hence those who consecrate themselves to carry on His work should also fight sin wherever it be found and help to deliver the afflicted from the grip of disease. This programme is the preventive form of his charge "Heal the Sick".

Sin. What then is sin? Of God's creatures man is distinguished by his free will. When man, forgetting his dependent position as a creature, deeming himself the creator, exercises his will to cut across the will of the Father, he commits sin and goes off the rail. This deviation from the divine path results in disease and death—the wages of sin. When he is set back on the original course he is saved. Therefore, the idea of sin is not confined to the transgression of moral and ethical rules only but extends over the whole gamut of nature. When man's life is in tune with the Infinite he obeys God and realizes himself, or else disharmony and discord is caused. Conversely, where there is disharmony of any kind it is symptomatic of sin and disobedience. A clash of man's will with God's purpose caused by the animal in us desiring something that goes against the dictates of the Spirit is *temptation*. When we yield to it we sin. Let us now consider a few examples of such sins in detail in various walks of life in the modern world.

Sex Relations. God has placed the sex mechanism in all creatures for the continuation of the species. When this function is used for the flesh it is a sin, whether it takes place within wedlock or outside. Perhaps there will be no difficulty in accepting such a glaring example. Similarly, in other departments of life also sin is found but often it escapes recognition as such.

Nutrition. For instance, in the matter of food, the grain of rice is made up of the germ, the pericarp, the bran and the starch. For various man-made purposes—commercial and aesthetic—these component parts are separated by polishing the rice. This disturbs nature's provision, hence when the polished rice is consumed without being balanced by other items of diet to replace the constituents lost by polishing, as is done by the poor people, the dire disease of Beriberi appears, with its attendant death, to punish the sinner.

In all animals the instinct of hunger is present to regulate the supply of fuel and to build the body. Man sins when he uses this function to pander to his palate.

---

[1] Matthew 9:13;18:11

He over-eats highly seasoned and overcooked processed food, causing most of the ailments human body is heir to, and receives the wages of sin.

Work. All rights carry with them certain duties. Separation of these so as to enjoy the rights to the exclusion of the duties is sin. Creative work has in it the elements of both work and leisure. Exploiters seek to pass on the work to labourers and enjoy the leisure themselves. Poverty, unemployment, famines, etc. are social diseases caused by our sin of splitting up what God ordained as wholesome work.

Exploitation of nature such as the unrestricted cutting down of trees for timber, without a proper plan of reforestation, leads to floods and soil erosion.

Railway freight rates, devised to export raw materials and to import finished goods, deprive people of their inherent right of work and occupation and cause poverty while they also impoverish the land by the loss of natural manures, as when oil seeds are exported, since this breaks the cycle of nature's economy. Similarly, large towns and cities, where the night soil is wasted, are carbuncles of nature, starving and destroying the fertility of the land.

Finance. The device of money which tempts the farmer to abandon food crops and shift to money crops, like the cultivation of tobacco, in a country like ours where people are dying of starvation, is a sin. When by the temptation of cash gains, eggs, milk, honey and such nourishing food products are snatched away to distant markets without being available to the producers themselves, the medium of exchange is used as an instrument of sin.

State. When the social and political organization is such that it prevents the natural development of the children of God to their full stature, denying to them freedom and opportunities of education, it becomes an arm of Satan. The State has to be the servant of the people and not their master. The State is created for the people, and not the people for the State. When the creative faculty bestowed on man for his progress is directed by the State to build engines of destruction, it becomes a veritable abomination of desolation.

The Army, Navy, and other destructive forces are occupations conceived by Moloch for his own followers, forming gangs for organizing murder. There can be no room in these for the followers of "the Prince of Peace" whose banner is love. Wars should be no more and all swords should be beaten into plough-shares in every land where Jesus reigns.

To attain all these, those who have dedicated themselves thus to serve God in the needs of their neighbours will have to render their devoted service as a chosen generation and a holy group of workers, without fear and seeking no favours. They will turn away from the darkness caused by man-made sophisticated doctrines to the simple teachings of the Nazarene, the carpenter's son, and by their relentless fight against sin schew forth the glory of God who has called them out of darkness into His marvellous light to be the light of the world, to dispel the darkness of sin and ignorance in national life from all shady corners, and as the salt of the earth they will keep the streams of life pure throughout the land in the midst of vital activities. Behold the fields are white already to harvest, but such labourers as we need are few. May we, therefore, pray fervently that the Lord of the harvest would send forth His workers imbued with His Spirit for the task before them.

Chapter 7

Commandments of Men

Jesus makes a distinction, as to their claims over us, between the commandments of God and the laws laid down by men. The former have to be obeyed always, while the latter, being limited by time and space, are to apply only in so far as they are not in conflict with the spirit of the former and as circumstances permit.[1] As Peter puts it, "We ought to obey God rather than men."[2]

Paul also constantly distinguishes between the rules and suggestions he makes "by permission" as being quite distinct from those he lays down "by commandment of the Lord".[3] Sometimes the line of demarcation is very thin and so one has to be always on his guard lest by mistake a commandment of man be given precedence over a divine one. The Spirit of Truth, our Comforter and Teacher, is the only reliable Guide at such times. No earthly body, however eminent, can speak with greater authority than this Spirit within us. Neither "His Holiness" nor the Acts of the Houses of Parliament, nor the decisions of the Privy Council, can make us do things contrary to this supreme Voice within. Hence, so as to be forewarned, it is expedient for us to consider, in this chapter, a few matters on which much misunderstanding exists, especially in regard to the position of women, marital relations and the powers that be, by way of samples. Life is replete with such problems, especially as society gets more and more complex. No earthly conclave can lay down the laws in detail for all times in such matters.

Jesus was content with enunciating the basic principles, which, of course, hold good always and He left further advances and details to be filled in by the Spirit of Truth.

As we have already been in the third chapter, according to Jesus the sinful thought and desire that precede the act constitute the transgressions just as much as the deed consqeuent on them—anger as much as murder, sensual thought or even lustful look as much as adultery. While opening the gates wide to receive large number into the fold, the early churches lowered this standard from the sinful spirit to sin in the flesh itself. Their condition of membership was "that ye abstain from meat offered to idols and from blood and from things strangled and from fornication."[4] It did not seem wise to them to lay heavier burdens on the early converts from the Gentiles who were as yet weak spiritually.

Where the modern churches have gone off the line is in accepting these special concessions made by Peter, Paul, and the early Church, to conditions that prevailed two thousand years ago in certain localities and in peculiarily situated congregations, to be final rulings that were to govern all cases everywhere and at all times, instead of looking to Jesus and the Spirit of Truth—the original Fountainhead.

---

[1] See Matthew 23:23 and Mark 7:8,13.   [2] Acts 5:29   [3] See 1 Corinthians 7:6,12,25 and 2 Corinthians 8:8,10;11:17.   [4] Acts 15:29

Positions of Women. This error in fundamental approach has led to many ludicrous situations under differing climes and circumstances. For instance, in this modern age of women's emancipation when, Miss Maud Royden went into the pulpit of the City Temple in London, there was a furor and some men of orthodoxy rose in horror as it was thought contrary to Paul's direction in the first century to the churches at Corinth and at Ephesus that "it is a shame for women to speak in the church"[1] and that women were not to be permitted to teach.[2] This attitude was based on the story of the curse of God on Eve for tempting her husband, Adam, in the Garden of Eden, when she was told that as a consequence of her evil deed she would always be ruled by Adam.[3]   With the upholding of such an anacrhonism what will schools do without women teachers? Today in America, the teaching profession is practically a monopoly of women especially in their earlier grades. Such orthodox persons, who wish to promulgate the superior rights of man, conveniently forget that the same Paul had told the churches of Galatia that "there is neither male nor female in Christ Jesus".[4]

Husbands and Wives. In writing to the church at Corinth about marital relations, Paul was dealing with the local prevalent problem of fornication among them, which question was specifically referred to him[5] and even then he dealt with the husbands and wives on the same level and, what is more, he definitely states that he was not speaking by commandment. On the other hand, in his letter to the Ephesians 5:23,24, he did hold that "the husband is the head of the wife". This again, as we have already noticed, has reference to the curse on Eve, and was undoubtedly, an outcome of Paul's early training as an orthodox Pharisee.

The same Jewish influence led him to advocate that women must cover their heads as a sign of their subjection to man.[6]   To this day, the churches enjoy this custom on the women of their congregations! And still Paul did recognize the equality of men and women before God.[7]

As regards Peter, we must not forget that he was the Apostle detailed out to shepherd the Jewish congregations, amongst whom some wives had accepted the Christian belief while their husbands were still Jewish and vice versa. Therefore, when he suggests wives be in subjection to their husbands he is dealing with a peculiar problem confronting him.[8]   He wants these wives to win over their husbands by their meekness, chastity, and quiet spirit. It is the method of "Satyagraha" that he is advocating. There is no inference of inferiority as he recommends a similar course to the believing husbands also.[9]   Paul also writes to the Corinthians in the same fashion.[10]

Jesus holds the sexes in complete equality; in fact He makes no sex distinctions, for He says, "They are as angels of God in heaven,"[11] i.e. sexless, when they become children of God. Sex differentiation belongs to the animal kingdom—the physical world—for reproduction and preservation of the species. In man it is the remnant of the instinct of the brute worsened by the possession and misuse of free will. This will be completely erased on being born again.

---

[1] 1 Corinthians 15:35   [2] 1 Timothy 2:11   [3] Genesis 3:16   [4] Galatians 3:28   [5] 1 Corinthians 7:1-6   [6] 1 Corinthians 11:5-10   [7] 1 Corinthians 11:11   [8] 1 Peter 3:1-4   [9] 1 Peter 3:7   [10] 1 Corinthians 7:14   [11] Luke 20:36

The Authoritarian Church. In like manner, in matters pertaining to church doctrine, interpretation and government, the churches claim implicit obedience basing their right on the writings of Peter and Paul.

Romans 13:1–6 is the charter of the powers that be. But the very first qualification implied in Paul's writing that "the powers that be are of God" is often slurred over. All powers are not clothed with the same authority. If they were, regardless of individual allegiance, the Shankaracharyas or the Jagadgurus of the Hindus, the Dalai Lamas of the Buddhists and the Caliph of the Muslims should claim the obedience of the Pope and the Archbishop of Canterbury! What powers we choose to obey is subject to the spiritual guidance within us.

Paul, himself a Pharisee, rebelled against the Jewish authorities when he saw the light. Later the Apostles broke away from the fundamental Mosaic law of circumcision.[1] In spite of this, when circumstances seemed to demand it, Paul circumcised Timothy.[2] Paul's appeal to Caesar was to avoid being brought under the clutches of the Jewish religious authorities.[3]

Jesus is often cited as advocating obedience to authority as represented by the scribes and Pharisees and the passage relied on to support this contention is Matthew 23:2,3. The crucial qualifying clause, "the scribes and Pharisees sit in Moses' seat", is ignored. Moses was the leader chosen by God and accepted by the people. In a patriarchal community this comes nearest to the natural leaders elected by the people in a modern democracy. Therefore, what Jesus enjoins is obedience to God-sent leaders. Those who claim obedience must first produce reliable credentials of being God-sent representative of the people.

Besides, the word "observe" in the above passage probably indicates that Jesus was dealing mainly with rites rather than with matters of conscience. We know that He had directed the lepers, when healed, to offer for their cleansing as required by the Mosaic law.[4] If this reading is correct, apart from ceremonial observance, no abject obedience to priesthood is enjoined by this passage. He characterized the scribes and Pharisees as "blind guides".[5] Surely, He cannot advocate people following such guides unquestioningly!

Jesus was neither a fanatic nor a bigot. He showed sympathy and courtesy towards those of other faiths.[6] In practice, Jesus himself never gave Jewish authorities implicit obedience. We have several instances of Jesus setting aside Mosaic law when circumstances deamdned it. He again and again broke the laws of the Sabbath, as the Pharisees interpreted it, when the occasion called for such action. He taught that the Sabbath was made for man and not man for the Sabbath.[7] In all his actions the overriding consideration was not the Mosaic law but the, "will of the Father". Hence the Spirit of Truth within us is the supreme court of appeal and we have to answer to that even at the cost of our lives.

Powers Temporal. In this sphere also, to enforce implicit obedience, Paul's authority is invoked with the suppot of Peter's, too.[8]

Let us deal with Peter first. His is not a general charge to submit to temporal authority at all costs but it has a specific reference. These two verses are qualified

---

[1] See Acts 15:23–29 and Galatians 5:6.   [2] Acts 16:3   [3] Acts 25:11   [4] Matthew 8:4   [5] Matthew 23:16   [6] See Matthew 8:10–11.   [7] Mark 2:27   [8] 1 Peter 2:13,14

by the very next verse which, according to Dr. Moffatt, forms but a clause of the sentence beginning with the 13th verse and runs on: "...for it is the will of God that by your honest lives you should silence the ignorant charges of foolish persons;" i.e. , just as Jesus submitted to Pilate's jurisdiction to vindicate Truth.

As regards Paul, it is well to recall his antecedents. Like many of us, Indian Christians, who are thoroughly denationalized even to the extent of making English almost our mother tongue, and are taught from childhood to be loyal citizens proud of being British born subjects, Paul too, being by birth a roman citizen, a proud privilege[1] and a coveted distinction held in much honour in those days[2] was brought up in a tradition of loyalty to a foreign power. Again, like us he must have been steeped in Western lore and, no doubt, his acquaintance with the Aristotelean doctrine of the subordination of the individual to the State had greatly influenced him. This, of course is repugnant to Jesus' teaching of the freedom or sovereignty of the individual personality of the child of God. With such a background Paul's authority to guide us in such matters cannot carry much weight. His reasoning is definitely weak in the passage relied on[3] where he states, "For there is no power but of God: the powers that be are ordained of God." If this sweeping statement were to be accepted without any qualification should we not be "kicking against the pricks" by waging war on Hitler and Mussolini? Who wields greater power than these dictators? Besides, Paul himself on another occasion recognizes the existence of earthly authority other than those from God.[4]

To make matters worse, the Authorized Version gives a cross reference to the answer of Jesus to Pilate[5] as though to prop up this case with the supreme authority of Jesus. Here again, we have to bear in mind the context. Pilate haughtily tells his prisoner, Jesus, "Knowest thou not that I have power to crucify thee, and have power to release thee?" Jesus promptly brings him down a peg or two and puts him in his place by retorting, "Thou couldst have no power at all against Me, expect it were given thee from above." That is, Pilate would be like any other man in the street if he were divested of the judicial authority conferred or delegated to him by Caesar. The word "above" refers naturally to his official superior and not to God. If it had been a reference to God, Jesus would have used the term, as He usually does, of "My Father" or "Heaven".[6]

gain, we are provided with a cross reference, a few verses lower down[7] to Jesus saying, "Render unto Caesar the things which are Caesar's and unto God the things that are God's."[8] To appraise correctly the significance of this passage, once more we have to recall to our mind the circumstances which called forth this statement from Jesus. "Then went the Pharisees, and took counsel how they might entagle Him in his talk"[9] and sent to Him their Gestapo or C.I.D. men who plotted to trap Him into a seditious statement against Caesar by asking Him if it was lawful to pay tribute to Caesar. "But Jesus perceived their wickedness, and said, why tempt ye me, ye hypocrites?"[10] Thus Jesus was presented with a premeditated, well-conceived dilemma. He skillfully fenced with His inquisitors by referring to the two currencies in which the Roman tribute and the Temple

---

[1] Acts 16:37,38   [2] Acts 22:25,28   [3] Romans 13:1   [4] 1 Corinthians 11:6–8   [5] John 19:11
[6] See Matthew 22:53 and Luke 9:54.   [7] Vs. 7   [8] Matthew 22:21   [9] Matthew 22:15
[10] Matthew 22:18

dues had to be paid and so nonplussed them with the above sententious pithy saying under the consideration. Is it fair to Jesus to hang a whole system of State philosophy upon an oracular statement extracted from Him under duress?

Even granting we might do so, it is possible logically to prove quite the contrary of the opinion sought to be established. For we are told, "All things were made by Him; and without Him was not anything made that was made."[1] Therefore, if God "had made heaven and earth, the sea, and all that in them is", where does the poor worm of a Caesar get a look in? All things (including Caesar himself) belong to God and so have to be rendered to Him and hence Caesar gets nothing!

The only recorded occasion where Jesus in the course of His brief earthly life was confronted with the quesiton of tax was at Capernahum when enquiries were made if He too would pay the Temple Tax. Though He was of the opinion that only aliens were to be taxed by earthly powers, yet, rather than cause any offence, He directed Peter to pay it.[2] We hardly need this incident to provide all our inspiration for formulating the principles of Public Finance needed to run a modern State.

Jesus' whole life was a continuous fight against usurpation and unreasoning authoritarian rule and a heroic attempt to assert the divinity of man and the absolute supremacy of the Spirit of Truth within Him. In this struggle He was nobly followed and supported by an army of early Christian martyrs who faced the most diabolical tortures rather than let their spiritual personality be subdued by brute force or earthly power. With such undying and unmistakable evidence before us, can we escape or shirk our God-imposed responsibilities by passing it on to an outside authority or power? We may follow the latter only in so far as their requirements are in perfect alignment with the dictates of our soul. We have to discharge the duties devolving on us primarily to the satisfaction of God. No excuses or substitutes will be accepted. "Watch ye, therefore, and pray always, that ye may be accounted worthy to escape all these things."[3] "For there shall arise false Christs, and false prophets, and shall shew great signs and wonders; in so much that, if it were possible, they shall deceive the very elect."[4]

"My sheep hear My voice, and I know them, and they follow me."..."My Father, which gave them Me, is greater than all; and no man is able to pluck them out of My Father's hand."[5]

---

[1] John 1:3   [2] Matthew 17:26,27   [3] Luke 21:36   [4] Matthew 24:24   [5] John 10:27,29

Chapter 8

A Parable—Recapitulation and Summary

Whereunto shall we liken man with the spark of the Divine and the gift of free will? With what comparison shall we compare him?

Man is like a sailing boath on the ocean of life. He is equipped with a compass—the Spirit of Truth—to indicate the cardinal points by which to direct his course, he is fitted with a rudder—the gift of free will—by means of which to regulate and control his life.

The Spirit of Truth being absolute, and not relative to each individual, is the same in all men, and true for all time. But the steering gear varies. Its position with reference to the hull is dependent on the nautical bearing of the ship—latitude and longitude, the conditions, obstructions and currents in the sea and the direction of the wind.

The Compass. Though the compass is on the ship, yet it is not a part of the ship as it works within the great magnetic field of the earth. The ship's hull may pitch and roll on the waves and its bow may shift and change its direction from moment to moment, but the compass being mounted suitably on an universal swivel point or kept floating on a liquid, maintains its level position irrespective of the motion of the ship, and the needle being under the influence of the magnetism of the earth, remains constantly pointing to the North Pole. Thus being independent of the movements of the boat, it is capable of pointing to the true north, in all weathers and under varying circumstances. Hence, it is made possible to obtain the actual direction of the ship's course and regulate and control its movements accordingly.

Similarly, man, though from the world, is not of it. His spirit being part of the divine is capable of detachment from the things of the earth, gazing always on the eternal purposes of the Creator and forming a part—however minute—of God Himself, just as the magnetic needle itself forms part of the huge magnet—the earth. The Spirit of Truth, being not of the body, is detached from the animal in man and guides him into the ways of God. If man submits himself to it he will bring his own free will into alignment with the will of God.

The Rudder. Unlike the compass, the rudder is firmly attached to the ship and revolves freely on its pivot or hinges and functions so as to change the course of the ships. Its movements may set the ship on its purposeful and chartered course or may lead it to its destruction, according to whether the rudder is steered in definite relation to the readings indicated by the needle of the compass or not.

When the rudder—the free will of man—is set in full alignment with the will of God, man attains salvation and eternal life by his union with God as his life is regulated, controlled and disciplined according to God's purposes. If the gift of free will is not so controlled, the life of man deviates from the divine course set for him and becomes purposeless like a boat that has lost its rudder and compass and is tossed about by the wind and currents helplessly on an uncharted sea.

The rudder cannot function as the compass. We cannot determine the course of the ship by mere knowledge of the angle the rudder makes with the hull. The two boats may be making for the same port. Their magnetic needles will point in the same direction—due north—while the position of their rudders will differ according to conditions obtaining in the neighbourhood of each boat. Even if two boats be sailing parallel to each other and if they encounter a sandbank ahead, one may round it to the east of the sandbank and the other to the west and though for a while they seem to be going in diametrically opposite directions yet they will again come together on the other side of the bank. In the same way, two men or two groups of men may appear to act differently, but this fact in itself is no ground for pronouncing judgment on them. If they are guided by the same Spirit of Truth and regulate their rudders—their will—accordingly, they will ultimately reach the same goal. The apparent contradictions are but adaptations in details called for by varying local circumstances. Rudders of all boats sailing into the same harbour are not allf ixed in exactly the same relationship to their respective hulls. In fact, from moment to moment, the angle the rudder makes with the hull will vary. The rudder is not rivetted or screwed on to the hull but has to be moveable to perform its function satisfactorily.

The goal of all religions, as long as the Spirit of Truth pervades their atmosphere, is the same, though for the moment their rudders—free will and commandments of men—may differ widely. This is no cause for differentiation or condemnation.

The Old Covenant. Before the advent of Jesus, the Jews had mistaken the rudder—the mosaic Law—for the compass, and emphasized the position of a fixed rudder in relation to the hull rather than in relation to the needle of the compass. Jesus came to set them right and shew them the relative functions of these indispensable instruments to enable them by the proper use of these to attain life abundant and life everlasting.

The New Covenant. Leaving aside the idea of a permanently fixed rudder—of the literal obedience to the Law and the tradition of the Elders emphasizing the act rather than the spirit—Jesus pointed to the root cause of evil in the very thought, before even the deed is done. He taught how to read the compass from the position of the needle and direct, regulate and control the course of our lives so as to fulfil the will of the Father.

Prayer. If we may carry the comparison further, the first three-sections of "the Lord's Prayer" contemplate the compass—the eternal values that should govern our lives—and the later ones the rudder—the conduct and control of the course of our earthly lives.

Temptation. When the vital connection between the functions of the compass and the rudder is broken, thereby having lost touch with the divine, we fall into temptation and are tossed about on the billows of desire, ignoring all absolute values. Salvation lies in returning back to the never failing guidance of the compass, so falling in line with the chartered course, and abandoning the previous life of selfish gratification of physical desires.

The Task. Our mission in life is to study the charts of the sea of life, learn of its dangers and be warned ahead of the unseen submerged rocks hidden by the tempting placid waters, to guard against being drawn away by the seemingly easy sailing over shallow seas—over sandbanks, etc.—and to guide our lives as well as those of our neighbors so as to ward off these dangers and set sail steadfastly towards the haven of eternal rest. Those who undertake this responsibility can neither slumber nor sleep.

Man-made Rules. Like the Jews of old, the modern churches too have made the mistake of clinging to the policy of fixed rudders. Peter, Paul, and other Apostles steered the early church through Euroclydons, storms and shoals that were peculiar to their seas. The present churches carefully measure the angle the rudders of the Apostles made to the old hulls and have rivetted their own rudders immoveably to their hulls and are attempting to set sail dispensing with the compass as being cumbersome. Hence, this caatastrophic shipwreck of Europe.

May we take this lesson to heart and assign to the rudder its proper place, restoring to it its mobility and adjustability in relation to the control and satisfaction of his desires, subject to the discipline of the Spirit of Truth, calls for the everlasting vigilance which Jesus enjoins. Satan will snatch any unguarded moment and divert our course to destruction.

Suggested Readings from Apostolic Writings on Matters Considered in the Book

- **On Chapter 1**, The Epistles to the Romans and Hebrews.

- **On Chapter 2**

    - *Ceremonials and Rituals:*
      Acts 40:17;15:8,9.
      Romans 4:12;9:7.
      1 Corinthians 1;17.

    - *Worship and Religion:*
      Romans 12:1,2.
      James 1:27.

    - *Raised in the Spirit:*
      Romans 6:4–6.
      Colossians 2:11,12,13.
      1 Peter 3.

    - *Contentment:* 1 Timothy 6:6–10.

- **On Chapter 3**, *Causes of Conflict:* James 4:1–4.

- **On Chapter 4**

    - *Sonship of God:*
      Romans 8:14–17,29,30.
      Galatians 4:6–7.
      1 John 2:28,29;3:1–3,9–11.

    - *Service:*
      1 Corinthians 4:1–5.
      Hebrews 6:7,8.
      James 2:14–26.
      1 John 3:16–18.

- **On Chapter 5**, *Free Will:*
  1 Corinthians 6:12–20;10:23,24.
  2 Corinthians 3:17.
  1 Peter 2:16.

- **On Chapter 6**

  - *Self-Control and Discipline:*
    Romans 6:12–23;7:13–25;8:1–13.
    Galatians 5:16–24;6:8.
    Hebrews 12:7–13.
    James 3:1–12.
    1 Peter 4:1–6.
    1 John 2:15–17.

  - *Trouble:* Romans 5:4,5.

  - *Detachment:* 2 Corinthians 6:8–10.

  - *Kinds of Service:*
    Romans 12:3–21.
    1 Corinthians 12;13.
    1 Peter 4:10–11.

  - *Tactfulness:* Acts 21:22–24.

  - *Gentleness:*
    1 Corinthians 3:1–3;8:8–13;10:25–33.
    Galatians 5:25;6:3.

  - *Sympathy with Other Faiths:*
    Romans 14:1;15:7.
    Ephesians 4:6,7.

  - *Non-Co-operation with offending brethren:* 1 Corinthians 5:9–13.

- **On Chapter 7**, *Rules, etc.:* Colossians 2:20;3:17.

Activist Writings
by Bayard Rustin

Editor's Forward

The more one learns of Bayard Rustin, the harder it is to avoid superlatives. He was instrumental in the American Civil Rights Movement, including bringing Gandhi's method of resistance to the black church leaders at the time. He noticed the talents of a young preacher, Martin Luther King, Jr., and taught King how to practice nonviolence during the Montgomery Bus Boycott. Afterwards, he helped to organize the Southern Christian Leadership Conference. He was the tactician who organized the first of the Freedom Rides to test the Supreme Court's ruling against interstate travel discrimination, and would later be tapped to organize the march on Washington. However, his role was largely downplayed in public because of his homosexuality, and this American hero was tragically anonymous when he died in 1987.[1]

It was rather difficult to select texts from Rustin, since he wrote passionately for his moment in history. He did not tend to write in a detached way for an abstract audience: rather, he wrote from his position to a specific audience. In many ways, his essays read more like blog posts than tracts. Reading anything from Rustin draws you into his moment and certainly draws you into his passion.

The three essays included here are simply samples of his thought, and each is included for a slightly different reason. In *"In Apprehension How Like a God!"*, Rustin lays out both practical and moral arguments against relying on increasing militarization in pursuit of peace, modernizing the arguments made by Tolstoy and Kumarappa for the nuclear age. In *The Meaning of Birmingham*, Rustin lays out the significance of the Birmingham protest, the meaning of the violence suffered by the nonviolent protestors, and the future of the movement in general. Finally, in *Twenty-Two Days on a Chain Gang*, Rustin reveals not only how horrific the conditions were for the arrested civil rights protestors, but he demonstrates how commitment to Christian virtues and to the strength within vulnerability worked to transform even that brutally inhumane environment. All in all, these essays should combine to show how Rustin as a Christian role model in both word and deed.

---

[1] In 2013, President Obama posthumously awarded Rustin the Presidential Medal of Freedom, and presented the award to Rustin's surviving partner.

Twenty-Two Days
on a Chain Gang

Late in the afternoon of Monday, March 21, 1949, I surrendered to the Orange County court at Hillsboro, North Carolina, to begin serving a thirty day sentence imposed two years before for sitting in a bus seat out of the Jim Crow section. As afternoon waned into evening, I waited alone in a small cell of the county jail across the street. I had not eaten since morning, but no supper was forthcoming, and eventually I lay down on the matressless iron bed and tried to sleep. Next morning I learned that only two meals were served daily—breakfast at seven A.M. and lunch at noon.

That morning I spent reading one of the books I had brought with me and wondering where I would be sent to do my time. At about two P.M. I was ordered to prepare to leave for a prison camp. Along with two other men I got into the "dog car"—a small, brown enclosed trunk with a locked screen in teh rear—and began to travel through the rain. An hour later we stopped at the state prison camp at Roxboro, and through the screen I could see the long, low building, circled by barbd wire, where I was to spend the next twenty-two days.

The camp was very unattractive, to put it mildly. There were no trees, grass only near the entrance and to one side. There was not one picture on the walls and no drawer, box, or container supplied for storing the few items one owned. While an effort was made to keep the place clean, there was always mud caked on the floor as soon as the men got in from work, since there was no change of shoes. Roaches were everywhere, though I never saw a bedbug. Once a week the mattresses were aired.

In the receiving room, under close supervision, I went through the routine of the new inmate: receiving a book of rules and a change of clothing, fingerprinting, and—"You'll have to have all your hair cut off."

An inmate barber gleefully shaved my head and, with an expression of mock sadness, surveyed me from various angles. Finally he brought a small mirror and ceremoniously held it up for me. The final touch was his solemn pretense of brushing some hairs from my shirt. Then he told me to go out to the corridor, where an officer would show me to my bed. As I left, the three inmates who were in the room doubled up with laughter. Apparently they had discovered the reason for my schoolboy nickname, "Pinhead"!

Wordlessly the officer outside unlocked the dormitory door and motioned for me to go through.

Inside I found myself in one of two rooms into which a hundred men were crowded. Double-decker beds stood so close together that one had to turn sideway to pass between them. Lights bright enough to read by remained on all night. The rule book states: "No inmate may get out of bed after lights are dimmed without asking permission of the guard," and so all night long men were crying out to a guard many yards away: "Gettin' up, Cap'n,", "Closing the window, Cap'n", "Goin' to the toilet, Cap'n." I did not sleep soundly one night during my whole stay at Roxboro, though I went to bed tireder than I had ever been before.

The camp schedule at Roxboro began with the rising bell at five-thirty. By seven beds had been made, faces washed, breakfast served, and lines formed for leaving the camp for the ten-hour-day's work. We worked from seven until noon, had a half-hour for lunch, resumed work at twelve-thirty, and worked until five-thirty. Then we were counted in and left immediately for supper, without so much as a chance to wash hands and face. From six o'clock we were locked in the dormitory until lights were dimmed at eight-thirty. From then until five-thirty A.M. we were expected to sleep.

On the morning of March 23, my second day at camp, I shaved hurriedly. When I had finished, Easy Life, an inmate who had a nearby bed, apologetically asked if he might borrow my razor. He had a week's growth of hair on his face.

"Most of us ain't got no razors and can't buy none," he said. "But don't they give you a razor if you can't afford one?" I asked.

He looked at me and smiled. "We don't get nothing but the clothes we got on and a towel and soap—no comb, no brush, no toothbrush, no razor, no blades, no stamps, no writing paper, no pencils, nothing." Then he looked up and said thoughtfully, "They say, 'Another day, another dollar,' but all we get for our week's work is one bag of stud."

I suppose my deep concern must have been reflected in my face, for he added, "Don't look so sad. T'ain't nothin! The boys say, 'So round, so firm so fully packed,' when you roll your own."

The guard swung open the doors for breakfast, and as Easy Life rushed to the front of the line he yelled back, "But the damn stuff sure does burn your tongue—that's why I like my tailor-mades," meaning factory-made cigarettes. He winked, laughed heartily, and was gone. I picked up my toothbrush and razor, and slowly walked to my bed to put them away.

A week later I was to remember the conversation. The one towel I had been given was already turning a reddish gray (like the earth of Persons County) despite the fact that I washed it every day. That towel was never changed as long as I stayed at Roxboro. Some of the men washed their towels but once a week, just after they bathed on Saturday.

Each week we were given one suit of underclothing, one pair of pants, a shirt, and a pair of socks. Even though we worked in the mud and rain, this was the only clothing we would get until the next week. By Tuesday, the stench in the dormitory from sweating feet and encrusted underclothing was thick enough to cut. As one fellow said, "Don't do no good to wash and put this sweat-soaked stuff on again."

Two weeks later I saw Easy Life borrowing my toothbrush. "My old lady's coming to visit today and I gotta shine my pearls somehow," he apologized.

I offered him thirty-five cents for the toothbrush. He accepted the money, thanked me, and said, "But if you don't mind I'll buy stamps with it. I can write my old lady ten letters with this. I can borrow Snake's toothbrush if I wanna, but he ain't never got no stamps, and I ain't never got no money."

I started from the camp for my first day's work on the road with anything but an easy mind. Our crw of fifteen men was met at the back gate by the walking boss, who directed the day's work, and by a guard who arried both a revolver and a shotgun. We were herded into the rear of a truck where we were under constant scruinty by the armed guard, who rode behind in a small, glass-enclosed trailer. In that way we rode each day to whatever part of Persons County we were to work in. We would leave the truck when we were ordered to. At all times we had to be within sight of teh guard, but at no time closer than thirty feet to him.

On this first day I got down from teh truck with the rest of the crew. After several moments of complete silence, which seemed to leave everyone uneasy, the walking boss, whom I shall call Captain Jones, looked directly at me.

"Hey, you, tall boy! How much time you got?"

"Thirty days," I said politely.

"Thirty days, Sir."

"Thirty day, Sir," I said.

He took a newsclipping from his pocket and waved it up and down.

"You're the one who thinks he's smart. Ain't got no respect. Tries to be uppity. Well, we'll learn you. You'll learn you got to respect us down here. You ain't in Yankeeland now. We don't like no Yankee ways." He was getting angrier by the moment, his face flushed and his breath short.

"I would as lief step on the head of a damyankee as I would on the head of a rattlesnake," he barked. "Now you git this here thing straight," and he walked closer to me, his face quivering. "You do what you're told. You respect us, or..." He raised his hand threateningly but, instead of striking me, brought the back of his hand down across the mouth of the man on my left. Then he thrust a pick at me and ordered me to get to work.

I had never handled a pick in my life, but I tried. Captain Jones watched me sardonically for a few minutes. Then he grabbed the pick from me, raised it over his head, and sank it deep into the earth several times.

"There, now," he shouted, "Let's see you do it."

I took the pick and for about ten minutes succeeded in breaking the gorund. Then my arms and back began to give out. Just as I was beginning to feel faint, a chain-ganger called Purple walked over and said quietly, "O.K. Let me use dat pick for a while. You take the shovel and, no matter what they say or do, keep workin', keep tryin', and keep yo' mouth shut."

I took teh shovel and began to throw the loose dirt into the truck. My arms pained so badly that I thought each shovelful would be the last. Then gradually my strength seemed to return.

As Purple began to pick again, he whispered to me, "Now you're learnin'. Sometimes you'll give out, but you can't never give up—that's chain-gangin'!" An hour later we moved to another job. As I sat in the truck I racked my mind for some way to convince Captain Jones that I was not "uppity", and at the same time to maintain self-respect. I hit upon two ideas. I would try to work more willingly and harder than anyone in the crew, and I would be as polite and considerate as possible.

When the truck stopped and we were ordered out, I made an effort to carry through my resolution by beginning work immediately. In my haste I came within twenty feet of the guard.

"Stop, you bastard!" he screamed, and pointed his revolver at my head. "Git back, git back. Don't rush me or I'll shoot the goddamned life out of you."

With heart pounding I moved across the road. Purple walked up to me, put a shovel in my hand, and said, "Follow me and do what I do."

We worked together spading heavy clay mud and throwing it into the truck. An hour later, when the walking boss went down the road for a Coca Cola, I complained to Purple about my aching arms. Purple smiled, patted me on the back, and said as he continued to work, "Man born of black woman is born to see black days."

But my first black day was not yet over. Just after lunch we had begun to do what the chain-gangers call "jumpin' shoulders", which means cutting the top from the shoulders of the road when they have grown too high. Usually the crew works with two trucks. There is scarcely a moment of delay and the work is extremely hard. Captain Jones was displeased with the rate of our work, and violently urged us to greater effort. In an attempt to obey, one of the chain-gangers struck another with his shovel. The victim complained, instantly and profanely. The words were hardly out of his mouth before the Captain strode across the road and struck the cursing chain-ganger in the face with his fist again and again. Then Captain Jones informed the crew, using the most violent profanity, that cursing would not be tolerated. "Not for one goddamned moment," he repeated over and over.

No one spoke; every man tried to work harder yet remain inconspicuous. The silence seemed to infuriate the Captain. He glared angrily at the toiling men, then yelled to the armed guard.

"Shoot hell out of the next one you find cursin'. Shoot straight for his feet. Cripple 'em up. That will learn 'em."

The guard lifted his rifle and aimed it at the chest of the main nearest him.

"Hell, no!" he drawled, "I ain't aimin' fer no feet. I like hearts and livers. That's what really learns 'em."

Everyone spaded faster.

On the ride back to camp that evening, I wondered aloud if this were average behavior for Captain Jones.

"Well," said Easy Life, "that depends on how many headache powders and Coca Colas he takes. Must have had a heap today."

Back in camp Easy Life continued the conversation.

"Dat was nothin', really," he said, "Cap'n might have done them up like the Durham police did that old man over there."

He pointed to a small, thin man in his middle fifties, dragging himself slowly toward the washroom. His head was covered with baandages and one eye was discolored and bruised.

"Dad," as the men already were calling him, had come up from the country to Durham a few days before for a holiday. He had got drunk, and when the police tried to arrest him he had resisted, and they had beaten him with blackjacks. After three days in jail he was sentenced to Roxboro. When he got to the prison camp he complained that he was ill, but nonetheless was ordered to go out on the job. After working an hour, Dad told the walking boss that he was too sick to continue and asked if he could be brought in. He was brought in and the doctor was summoned, but he had no temperature and the doctor pronounced him able to work. When he refused to go back to his pick and shovel he was ordered "hung on the bars" for seventy-two hours.

When a man is hung on the bars he is stood facing his cell, with his arms chained to the vertical bars, until he is released (except for being unchained periodically to go to the toilet). After a few hours, his feet and often the glands in his groin begin to swell. If he attempts to sleep, his head falls back with a snap, or falls forward into the bars, cutting and bruising his face. (Easy Life told me how Purple had been chained up once and gone mad, so that he began to bang his head vigorously against the bars. Finally the night guard, fearing he would kill himself, unchained him.)

The old man didn't bang his head. He simply got weaker and weaker, and his feet swelled larger and larger, until the guard became alarmed, cut the old man down, and carried him back to bed.

The next day the old man was ordered out to work again, but after he had worked a few minutes he collapsed and was brought back. This time the doctor permitted him to be excused from work for a week. At the end of the week, when Dad came back to work, he was still very weak and tired but was expected to keep up the same rate of work as the other members of the crew.

A few days later, I told several of the boys that I had decided to talk to the Captain to try to improve relations on the job, since I was sure the guards were taking it out on the men because of me. They urged me to keep still. "Quiet does it," they said. "No need to make things worse," they admonished. "He'll kick you square in the ass," Purple warned.

Nevertheless I stopped the Captain that morning and asked to speak with him. He seemed startled. I told him that I knew there were great differences in our attitudes on many questions but that I felt we could be friends. I said that on the first morning, when I had failed to address him as "Sir", I had meant no disrespect to him and if he felt that I had been disrespectful I was willing to apologize. I suggested that perhaps I was really the one who deserved to be beaten in the face, if anyone did. I was willing to work as hard as I could, and if I failed again at my work I hoped he would speak to me about it and I would try to improve. Finally i said I could not help trying to act on the basis of my own Christian ideals about people but that I did try to respect and understand those who differed with me.

He stared at me without a word. Then after several moments he turned to the gun guard and said in an embarrassed tone, "Well, I'll be goddamned." Then he shouted, "O.K., if you can work, get to it! Talk ain't gonna git that there dirt on the truck. Fill her up." (Later I learned that the Captain had said to one of the chain-gangers that he would rather I call him a "dirty-son-of-a-bitch" than to look him in the face "and say nothin'.")

That evening he called us together.

"This Yankee boy ain't so bad," he said. "They just ruined him up there 'cause they don't know how to train you-all. But I think he'll be all right and if you-all will help him I think we can learn him. He's got a strong back and seems to be willing."

The chain-gangers glanced at one another. As we piled into the truck one of them turned to me and said, "When he says he'll learn you, this is what he means:

"When you're white you're right,
When you're yellow you're mellow,
When you're brown you're down,
When you're black, my God, stay back!"

The chain-gangers laughed. We pulle dthe canvas over our heads to protect us from the rain that had begun to pour down, and headed back to camp to eat supper.

The book of regulations said: "No talking will be permitted in the dining hall during meals." Not until I experienced it did I realize what a meal is like when a hundred men are eating in one room without a word spoken. The guards stood with clubs under their arms and watched us. I had the feeling they too were unhappy in the uneasy silence.

At one eavening meal, I was trying by signs to make the man next to me understand that I wanted the salt. I pointed toward the salt and he passed me the water, which was close by. I pointed again, and he passed the syrup. When I pointed again, he picked up the salt and banged it down angrily against my plate. Forgetting the rule, I said quietly, "I'm sorry." One of the guards rushed across the room to our table and, with his stick raised, glared at me and said, "If I catch you talking, I'll bust your head in." The spoons and forks were no longer heard against the aluminum plates. The dining room was perfectly quiet. The guard swung his club through space a couple of times, then retired to a corner to resume his frustrating vigil. The tin spoons and forks rattled again on the aluminum plates.

The morning after my conversation with Captain Jones we were instructed to go to the cement mixer, where we were to make cement pipe used in draining the roads and building bridges. We had been working twenty minutes when the Captain came to me carrying a new cap. He played with the cap on the end of his finger for a while and stared at my shaved head.

"You're gonna catch your death of cold," he said, "so I brought you a cap. You tip it like all the other boys whenever you speak to the Captain and the guards, or whenever they speak to you."

I had noticed the way the men bowed obsequiously and lifted their hats off their heads and held them in the air whenever they spoke to the guard. I had decided I would rather be cold than behave in this servile way. I thanked the Captain, put the cap on my head, and wore it until lunchtime. After lunch I put it in my pocket, never to wear it again in the presence of the Captain or the guards.

Some of the men left their caps in the camp rather than wear them on the job, and for good reason. There was a rule that when leaving for work in the morning a man was not permitted to wear his hat until he was beyond the barbed-wire fence that surrounded the camp. On several occasions, men going to or coming from work would rush thoughtlessly through the gates with their caps on, and be struck severely on the head with a club. As Softshoe, a chain-ganger distinguished for his corns and bunions, said, "No use courting trouble. If you don't wear no hat, you ain't got to doff it."

One day the chain-gangers were on fire with the news that an old prisoner had returned. Bill was slender, tall, good-looking, and sang very well. Some three years before he had raped his own three-year-old daughter and been put in jail for a year. This time he was "up" for having raped his eight-year-old niece.

It was difficult to believe all the tales the men told about Bill. One evening he came to me and asked me if I had time to talk with him. We talked for almost two hours. He was quite different from the description I had heard. He had provided well for his family, he had gone to church, but, as he pathetically admitted, he had "made some terrible mistakes". It was apparent that he wanted to wipe the slate clean, but in Roxboro jail he could never discover the reason for his unhappiness and troubles.

As I lay awake that night I wondered how ten hours a day of arduous physical labor could help this young man become a constructive citizen. The tragedy of his being in the prison camp was highlighted by the extraordinary success that good psychiatrists and doctors are having today with men far more mixed up than Bill. I thought of the honesty with which he had discussed himself, of the light in his eyes when he had heard for the first time of the miracles modern doctors perform—and I knew that Bill deserved the best that society could offer him: a real chance to be cured, to return to his wife and children with the "devils cast out".

Then there was a young boy who had been arrested for stealing. It was obvious from his behavior that he was a kleptomaniac. I would see him spend half an hour going form one section of the dormitory to another, waiting, plotting, planning, and conniving to steal many small and useless items. Although he did not smoke, I saw him spend twenty minutes getting into a position to steal a box of matches, which he later threw away.

One day, after I had written a long letter for him, he began to tell me that he had stolen even as a child but that now he wanted to stop. As tears came to his eyes, he explained that he had been able to stop stealing valuable things but that he could not stop stealing entirely. I asked him if he really wanted to change. He said he thought so. But he added: "It's such a thrill. Just before I get my hands on what I'm gonna take, I feel so excited."

After that, as I watched him evening after evening, I wondered how many men throughout the world were languishing in jails—burdens to society—who might be cured if only they were in hospitals where they belonged. One thing was clear. Neither this boy, who reluctantly stole by compulsion, nor Bill could be helped by life on the chain gang. Nor could society be protected, for in a short time these men and thousands like them return to society not only uncured but with heightened resentment and a desire for revenge.

Early one morning Easy Life was talking with one of his friends, who had done time for stealing and was to be released that day. To the despair of those trying to get a few last winks, Easy Life was singing:

"Boys, git up, grab your pone,
Some to the right-a-ways, some to the road—
This fool's made it and he's headin' home."

Easy Life's companion smiled and said for all to hear:

"Boys, you stole while I took, Now you roll [work hard] while I look."

"I can work," Easy Life said, "and I can work plenty, for work don't bother me none. No sir! Boys, it's the food that gits me down." And he went to rhyming one of his spontaneous verses:

"Kick me, shout me, pull ma teet',
But lemme go home where I can eat."

As I lay in bed for a last few minutes' rest, I began to think about the food. We had beans—boiled beans, red beans, or lima beans—every day for lunch. Every day, after five long hours of hard physical labor, we had beans, fatback (a kind of bacon without lean meat), molasses, and corn pone. Many of the men who had spent years on the road were no longer able to eat the beans at all, and I saw several men, working for ten hours day after day, with nothing to eat after breakfast for the entire day but molasses and corn pone. One of the most frequently quoted bits of folk poetry described the lunch:

Beans and cornbread
Every single day.
If they don't change
I'll make my getaway.
How long, Oh Lord,
How long?

For breakfast we usually had oatmeal without sugar or milk, a slice of fried baloney, stewed apples, and coffee. In the evening the two typical meals were cabbage and boiled white potatoes, and macaroni and stewed tomatoes. On Sundays the meal consisted of two vegetables, Argentinean corned beef, and apple cobbler. Except for being struck with clubs, the thing that the men complained most about was the food. They often recited another bit of folk poetry:

The work is hard,
The boss is mean,
The food ain't done,
And the cook ain't clean.

Actually both the cooks and the dining room were relatively clean; the protest was against the monotony of the food.

The hour was getting near for Easy Life's companion to depart. They brought in the pillowcase in which his clothes had been stored three months earlier. As he dumped his clothes onto the bed, they made one shapeless lump. He opened out his pants and began to get into them. They had a thousand creases. Then he put on the dirty shirt he had worn when he came in, and dressed in this way he left to begin a new life. He had no comb or toothbrush or razor, nor a penny in his pocket. The "dog cart" would come to pick him up and drop him somewhere near the railroad station in Durham.

I looked at him, his face aglow, happy that he would once again be "free", and wondered how he could be so happy without a cent, with no job, and with no prospects. I wondered what he would go through to get his first meal, since he had no home. I wondered where he would sleep. He said he knew a prostitute who might put him up. Prostitutes and fairies, he said, "will always give a guy a break". I wondered where he would find a decent shirt or a pair of paints. Would he beg or borrow or steal?

I wondered if he would return. One day on the job the Captain had offered to bet ten to one that the man would be back before the week was up. As I saw him start forth, so ill prepared to face life in the city, I too felt that he would return. I asked Easy Life what he thought his friend would do when he got to town. Easy Life said, "He'll steal for sure if they don't get him first." I asked what he meant. He said, "If the bulls don't get him for vagrancy 'fore sundown, he'll probably snatch something for to eat and some clothes to cover his ass with for the night."

"For vagrancy?" I asked.

"For vagrancy! Sure enough for vagrancy, " Easy underlined. He then told me the story of a friend from South Carolina who had been on the chain gang. He, like all the others, was released without a penny in his pocket. While thumbing his way home, he was arrested for vagrancy soon after he crossed into South Carolina, and was back in jail for ninety days, less than two days after being released.

Between supper and "lights out" was our time for recreation. But for most men it was not a creative period. The rules permitted "harmless games", but there was not one set of checkers or chess or dominoes available, no material for the development of hobbies, and no books, only an occassional comic book. One newspaper came into the place, and few men had access to it. There were no organized sports, no library, no entertainment other than one motion picture a month.

Under these circumstances, recreation was limited to six forms, five of them definitely destructive. The first of these was "dirty dozens", a game played by one or two persons before an audience. Its object was to outdo one's opponent in grossly offensive descriptions of the opponent's female relatives—mother, sister, wife, or aunt. If a "player" succeeded in making a clever combination of obscene and profane words, the audience burst into laughter, and then quieted down to await the retaliation of the opponent. He in turned tried to paint a still more degrading picture of the relatives of his partner. No recreation attracted larger crowds or created more antagonism, for often men would be sucked into the game who actually did not wnat to play and became angered in the course of it.

Another form of recreation was the *telling of exaggerated stories about one's sex life.* These included tales of sexual relations with members of the same sex, with animals, with children and close relatives, and with each other. It was generally recognized that 70 percent of these tales were untrue, but the practice led to lying, to experimentation in abnormal sex relations, and to a general lowering of the moral standards of younger inmates, who continually were forced intot he positions of advocating strange practices as a means of maintaining status with the group.

Stealing "for the thrill of it" was yet another way in which numbers of men entertained themselves. One of the best friends I had in the camp had stolen stamps from me, returned them, and then described to me how he had done it. He had sent a friend to talk with me and had given the man who slept in the bed next to mine an old comic book to reduce the possibility of being detected. I asked him why he went to all that trouble, only to return my stamps. He explained that he had stamps, but, having nothing else to do, he wanted to "keep my hands warm."

Gambling was perhaps the chief form of recreation for those who had anything to gamble with. Men gambled for an extra sock stolen on the day of clothing exchange, or a sandwich smuggled from the kitchen, or a box of matches. The three games most widely used for gambling were Tonk and Skin, games played with an ordinary deck of cards, and throwing dice. Cheating was simple and common and led to constant arguments.

There was little or no effort to control the gambling, though it was against the rules. When a new night guard came on duty and complained to an old hand that the boys were playing dice in the rear of the dormitory, the older guard was overheard to say, "What da hell do I care! They gotta do sumpin, and dice keep 'em quiet."

Gossip and talking about one's sentence also consumed a great deal of time. Over and over again men related the story of their trial and told one another how they were "framed on bum raps." The gossip session was a stool pigeon's chief means of getting information to carry "up front." Even though men feared talking about one another, they did so because they felt that the gossip-mongers had to have something to tell the superintendent. As one of the chain-gangers expressed it, "That stool pigeon has got to sing sumpin, so it's better for me to give him sumpin good [i.e. helpful information for the authorities] to carry about somebody else, before somebody gives him sumpin bad to carry about me." This created an atmosphere of universal mistrust.

The most creative form of recreation was *rhyming and singing*. There were several quartets and trios and much informal singing, both on the job and in the dormitory. The poetry was almost always a description of life in the camp or of the desire for women or of the "fear of time". Occassionally it was the bragging of a tough guy:

> I was born in a barrel of butcher knives,
> Sprayed all over with a forty-five.
> Bull constrictor bit me.
> He crawled off and died.
> I hoboed with lightnin'
> And rode the black thunder,
> Rode through the graveyards
> And caused the dead folks to wonder.
> Sixty-two inches across my chest,
> Don't fear nothin' but the devil and death.
> I'll kick a bear in the rear
> And dare a lion to roar.

Much of the poetry was directed against those who complained. The following is an excellent example:

> Quit cryin'!
> Quit dyin'!
> Give dat white man
> Sumpin on your time.
>
> I would-a told you,
> But I thought you knowed,
> Ain't no heaven
> On the county road.
>
> Six months ain't no sentence,
> Twelve months ain't no time,
> Done been to penitentiary
> Doing ninety-nine.
>
> Quit cryin'!
> Quit dyin'!
> Give dat white man
> Sumpin on your time.

The following verses are some of the more imaginative statements about the relationship between the chain-gangers and the walking bosses and guards.

> Cap'n got a pistol and he thinks he's bad;
> I'll take it tomorrow if he makes me mad.

What I want for dinner they don't serve here.
Thirty-two thirty and some cold, cold beer.

Cap'n says hurry. Walker say run.
Got bad feet—can't do more 'n one.

One of the most stifling elements of life on the road gang is the authoritarianism. The prisoner's life is completely regulated. He is informed that obedience will be rewarded and disobedience punished. Section 1 of the rules and regulations makes this clear.

> Every prisoner upon arrival at any prison after being sentenced by the court shall be informed of the rules and regulations of the camp and advised what the consequences will be if he violates these rules. He shall also be informed as to what privileges he will receive if he obeys the rules and conducts himself properly.

Such unquestioning obedience may appear to be good and logical in theory, but in experience authoritarianism destroys the inner resourcefulness, creativity, and responsibility of the prisoner and creates, in wardens and prisoners alike, an attitude that life is cheap. The following illustrations indicate the degree to which respect for personality is violated.

—One day when we were digging ditches for draining Highway 501, we were working in water about a foot deep. A chain-ganger who had very large feet could not be fitted to boots. After attempting to do as much as he could from the dry banks of the ditch, he finally tried to explain to the Captain that he could not work in water over his shoe tops. "Get the hell in that water—I don't give a good goddamn if it is up to your ass," the Captain yelled at him. "You should have thought about that before you came here. The judge said ninety days, and he didn't say nuthin' about your havin' good ones."

—The walking boss was heard commenting on one of his ace workers who had come back for the third time. "Now ain't that a shame—and he only got a year. I sure wish he had ten or more."

—Every day after lunch the walking bosses and armed guards would send the food remaining in their lunch kits to the chain-gangers. After the kits had been emptied, I noticed that the water boy always filled them with the corn pone from the prisoners' meal. One day I asked the water boy why he did this. He explained that the Captain fed that "stinkin' pone to hispigs." For a moment no one spoke. Then Softshoe said, "Pigs and convicts."

—Visiting days were the first and third Sundays of the month; visiting hours, from one to four. The visiting took place in the prison yard. There were two wire fences about five feet apart. The voncits stood in front of one, the visitors behind another. There in the yard, in summer, winter, rain, snow, sleet, they talked—if they could be heard. Visiting day was an event both longed for and dreaded because, as one of the chain-gangers so aptly put it, "We gotta meet the home folks like animals in the zoo."

— The supreme authority in a state prison camp is the superintendent. The superintendent at Roxboro was a silent man who appeared chiefly at mealtimes. His major contacts with the men came when he observed them as they ate and when he directed them to their work in the morning. One of the few times I heard him speak to the men was when a newly arrived inmate violated one of the many petty rules of the dining hall and came down the wrong aisle. The superintendent raised his club and said, "Get around there before I knock the shit out of you."

We must bear in mind that one result of the authoritarian system is to develop in the prisoners many of the same attitudes they themselves decry in the officials. The majority of the prisoners accept the idea that punishment can be just. In fact they share this basic premise with most of the judges whom they eternally criticize. Many prisoners would be more severe than judges in making the punishment fit the crime. In discussing a young man who had raped two children I heard Easy Life say, "The no-good bastard should have got ninety-nine years and one dark day." When a young man came into the camp who reportedly had stolen eight hundred dollars, his mother's life savings, a prisoner suggested, "They should have built a jail on top of him." To which another replied, "That's too damn good for the bastard. They should have gassed him, but quick."

The prisoners, like the judges, hold the superstition that two wrongs can make a right. A chain-ganger claims that his incarceration clears him; hence the deprivations of prison life are equal to his crime. He feels he is doubly absolved when he gets the worst of the bargain. But any punishment that affects his body or causes him to fear while in prison, he looks upon as unjustified. Consequently he feels, often while in prison and certainly upon release, that he is entitled to avenge this injustice by becoming an enemy of society. Thus the theory that two wrongs make a right becomes a vicious circle, destructive to wardens, prisoners, and society.

Let us see what the punishments are on the chain-gang. Section 5 of the rules book states:

> *For Minor Offenses*—[The superintendent will be permitted to] hand-cuff [the prisoner] and require [him] to remain in standing or sitting position for a reasonable period of time.

This form of punishment produces swollen feet and wrists, muscular cramps, and physical fatigue. During the period, if the perisoner is standing up, he does not eat but is taken down for fifteen or twenty minutes every few hours to urinate, defecate, and relax.

> *For Major Offenses*—Corporal punishment, with the approval of the Chairman of the State Highway and Public Works Commission, administered with a leather strap *of the approved type* and by some prison officer other than the person in immediate charge of said prisoner and

only after physical examination by a competent physician, and such punishment must be administered either in the presence of a prison physician or a prison chaplain.

Another section of the rules book dealing with punishment and discipline states that the superintendent may place a prisoner on "restricted diet and solitary confinement, the period of punishment to be approved by the disciplinarian."

One chain-ganger whom I got to know very well had recently finished a period of such confinement in "the hole." For fourteen days James had been without any food except three soda crackers a day. "The bastards gave me all the water I could drink, and I'll be damned if I wasn't fool enough to drink a lot of it. Soon I began to get thinner, but my gut got bigger and bigger till I got scared and drank less and less till I ended by drinking only three glasses a day."

Although he was very weak, he was forced to go to work immediately. He was expected to work as hard as the others and be respectful to the same captain he felt was responsible for his hardship.

James had been sentence to sixty days for larceny, which good behavior would have reduced to forty-four days. Because of one surly remark he not only had to spend fourteen days in that unlighted hole, on crackers and water, but also lost the sixteen days of good time. Actually James had begun to hate himself as much as he hated the Captain. "A man," he said, "who tips his hat to a son-of-a-bitch he hates the way I hate him ain't no man at all. If I'd-a been a man, I'd-a split his head wide open the minute I got half a chance."

Some punishements were administered that were not listed in the rules book, as when officers kicked, punched, or clubbed the inmates.

One day when we were working at the cement mixer I heard the Captain yelling to an elderly man that he had better increase his rate and do more work. The old man attempted to work faster. "Cap'n says I'm lazy, but I'm plumb wore out," he complained. Then I ntoiced the Captain rushing toward him. "You goddamn lazy bastard," the Captain shouted. "I told you to get to work. When I work a man, I expect a man's work." As the old fellow turned to the Captain and began to explain that he was tired, the Captain kicked him heavily and said, "Don't talk, work." When the Captain had gone away, the old man said over and over, in mixed fear and resignation, "The Captain says I'm lazy, but I'm plumb wore out."

One chain-ganger, a man named Joe, aged about fifty-two, was at the camp for thirty days—his fifth or sixth time to receive that same sentence for drunkenness. He said he was tired all the time, that he had pains in his back. Some of the chain-gangers said he was "damn lazy." For two days the Captain urged him to work harder. "Get some earth on that spade. I'm getting tired of you, Joe. You'd better give me some work." All the second day the Captain kept his eye on Joe. In mid-afternoon he walked over to Joe and said, "You're not going to do no work till I knock hell out you." He calmly struck Joe several times vigorously in the face. "Now maybe that will learn you," the Captain said he walked away. Joe took off his cap, bowed obsequiously, and said, "Yessa, yessa, that sure will learn me." When the Captain had walked away Joe spat on the ground and said, "He's a dirty son-of-a-bitch and I hope he rots in hell."

The first thing a man did when he awoke in the morning was to look out the window. "How's the weather?" was always the first question. A heavy rain meant a day without work, and the fellows prayed for "sweet rain." It was not just because the work was hard but also for four other reasons, all having to do with working conditions:

1. The work was never done.

2. Thought and creativity in any form were not permitted.

3. Staying "under the gun" made for crowded, tense conditions.

4. The men felt like "things" rather than people on the job.

I believe they most disliked the feeling that no matter how hared they toiled, "the work on the highway wain't never done." When one job was finished there was always another. "Let's ride," the Captain would say, and off we would go. One fellow complained, "If we only knew we had so much to do in a day, then I wouldn't mind the aches so much 'cause I could look to some rest at the end."

I had never before realized the importance, even to men doing the most monotonous manual labor, of knowing clearly the reasons for doing a job, and the dejection of spirit that subconsciously creeps in when men cannot see a job completed. One day when we dug out patches in the road which another crew would fill in, Purple expressed this feeling: "I reckon these holes will be filled in by some fool 'rrested in Durham tonight, and he'll wonder where the hell they came from."

On the job the men were not permitted to use the kind of imagination that they put into their rhymes. Over and over again the walking boss would say, "Don't try to hink. Do what I tell ya to do." Once when a resourceful chain-ganger offered a suggestion that might have improved or simplified the task, the walking boss said, "I'm paid to think; you're here to work." Softshoe used to say:

"When you're wrong, you're wrong,
But when you're right, you're wrong anyhow."

On two or three occasions when the Captain was away, the assistant walking boss was in charge of the crew. He was quite inexperienced as compared with one of the chain-gangers, James, who knew almost as much about the job as the Captain. One day in the Captain's absence James suggested to the assistant that a ditch should be cut a certain way. The assistant captain ordered otherwise. So fifteen men spent three and a half hours in water and mud digging a ditch forty feet long, four feet wide, and in places five feet deep. The next day the Captain told us that the work would have to be redone. The men looked knowingly at one another and started digging.

There was a regulation that each prisoner, except the trusties, must at all times be within eyeshot and gun range of the armed guard. The prisoners called this "under the gun." Another egulation was that no time could a chain-ganger be seen to rest during his ten-hour day except during the two fifteen-minute smoking periods. These regulations made for continuous tension.

When digging or clearing ditches, our crew of fourteen to sixteen men was usually divided, half of them assigned to each side of the road. Since the amount of work on each side was seldom equal, the logical thing would have been for the crew that finished first to move on down the road. They could not do so because then they would not have been "under the gun." Or the crew that finished first could have rested for a few minutes and then moved on with the group. But the rgulation that "all must be busy at all times" precluded such a step. The solution accepted was to put all fourteen men on one side, where we were jammed in so tightly on one another that work was dangerous, slow, and inefficient. We got on one another's nerves and often struck each other with tools.

Certain men in the crew, to avoid hardship and to give the impression they were working harder than the others, indulged in hiding other men's tools, pushing, or criticizing one another's work in loud voices in order to place themselves in more favored working positions or to get in a good light with the Captain for informing. Whenever we worked on ditches, tensions in the evenings in the dormitory often ran high.

To me the most degrading condition of the job was the feeling that "I am not a person; I am a thing to be used." The men who worked us had the same attitude toward us as toward the tools we used. At times the walking bosses would stand around for hours while we worked, seeming to do nothing—just watching, often moving from foot to foot or walking from one side of the road to the other. It was under these conditions that they would select a "plaything." One boy, Oscar, was often "it." Once the bored gun guard ordered Oscar to take off his cap and ance. With a broad smile on his face, he warned Oscar, "I'll shoot your heart out if you don't." As the guard trained his rifle on Oscar's chest, Oscar took off his cap, grinned, and danced vigorously. The guard and the walking boss screamed with laughter. Later most of the crew told Oscar that they hated him for pretending he had enjoyed the experience. Bust almost any of them would have reacted the same way.

To return to the story of my relations with Captain Jones. He had learned of my case and knew I was from the North. Several chain-gangers agreed that the newsclipping he waved about on the day he first lectured me was the Durham *Sun's* article on my surrender. At any rate I am sure he felt that I was going to shirk and be difficult—that I would try to show off and challenge his authority.

My aims were really far different. I wanted to work hard so I would not be a burden to other chain-gangers. I wanted to accept the imprisonment in a quiet, unobtrusive manner. Only in this way, I believed, could the officials and guards be led to consider sympathetically the principle on which I was convicted. I did not epxec them to agree with me, but I did want them to believe I cared enough about the ideals I was supposed to stand for so I could accept my punishment with a sense of humor, fairness, and constructive goodwill.

It would ahve been easy to be either servile or recalcitrant. The difficulty was to be constructive, to remove tension, and yet to maintain my balance and self-respect, at the same time giving ample evidence of respect for the Captain's personality.

I found him to be a very fine craftsman, who knew well the skills of his trade. I noted, too, that when it began to rain hard he was much more careful to leave immediately for the dormitory than were most of the other captains. Soon after our first unfortunate encounter, I mentioned these facts to him.

One morning when he came toward me with what I considered a hostile expression on his face (I was unskillfully making cement pipe), I decided to take the initiative. Before he could teach me I called over to him, "Captain Jones, I need some help. Would you have the time to show...?" I could not finish my sentence.

"Damn well you need help," he said, but already I could notice a difference in his expression. He showed me how to scrape the steel forms and how to oil them. Thanking him politely, I told him that if he saw me doing poorly I hoped he would speak to me because I wanted to use the rest of my sentence to pick up as much knowledge as possible. He said, "Well, I can learn you," and walked away.

An hour later he returned, looked over my work, found it satisfactory, and said, "Well, Rusty, you're learnin'." That was the first time he had not called me "tall boy" or "hey-you-there".

For three days our relations improved, but on the fourth day when I reported for work he seemed very agitated. It turned out that an informer among the prisoners had told him I was urging the men not to wear caps so as not to have to tip them. Actually I did look upon the tipping of caps as degrading, for most of the men did it as a gesture of respect while inwardly they not only cursed the captains but also lost self-respect. When asked, I had told the men about my attitude but also had made it clear that my first concern was what the tipping did to them inside.

That same day I had another talk with the Captain. He seemed very impatient, but he did listen as I explained my position on wearing caps. Although he said nothing more to me, I later heard that he informed several men who had recently begun to go bareheaded that they should wear the caps year round or not at all. One of the perisoners said, "There is goin' to be some coldheaded spooks 'round here next January!" After that there was no further discussion of the caps and no effort to get men to wear them.

THe next morning the Captain offered us cigarettes during smoking period. Since I did not smoke, I felt I should not take any and attempted to return them. "Rusty," he said, "they're for you whether you smoke or not." I accepted the cigarettes and gave them to another chain-ganger. This seemed to me a logical way to behave, but the Captain attached real significance to my having offered to return the cigarettes. That afternoon he told one of the men that I was filled with a lot of bad ideas but at least I was polite. Later he said to the armed guard, in teh presence of Easy Life, that it was probably not my fault that I was "mixed up about so many things." He concluded, "Everything those damyankees touch the bastards spoil."

The Captain and I continued to disagree on many points, but as time went on, I felt, we came to recognize that despite our different attitudes we could work together and learn from each other.

One day toward the end of my stenence, the Captain stopped me.

"Well, how are you getting along, Rusty?" he said.

"Quite all right, Captain," I answered, "but I feel that some of the fellows need things. I hope to send in some toothbrushed, combs, and razors when I get home."

"Well, you got a surprised, didn't ya?" he asked.

"A surprise?" I said.

"Yes, indeed. you thought we was going to mistreat ya—but bad, didn't ya?"

"I didn't know what to expect," I said, "but I have learned a good deal here."

"Well, we can all learn something," he said, and walked away. That afternoon he treated the crew to a bottle of Royal Crown Cola.

Before I left, I decided to write the Captain a letter. The prisoners were astounded. "You can't write the Captain." "What do you think you're doin'?" "They ain't goin' to do nothin' but throw it in the shit pot."

I explained to the men that I was sure they could write anyone connected with the camp or the Prison Bureau. But even the more enlightened were skeptical. "I bet the Captain don't never get it," Purple said.

At any rate, I sat down and wrote the following letter to Captain Jones.

Camp #508
Roxoboro, North Carolina
Sunday, April 10, 1949

Dear Captain Jones:

If all goes well, I understand that I may be released this coming Wednesday morning. But before I go I want to say that I am pleased to have been placed in your work crew.

Never having done similar work before, I am afraid I was not very apt, so all the more I want to thank you for all the help you gave me on the job. I feel that I learned a great deal.

I want to thank you and Captain Duncan for teh treats to cigarettes and soft drinks. As you probably know better than I do, life has not always been easy for most of the men who come to this camp. And such kindness mean more to us than words can express.

I trust that your cold will have cleared up soon.

Sincerely, Bayard Rustin

The Captain's reaction to the letter was very interesting. He was seen passing it around to the other captains and to several guards. He never mentioned it to me, but he did seem to have an honest, friendly feeling toward me during my last days at the camp.

Now most of the inmates were pleased that I had written the letter. On my last night in camp one of the chain-gangers asked me if I would help him compose a letter to an official.

"Your letter sure done some good," he said. "Guess it won't hurt me none to try."

This one successful attempt to modify the authoritarian setup should not, however, carry undue weight. There was much working in my favor. Many persons wrote and visited me; people outside sent packages to the community kit; I had a short sentence; and I got on well with the other chain-gangers. All this made it easier for me to approach the Captain and to do so with some degree of confidence. On the other hand, this experience does indicate that even in trying circumstances (for both the Captain and me) it was possible to reach a working solution without losing one's self-respect or submitting compeltely to outside authority.

There are three methods of dealing with offenders against society once they are apprehended: retribution, deterrence, and rehabilitation. Prison officials and men generally lay claim more or less advocating all three. At present the public thinks that offenders should be punished. There are many different reasons why this is so, among them the belief that the average criminal responds to nothing but fear and penalties. Yet there is some real evidence that only through the very opposite of fear and punishment—intelligent good will—can men be reached and challenged and changes brought about.

Three experiences during my stay at Roxboro exemplify Auden's statement, "What can be loved can be cured," and suggest that we can expect true rehabilitation only when we have rejected punishment, which is revenge, and have begun to utilize the terrific healing and therapeutic power of forgiveness and nonviolence.

On my final Saturday of my stay, the Captain was away and his assistant directed the work. While the assistant was not so skillful as the Captain, he was more gentle, more considerate, and willing on occasion to consult the crew on procedure. Before we began work he explained clearly what was to be done. For five hours that morning, in the presence of a direcotr who was not tense, who did not curse, and who permitted the men to help plan the work, many constructive things occurred. The men were cooperative, they worked cheerfully, tension was reduced, and the time passed more quickly than usual. When we returned to the dormintory, Purple, who had a way with turning phrases, referred to the morning's work as a "halfday of heaven".

Stealing was the chief problem in the dormitory. The night I arrived, my fountain pen, stamps, razor, and twenty blades were stolen. The net morning my writing paper disappeared. All these things had been locked away in a box, so I decided to follow the policy of not locking up my belongings. I announced that in the future, all my stamps, money, food, writing paper, etc., were for the use of the community, but that in order to divide things according to need, I hoped that before anyone took anything he would consult me. As small boxes of food and other things were sent to me, they were added to the community kit. Gradually, the following things occurred:

1. After a week, except for four candy bars, there was no stealing from the community kit.

2. Other men made contributions to the community kit.

3. Inmates began to unlock their unsafe strongboxes and bring things to the open community kit for safekeeping. As one of the fellows said, "If anyone is caught snatching from that box, the boys won't think much of him."

4. Two packages of cigarettes were stolen from a chain-ganger. Then it was announced that unless they turned up, money would be taken from the community kit to pay for them. The ciagarettes were found on the floor the next morning.

Finally there is the example of our party. Near the end of my second week in camp several boxes of candy, cookies, cakes, dates, peanuts, and fruit juice were sent in to be added to the community kit. It was susggested that we have a party, but practically all the inmates were against it. They said, "The fellows will behave like pigs." It would be impossible to keep order, they added, and a few husky people would get all the food.

The decision was that I should select the committee to put on the party. I purposely chose the three men known to be the biggest thieves in the camp, and they accepted. The others were disheartened. "Now we know the party is wrecked. Those guys will eat half the stuff themselves before it even starts!" they groaned.

Nevertheless the boxes were turned over to them to be kept for two days until the party. Except for the disappearance of the four candy bars already mentioned, all the food was kept intact, and six candy bars were donated to replace the four stolen ones. The party itelf was well organized and orderly, and the left-over food was returned to the community kit. perhaps more significant was the fact that one man, noted for stealing, became known as one of the most capable men in the camp. He was so thorough that he appointed a sergeant-at-arms for the party, whose business was to patrol the floor to watch for stealing or disorder. Fortunately the sergeant-at-arms had no business at all and gave up his job before the party was half over.

I certainly do not want to imply that we had in any real sense dealt with the problem of stealing in the camp. However, the stimuli of expectancy, trust, and responsibility had, for the moment at least, brought about positive responses— faithfulness to duty, imagination, and sharing. Would more such gentle stimuli over longer periods of time, accompanied by proper diet, medical care, music education, good quarters, and respectful treatment, be more effective finally than retribution and punishment? If the law of cause and effect still operates in human relations, the answer seems clear.

The Meaning of Birmingham

Since the signing of the Emancipation Proclamation in 1863, the struggle for justice by Afro-Americans has been carried out by many dedicated individuals and militant organizations. Their ultimate aim, sometimes stated, often not, has always been total freedom. Many forms of strategy and tactics have been used. Many partial victories have been won. Yet the gradual and token "progress" that many white liberals pointed to with pride served only to anger the black man and further frustrate him. That frustration has now given way to an open and publicly declared war on segregation and racial discrimination throughout the nation. The aim is simple. It is directed at all white Americans—the President of the United States, his brother, Robert, the trade-union movement, the power elite, and every living white soul the Negro meets. The war cry is "unconditional surrender—end all Jim Crow now". Not next week, not tomorrow—but now.

This is not to say that many have not felt this way for decades. The slave revolts, the occasional resorts to violence in recent times, the costly fifty-year struggle that the National Association for the Advancement of Colored People has carried on in the courts, the thousands arrested throughout the South since the Montgomery bus boycott—all reveal an historic impatience and a thirst for freedom. What is new springs from the white resistance in Birmingham, with its fire hoses, its dogs, its blatant disregard for black men as people, and from the Afro-American's response to such treatment in "the year of our Lord" 1963.

For the black people of this nation, Birmingham became the moment of truth. The struggle from now on will be fought in a different context. Therefore, to understand the mood, tactics and totality of the black people's relentless war on Jim Crow, we must grasp fully what is taking place in this Southern industrial city.

For the first time, every black man, woman and child, regardless of station, has been brought into the struggle. Unlike the period of the Montgomery boycott, when the Southern Christian Leadership Conference had to be organized to stimulate similar action elsewhere, the response to Birmingham has been immediate and spontaneous. City after city has come into the fight, from Jackson, Mississippi, to Chesterton, Maryland. The militancy has spread to Philadelphia, where the "city fathers" and the trade-union movement have been forced to make reluctant concessions. It has reached the old and established freedom organizations. For example, Roy Wilkins, executive secretary of the NAACP, who only a year ago, from a platform in Jackson, Mississippi, criticized the direct-action methods of the Freedom Riders, was arrested recently for leading a picket line in that very city, after hundreds of NAACP members had been arrested in a direct action struggle.

Before Birmingham, the great struggles had been waged for specific, limited goals. The Freedom Rides sought to establish the right to eat while traveling; the sit-ins sought to win the right to eat in local restaurants; the Meredith case centered on a single Negro's right to enter a state university. The Montgomery boycott, although it involved fifty thousand people in a year long sacrificial struggle, was limited to attaining the right to ride the city buses with dignity and respect. The black people now reject token, limited or gradual approaches.

The package deal is the new demand. The black community is not prepared to engage in a series of costly battles—first for jobs, then decent housing, then integrated schools, etc., etc. The fact that there is a power elite which makes the decisions is now clearly understood. The Negro has learned that, through economic and mass pressures, this elite can be made to submit step by step. Now he demands unconditional surrender.

It is significant that in city after city where the spirit of Birmingham has spread, the Negroes are demanding fundamental social, political and economic changes. One can predict with confidence that in the future the scope of these demands will be widened, not narrowed, and that if they are not met in the North as well as in the South, a very dangerous situation will develop. Federal troops may well become a familiar sight in the North as well as the South, since the black community is determined to move vigorously and fearlessly arid relentlessly ahead.

Absence of Fear

Gandhi used to say that the absence of fear was the prime ingredient of nonviolence: "To be afraid is to be a slave." A.J. Muste frequently says that to be afraid is to behave as if the truth were not true. It was the loss of all fear that produced the moment of truth in Birmingham: children as young as six paraded calmly when dogs, fire hoses and police billies were used against them. Women were knocked down to the ground and beaten mercilessly. Thousands of teenagers stood by at churches throughout the whole county, waiting their turn to face the clubs of Bull Connor's police, who are known to be among the most brutal in the nation. Property was bombed. Day after day the brutality and arrests went on. And always, in the churches, hundreds of well-disciplined children eagerly awaited their turns.

While these youngsters, unlike Meredith, had the advantage of operating in groups, and while Meredith's ordeal must have been the most difficult borne by any freedom fighter short of death—the children of Birmingham, like no other person or group, inspired and shamed all Afro-Americans, and pulled them into a united struggle.

E. Franklin Frazier wrote in the past of the Negro bourgeoisie. He told of the efforts of the Negro upper classes to ape white people, of the exploitation of Negroes by wealthy members of their own race and of the absence of identity among Negroes. But had Frazier been alive to see Birmingham, he would have discovered that the black community was welded into a classless revolt. A.G. Gaston, the Negro millionaire who with some ministers and other upper-class elements had publicly stated that the time was not ripe for such a broad protest, finally accommodated himself, as did the others, to the mass pressure from below and joined the struggle. Gaston owns much property, including a funeral parlor and the motel that eventually became the headquarters for the Birmingham campaign. The bombing of his motel was one cause of the outbreak of rioting on the part of elements that had not come into the nonviolent struggle.

On the basis of the behavior of the black business community in the cities where protests have emerged since Birmingham, one can confidently predict that future struggle will find the Negro bourgeoisie playing a major role in social change and nonviolence. They know that unless they join in the struggle they will lose the business of their fellow Negroes, who are in no mood to tolerate Uncle Tom-ism.

Black people have waited a hundred years for the government to help them win their rights. President after President has made commitments before election and failed to use the executive power he possesses after election. Congress today, dominated by Southern Democrats, cannot pass any meaningful civil-rights legislation. The Supreme Court, from 1954 to 1963, took a gradualist approach, thereby putting its stamp of approval on "with all deliberate speed", which spells tokenism.

So the black people have looked elsewhere for allies, hoping to discover some major power group within American society which would join them not only in the struggle for Negro rights, but also in the struggle for a more democratic America. The trade-union movement and the churches have issued radical pronouncements but in fact have done precious little and on occasion have even blocked progress. Thus the black population has concluded that the future lies in casting not just a ballot, what Thoreau called "a piece of paper merely", but the total vote—the human person against injustice.

This is not to say that black people are not deeply appreciative of those few independent radicals, liberals and church people who have offered time, money and even their lives. They have nothing but admiration for people like Jim Peck, who was brutally beaten in Mississippi and Alabama during the Freedom Rides, Barbara Deming, who was arrested in Birmingham, Eric Weinberger, who fasted for a month in Alabama jails, and William Moore, the slain postman. One can be thankful that the number of such individuals is increasing. However, social change of such magnitude requires that major power groups in our society participate as meaningful allies.

Body Against Injustice

The use of the "black body" against injustice is necessary as a means of creating social disruption and dislocation precisely because the accepted democratic channels have been denied the Negro.

In practice, it works like this: having urged the social institutions to desegregate to no avail, having pleaded for justice to no avail, the black people see that the white community would rather yield to the threats of the segregationist (in the name of law and order) than change the social system. And so Negroes conclude that they must upset the social equilibrium more drastically than the opposition can. They place their bodies against an unjust law by sitting in a restaurant, or a library, playing in a park or swimming in a pool. The segregationists, frequently joined by the police, attack. Arrests and brutality follow. But the black people keep coming, wave after wave. The jails fill. The black population boycotts the stores. Businesses begin to lose money.

At this point the white community splits into two groups. On one side are the political and law-enforcement agencies, supported by the arch-segregationists, who fearfully resort to indiscriminate violence as a stop-gap measure. Then the more enlightened section of the community, including many business leaders, begin to act for the first time. They sense not only the rightness of the Negroes' demands but their inevitability. They realize that police violence may bring both a violent response from unorganized elements of the black population and increased economic reprisals. Thus the business community, previously having sided with the forces of reaction, at first quietly and then openly sue for discussion and negotiation with the Negro community, an approach they had earlier dismissed when it was proposed by Negro leaders.

This method of massive nonviolence has many dangers. The greatest threat is that violence, which has been smoldering beneath the surface for generations, will inevitably manifest itself. But the creative genius of people in action is the only safeguard in this period and it can be trusted to bring about, ultimately, a better community, precisely because the tactic of mass action is accompanied by nonviolent resistance. The protesters pledge themselves to refrain from violence in word and deed, thereby confining whatever inevitable violence there may be in the situation to an irreducible minimum.

The genius of this method and philosophy lies in its ability to destroy an old unjust institution and simultaneously create a new one. For finally the white community is forced to choose between closing down the schools, restaurants, parks, buses, etc., and integrating them. Faced for the first time with a choice that can impose discomfort, inconvenience and economic turmoil in the white community—that community discovers that it would prefer integrated institutions to no public institutions at all.

It is therefore clear that we can now expect, following Birmingham, a more sympathetic ear from the power structure, in both the North and the South.

Financial Tenderness of Segregation

Loss of money to retail stores throughout the country, the reluctance of many industries to move to Little Rock during the school integration struggle, the fear of capitalists to invest in Mississippi and Alabama now, and the disrupting of the economy in Birmingham have caused big businesses, including steel, to take a second look at the "Negro problem".

The nation gives Robert Kennedy credit for the fact that the real rulers of Birmingham sat down with representatives of the black revolution. But knowledgeable people realize that it was the withdrawal of black purchasing power in a city which is almost half black, and the militant, unconditional surrender policies of the nonviolent struggle that turned the tide.

Again, Birmingham is a turning point in that all significant elements of the power structure have now acknowledged that the white community must recognize the true nature of the black revolution and its economic consequences.

Therefore, in city after city, following Birmingham, the real powers have moved to convince the politicians that they should negotiate. Chain store, moving picture, hotel and restaurant executives have recently sought out representatives of the black community to ask for negotiations leading to nation-wide desegregation. This is new. It is a consequence of the handwriting they see on the wall. They see it in police brutality and the bombed-out homes and business establishments. They see it in the eyes of Birmingham's children.

The tragedy is that the trade-union movement, the churches and educational institutions which lay claim to freedom and justice, reveal that they have learned nothing from the Battle of Birmingham. This is especially sad since the great battle lies ahead. And this battle the black population is now prepared to wage. This is going to be the battle for jobs.

Negroes are finally beginning to realize that the age of automation and industrialization presents them with peculiar problems. There is less and less of a market where the unskilled can sell his labor. Inadequate, segregated schools increase the problem. The negative attitude of the trade unions compounds it further. The Cold War economy, geared to armaments production (perhaps the most automated of all industries) is throwing millions out of work, hut the minority groups are being hit hardest. For every white person unemployed, there are close to three Negroes without jobs.

In general, the unemployed, whether white or black, are not yet prepared to take radical action to demand jobs now. However, unemployed black people are prepared to move in conjunction with the rest of the black community and its many white supporters, within the context of the broad civil rights upheaval. Since their most immediate ends are economic, their banner will be "Dignity of work with equal pay and equal opportunity". This agitation on the part of Negroes for jobs is bound to stimulate unemployed white workers to increased militancy. There will be sit-downs and other dislocating tactics. Nonviolent resistance will have to be directed against local and federal governments, the labor unions, against the AFL/CIO hierarchy and any construction plant or industry that refuses to grant jobs. Such mass disturbances will probably soon take place in the major industrial centers of the country and it is likely that they will be more vigorous in the North than they have been in the South. And they will have incalculable effects on the economic structure.

The great lesson of Birmingham is at once dangerous and creative; black people have moved to that level where they cannot be contained. They are not prepared to wait for courts, elections, votes, government officials, or even Negro leaders. As James Baldwin said in an interview published in the *New York Times* for June 3rd: "No man can claim to speak for the Negro people today. There is no one with whom the power structure can negotiate a deal that will bind Negro people. There is, therefore, no possibility of a bargain." The black people themselves are united and determined to destroy an unjust laws and discriminatory practices, and they want total freedom, including equal economic opportunity and the right to marry whom they damned well please. They know that at a time when the Kennedy brothers were fighting hard to maintain an aura of leaderhip and control of the civil-rights movement, the children of Birmingham, using methods of nonviolent resistance, restored the leadership to the black community. This was, as reported in the June 6th issue of *Jet*, a "terrible licking" for the federal government. If kids can revitalize the civil rights movement in Birmingham, the least we can do is to act like men and women and fight now to provide them with a decent future.

The mood is one of anger and confidence of total victory. The victories to date have given added prestige to the method of nonviolent resistance. One can only hope that the white community will realize that the black community means what it says: *freedom now.*

"In Apprehension How Like a God!"

> What a piece of work is a man! how noble in reason! how infinite in
> faculty! in form and moving how express and admirable! in action
> how like an angel! in apprehension how like a god!
> (*Hamlet*, Act II, Scene 2.)

On August 6, 1945, a bomb fell on Hiroshima. At that same moment a bomb
fell upon America, and its impact was felt around the world. Since that time,
there has been considerable discussion of the atomic bomb and its effect upon
man, and much of this discussion speaks of the bomb as a new factor in the
stream of history. In the physical sense this is no doubt true. However, in a
spiritual sense the atomic bomb is not new, but is merely another listing in the
encyclopedia of force which began with the club and the slingshot and which now
includes biological agents and chemical warfare. The atomic bomb has forced us
to raise a question: Will not those who rely on violence end not only in utilizing
any degree of violence, but in justifying it? If the answer to this question is Yes,
then the use of violent force becomes the greatest problem of our time. In his
book, *Thieves in the Night,* Arthur Koestler recognizes this fact when he says.
"We are entering a political ice-age in which violence is the universal language
and in which the machine gun is the esperanto to be understood from Madrid to
Shanghai."

The world over, suspicion is so intense, apathy so wide-spread and reliance
on old methods so established, that man has become cynical and frustrated. Yet,
when we look upon our scientific progress, we can, without worry, repeat the words
of Hamlet, "What a piece of work is a man! how noble in reason! how infinite in
faculty!" But, can we add, "in action how like an angel! in apprehension how like
a god!"? Many formerly trusting men, observing the manifestations of depravity
today, have begun to question whether that spark of God in each of us is not all
but completely smothered.

The spark, the potential, is indeed still within us, but in our reliance on violence
we have misused our energies and sapped the strength from our moral muscles.
At this moment each man in the world possesses a limited energy for social action.
Let us consider this quantity similar to the contents of a drinking cup. If we use a
portion of this energy in fear, another portion in frustration, and still another in
preparation for violent aggression, soon we shall discover that our power is greatly
diminished. But, if we can discipline ourselves—and that is a matter requiring
a practical, willing, and thorough-going devotion—we can remove fear, hatred,
bitterness and frustration. Then the cup will overflow with energy, a great deal
of which can be used in finding a creative solution to our problems.

On the other hand, placing our faith in weapons, no matter how reluctantly
we do so, and no matter how compassionately we rationalize, means that we are

using our energies in the hope that the Devil can cast himself out. Reliance on violence by inexorable logic leads to three conditions that are contrary to that community of spirit on which law and order are based. Violence leads to fear, to moral suicide and to nation-worship

May we begin with an examination of fear and certain of its effects upon human behavior? When we are frightened our behavior often becomes erratic and unaccountable. We may be petrified, or we may run about wildly, as men have done in a burning building. It might be a simple matter to walk directly to an exit. But frightened men behave as if the truth were not true.

So great has America's fear of the Soviet Union become that many people do not recognize the law of cause and effect still to be in operation. The argument runs that getting tough with the Russians will bring them to their senses and inspire in them a more reasonable attitude toward us; when, actually, a rather substantial case can be made that our present discord with the Soviet Union may be in large part the result of our own past policies and unfriendly acts. We are, in reality, in the present crisis precisely because the law of cause and effect has been and still is in operation—unfriendliness begetting unfriendliness, trust inspiring trust.

Many people today believe that the way to peace is to play upon the horror of modern weapons and the devastation of any future war. In an article, "Do People Like War?", published in *Look* on September 30, 1947, A.M. Meerloo, the Dutch psychologist, comments on the current notion that people will actually be forced by fear to build a constructive plan for peace: "Psychology tells us that this way of thinking is dangerous. We know that fear never evokes peaceful reactions in men. On the contrary, people react to fear by readying themselves for defense and attack. ... But we are not only children and fighting primitives. We still possess positive drives for peace. But they are based on love and social adaptation, not on fear of attack. ... The answer to how to build a positive peace cannot be found in military strategy and atomic science. The militant way of life always fails. It always turns into a vicious circle of defense, aggression, and renewed attack. 'To resist force inspires force.' Mobilization of armies in this country means counter-mobilization of armies elsewhere. This is an eternal law. But making peace without fear and suspicion encourages peace. That is the other aspect of the same eternal law." This is the kind of statement one had learned to expect only from the pulpit. Today men in all walks of life are deeply concerned.

At a meeting of the Emergency Committee of Atomic Scientists at Princeton on November 17, 1946, Dr. Albert Einstein addressed himself to the question of fear, and concluded that making peace is basically a psychological problem. He stated that today we have the profound dilemma of wanting to make peace at the same time we prepare for war. In conclusion, he said, "You cannot serve two masters. You cannot prepare for peace and for war at the same time. It's psychologically impossible." An indication of this lies in the fact that while the great majority of people in America cry "peace, peace" and truly desire peace, and while the Government claims that its first job is to insure peace, we go on spending 79 cents of every dollar paid into the treasury for war, present, past and future, while we spend a mere pittance in developing the functional agencies of the

United Nations which might lead to world government. We hope in one direction but follow the road that is diametrically opposed.

It was in fear that Congress, on August 2, 1947, placed its stamp of approval for the first time in American history, upon the creation of a secret police: the Central Intelligence Agency, with orders to operate throughout America and the entire world. This agency must now spend as much time watching our "trusted and essential" scientists as in observing individuals who may be engaged in sabotage. For in times when war is total, who, indeed, is to be trusted? It is fear which prompts us to permit the military to shackle research in physical sciences in our universities.

Our fears demand total preparedness, and such preparedness demands totalitarianism for American citizens. Cord Meyer, Jr., is a marine veteran who was wounded in the fighting in the Pacific, and who returned to serve as an aide to Commander Harold Stassen at the San Francisco Conference. The editor of *Harper's Magazine* describes him as adding up realistically, what it will cost America to disperse our industries, to move cities underground, and to build up stockpiles for atomic bombardment. In the June 1947 issue of *Harper's* Meyer wrote:

> ... Total preparedness means totalitarianism for American citizens. There is hardly an aspect of human life that will not have to be corrupted to the organized pursuit of force. Together with their loss of the democratic right to determine public policy, the large majority of American citizens stand to lose also their right to choose their work and to live where they please. It is unlikely that the freedoms of speech and assembly can be allowed to survive. Conscripted to serve in the defense forces or to labor in the subterranean factories, regulated by police restrictions in their attempts to travel, subjected to arbitrary search and arrest, forced to work longer hours at less pay, they will become mere instruments of the state. If there is complaint against these staggering sacrifices, the answer will always be that they are necessary in order to preserve the sovereign independence of the United States. This is the monumental irony inherent in the whole policy of modern preparedness. ...

In fear most Americans give passive support to totalitarian governments abroad at the very moment we protest totalitarianism. Fear of Russia dictates that we defend a government in Greece which follows the secret police techniques practiced for years in Nazi Germany. Fascist Italy and Spain, Japan, and the Soviet Union. On April 1, 1947, Arthur Krock, observer for the conservative *New York Times*, telegraphed his paper that between midnight and 5:00 A.M. on March 29, 1947, hundreds of innocent citizens had been arrested by the Greek Government. He then added:

> In one three-day period, after the United States said it would assume political responsibility, the Greek Government arrested about 600 persons in Athens, mostly professionals—doctors, lawyers, etc.—and sent

them away, frankly declaring there was no longer any need to exercise restraint. There is no doubt that the loudest shouters in support of the United States are Athens' three thousand wealthiest citizens whom the government continues to protect against any direct taxation and who, with their gold pounds, hardly realize there is any inflation. And the Rightists, and extremists, encouraged by the President's speech, now trumpet that the Center is almost as traitorous as the Left because it doesn't make humble obeisance to the government.

That one finally becomes the thing he violently fights is a fact that Hitler understood, in 1933, when he said, "The great strength of the totalitarian state is that it forces those who fear it to imitate it." It would be a tragic thing indeed if we Americans were stripped of our freedom by a foreign and aggressive power; it is all the more tragic that we gradually and somewhat unknowingly give up our freedoms, one after another, in the pursuit of that force which we claim will guard our liberty.

If it is true that violence destroys our liberty, it is also possible to offer some evidence that violence causes inconsistencies that are tantamount to moral suicide. The moral man is he who is opposed to injustice *per se*, opposed to injustice wherever he finds it; the moral man looks for injustice first of all in himself. But in the process of creating and utilizing modern weapons, one cannot really be concerned with injustice wherever it appears. Certainly, many who use violence wish to be so concerned, and begin with a broad sense of community; but they end in opposing injustice when it touches them, having become capable of rationalizing when they use it against others. An indication of this lies in some editorials which appeared in the *New York Times* in the year 1904, when the Japanese had "without warning" attacked Russia, as the United States was attacked at Pearl Harbor. In the editorial of February 9, 1904, the *Times* stated:

> Our Manchurian trade has, under Russian occupation, sunk from a very promising beginning to a condition which has brought American mills to bankruptcy. ... Japan stands for freedom, cultural enlightenment.

In the editorial of February 10, 1904, it continued:

> The blow came unexpectedly. ... As a matter of naval strategy and tactics, this prompt, enterprising and gallant act of Japanese arms will be memorable.

And on February 11, 1904, the editor concluded:

> It hardly becomes the dignity of a great nation to complain that it has been struck before it was quite ready. If Russia is caught unprepared, the fault is surely her own. To impute treachery to the Japanese because they took the promptest possible advantage, was a gloss reserved for the publicists at St. Petersburg.

Thus we observe that we are not opposed to sneak attacks; we are opposed to sneak attacks upon us, or when they are not to our advantage. We may justify a sneak attack according to its affect upon our "Manchurian trade."

Or, let us consider the efforts of a large segment of our leadership and citizenry to pass the Universal Military Training bill. In the thirties, we argued that conscription in peacetime was wrong in principle, that Italy and Germany, by conscription, were depriving young men of a most sacred freedom—freedom from military domination. Arguments which appeared in American newspapers and journals condemned totalitarian leadership which then conscripted youth. Yet today, many responsible men would conscript our young men in peacetime, and would be embarrassed to reread the things they once wrote. Military preparedness has led to its logical conclusion, as it did in Germany and Italy. We are opposed to conscription when others prepare to fight us, but can justify it when we are preparing to fight them.

When Vittorio, son of Benito Mussolini, returned from Addis Ababa and described to newspaper correspondents the effects of Italian flame-throwers, the American public was justly incensed that such a weapon had been used upon barefooted and ill-equipped Ethiopians. The American papers used such words as "cruel," "barbaric," and "uncivilized," in describing Italy's use of the flame-thrower against defenseless women and children. Yet scarcely ten years had passed before we destroyed hundreds of thousands of defenseless women and children by dropping bombs into Japan and Germany. Now it would he an easy mistake to call men in responsible positions evil because such bombs were dropped, but it is a more complicated problem than that. Such acts lie in and are the direct result of, dependence upon violence.

On November 4, 1947, the United Press reported from Tokyo that the United States Government had placed on trial several Japanese generals who had participated in the bombing of Chinese cities in 1937. In presenting its case, the American Government took the "view that any general bombing of extensive areas wherein resides a large population engaged in peaceful pursuits, is unwarranted and contrary to the principles of law and humanity." Since then, several of these Japanese generals have been hanged. One may ask why have we not hanged Eisenhower and the other American generals who engaged in the "general bombing of extensive areas wherein resides a large population engaged in peaceful pursuits"? We have not done so because we are not opposed to indiscriminate bombing. In addition, we have reached that stage in history where the choice must he between total war and total peace, since it may now he argued that all pursuits in wartime in some way, directly or indirectly, are connected with the war effort. Where does this process lead?

There is some indication that even military men are concerned to answer this question. On September 21, 1946, an Associated Press dispatch reported in the *Herald Tribune* for September 22, quoted Admiral Halsey as having said that the dropping of the bomb on Hiroshima was a "mistake" and an "unnecessary experiment" because the Japanese had already put out peace feelers. Halsey also indicated that he was sorry the bomb had been invented and used, and he deplored "exaggerated statements that the atomic bomb was responsible for the collapse of Japan." Even those who put pressure upon Admiral Halsey to change his statement could not, on the other hand, suppress *"The United States Strategic Bombing Survey,"* an official Government document published July 1, 1946, under the editorship of Commander Walter Wilds, United States Naval Reserve, which, in discussing the atomic bomb, concluded:

> Based on a detailed investigation of all the facts and supported by the testimony of the surviving Japanese leaders involved, it is the Survey's opinion that certainly prior to 31 December 1945, and in all probability prior to 1 November 1945, Japan would have surrendered even if the atomic bombs had not been dropped, even if Russia had not entered the war, and even if no invasion had been planned or contemplated.

We thus observe the eternal truth proclaimed by Laotse, Buddha, Jesus, St. Francis, George Fox and Gandhi: the use of violence will destroy moral integrity—the very fundamental of community on which peace rests. We cannot remain honest unless we are opposed to injustice wherever it occurs, first of all in ourselves.

Further, there is real evidence in history that those nations which have defended themselves by physical force have produced citizens whose final allegiance is to the political state rather than to principle, to truth, or to God.

On May 28, 1946, the Emergency Committee of Atomic Scientists set out to raise $200,000 for a Campaign of Education on the Atomic Bomb. The Committee stated in its press release that the time had come to "let people know that a new type of thinking is essential in this atomic age" if mankind is to survive and move toward higher levels. On the day following this urgent appeal the Federation of American Scientists said, "Scientists seek by education to teach men that they must abandon atomic weapons to preserve civilization." But there is some reason to question whether scientists who are building stockpiles of atom bombs can "teach men that they must abandon atomic weapons to preserve civilization." How can scientists expect the man on the street to follow their leadership? Would not ordinary human beings conclude that the matter is not so serious after all, and that the thousands of dollars which the scientists are attempting to raise will have little effect? It would seem that the only logical conclusion many could reach in observing the scientists continue to make what they describe as "utterly dangerous and destructive" would be that these scientists are "afflicted with insanity."

The campaign of education on the atom bomb was addressed to those "possessing the power to make decisions for good and evil." It announced that "our modes of thinking must be changed," and yet the atomic scientists themselves are still addicted to outmoded thinking, and the Federation of Atomic Scientists expressed it most frankly in their statement made on May 26, 1947, to which we have referred, by admitting that in these matters "we must submit to *the guidance and orders of the military.*" The behavior of these scientists is symbolic of many Americans' basic allegiance. Although these scientists claim that the atom bomb will destroy civilization, and although they sincerely appeal for funds in order that this calamity shall be avoided, they end in foregoing the dictates of their conscience, and, in the interests of national defense, "submit to the orders of the military." A few days after the Emergency Committee of Atomic Scientists issued their appeal for funds, A.J. Muste of the Fellowship of Reconciliation wrote Dr. Einstein and said, in part:

> You and your colleagues seek to draw a line between yourselves and the military. You speak of them as "fantastic and shortsighted" in the estimation of "reasonable men." Some of you have said even harsher things than this of General Groves and other military men. But plainly you are subservient to the military, as you were during those years when, without the knowledge of your fellow citizens, you made the first atomic bomb. The military say they must have atomic bombs, which will wreck civilization, and you make them! You are cogs in the same machine as they are. If you think there are not some of them who also work with heavy hearts and without enthusiasm, you are surely mistaken and lacking in the grace of humility. They have not changed their mode of thinking—the habit of command. You have not changed your mode of thinking—the habit of subservience to the military and to the State—when it comes to a showdown. In the final analysis, they practice the Fuehrer principle, and you submit to it.

Mr. Muste ended his statement by urging the scientists to forsake being merely scientists, and to become prophets, persons, whole human beings, and not technicians or slaves of a war-making state. He urged them to become conscientious objectors, and to refuse to make weapons of destruction. On June 10, 1946, Dr. Harold C. Urey, who had received a copy of the Einstein letter, wrote Muste from the University of Chicago Institute of Nuclear Studies. He began by saying, "In the first place, neither Dr. Einstein nor I myself nor anyone else has the power to prevent some scientists from working on military weapons if they wish to. We have only control over our own actions and no others." He then said, "I personally believe in obeying the laws of this country, and in aiding its efforts in whatever direction my own government and the responsible officials believe that we should go."

Thus, men who cry out that atomic weapons will destroy civilization continue to make them, because national allegiances demand it. They announce that they work with "heavy hearts and without enthusiasm" but they do not answer the heart. They answer the demands of the state. It may be true, of course, that men continue to depend upon guns because they see no other way. Faced with tyranny within and without, we have begun to question man's ability to reach peaceful solutions. One of the chief causes of dictatorship and war may be the readiness of the average citizen to go into uniform. How difficult it must be for leaders in government to make a sacrificial effort to avoid hostilities, when men and women doubt the efficacy of demanding that their leaders find a real way to peace. The hearts of thousands of men cried out against participation in the last war, yet they who protested against the useless order of a life at variance with the centers of their beings, had been so conditioned by nationalism that they could not use the unique and powerful weapon within their own hands—civil disobedience. We find many reasons for our failure to use this weapon. As Tolstoi pointed out in his book *Christianity and Patriotism:*

> One man does not assert the truth which he knows, because he feels himself bound to the people with whom he is engaged; another, because the truth might deprive him of the profitable position by which he maintains his family; a third, because he desires to attain reputation and authority, and then use them in the service of mankind; a fourth, because he does not wish to destroy old sacred traditions; a fifth, because he has no desire to offend people; a sixth, because the expression of the truth would arouse persecution, and disturb the excellent social activity to which he has devoted himself.

For these and other reasons, we have failed, in the past, to identify ourselves with all men. Now we have no choice but to do so if we are to survive. We have reached that stage where only a miracle can save us—the miracle of individual responsibility. Individual responsibility is the alternative to violence; individual responsibility is capable of overcoming fear; it is capable of converting nation-worship back to the Judaeo-Christian tradition and ethic; it is capable of re-establishing moral integrity. How can we begin? We can begin by opposing injustice wherever it appears in our daily lives. As free men we can refuse to follow or to submit to unjust laws which separate us from other men no matter where they live, nor under what government they exist. As the now-famous editorial in *Life Magazine* pointed out, in our time it is "the individual conscience against the atomic bomb." In the parochial states of the world today, it is the responsible man, the man against all injustice, who can save us, and this in a very real sense means man against the state.

Justice Jackson of the United States Supreme Court, in his opening statement at the Nuremberg trials, addressed to the people of the civilized world, castigated the German people for refusing to recognize this principle. Mr. Jackson said over and again that German citizens had been irresponsible in following the cruel and antisocial directives of the Hitler government. He reiterated that responsible people would have resolved to end the Nazi regime and its wide-spread injustice, even though they were aware that to have done so would have meant severe punishment or even death for many of them and their families. There is some question in my mind that Mr. Jackson understood the total implication of his words, since he had issued no such statement in defense of the conscientious objectors in this country, who refused to register under what they considered the antisocial Selective Service and Training Act. I agree with him, however, that the failure of the German citizens to resist unjust laws from the beginning of Hitler's regime logically ended in their placing Jews in gas furnaces and lye pits, although many who did these things, no doubt, worked with "heavy hearts and without enthusiasm."

It would, however, be a mistake to make simple the matter of resistance to the state. Several of the greatest teachers of the past, and such practicers of civil disobedience as Mahatma Gandhi, have never taken lightly their inability to follow the directives of governmental officials, and have with intense study and grave concern for all persons involved, weighed many aspects of the question under consideration before appearing to set themselves off from the will of an organized social group. Although there has not been complete agreement among those who have practiced civil disobedience, most leaders have generally adhered to certain very basic principles. The chief of these is that no individual has the right to rebel against the state. One has not the right to resist the social group of which he is a part. This is particularly true where decisions made have been reached after extensive democratic discussion. One has, on the other hand, a duty to resist, and one resists because the state is poorly organized and one's everlasting aim is to improve the nature of the state, to disobey in the interest of a higher law. Hence, one has the duty but not the right to rebel. But before rebelling, one must clearly examine the questions outlined by the British scholar, T.H. Green, in his *Lectures on the Principles of Political Obligation:*

I must ask:

(a) Have I exhausted all possible constitutional methods of bringing desired change?

(b) Are the people I ask to rebel keenly conscious of a flagrant wrong to them? Or do I excite their passions?

(c) What is likely to be the effect of the resistance? Will the new state be worse than the first?

(d) What of my own motives? Have I removed all ego?

To these one must add another: Can I accept punishment, prison, or even death, in that spirit which is without contention? It is most important to examine one's own motives, for even if a given resistance fails, this does not disprove its validity; repeated attempts and repeated failures may be necessary to success. But, since it is not possible to see completely what the results of any given resistance will be, one must therefore be careful that one's character and motives are clear. Henry Thoreau, sitting in prison, was visited by Ralph Waldo Emerson, who urged him to forego his useless efforts to stop slavery and an unjust war. But Thoreau, whose aim was clear, held to his belief and action. Little did Emerson realize that Thoreau's action was to be one of the chief factors in the development of the life and spirit of Mahatma Gandhi, and that Thoreau's resistance was to move through history and help bring freedom to four hundred million people, far exceeding the number Thoreau attempted to free in the middle of the 19th century.

There have been many great men in history who have been civil resisters. All who have resisted have seen clearly that social progress is made through simultaneous change in men and in the environment in which men find themselves. Thus, these men have not only sought to behave with integrity, but they have resisted secure in the faith that their opposition ultimately would influence society in the direction of those conditions which make it possible for other men to see issues clearly enough to press for a more abundant economic, social, and political life. These men recognized that there is "individual responsibility for collective guilt." Among these have been Socrates, Henry Thoreau, and more recently, Norbert Wiener, the American scientist.

Plato describes in the *Apology* a scene in which Socrates is on trial for the practice of philosophy. In that great work Socrates, having heard an indictment against himself by Anytus, turns to the Athenian court, and says:

> If you say to me, Socrates, this time we will not mind Anytus and you shall be let off, but upon one condition, that you are not to inquire and speculate in this way any more, and if you are caught doing so again, you shall die—if this was the condition on which you let me go, I should reply: Men of Athens, I honor and love you; but I shall obey God, rather than you, and while I have life and strength I shall never cease from the practice and teaching of philosophy, exhorting anyone whom I meet and saying to him after my manner.
>
> I tell you that virtue is not given by money but that from virtue comes money and every other good of man, public as well as private, this is my teaching: this is the doctrine which you say corrupts the youth — For I do nothing but go about persuading you all, old and young alike, — not to take thought of your persons, or your properties, but first and chiefly to care about the greatest improvement of the soul — I shall never alter my ways, not even if I have to die many times. — For I will obey God rather than you ... and so I bid you farewell — to die, you to live; which is better, God only knows.

Centuries later, the United States government, which at the time condoned slavery, called upon Henry Thoreau to contribute his share into the tax-box to support the war with Mexico. Thoreau, as you know, refused to pay such taxes, and in his *Essay on Civil Disobedience*, which Mahatma Gandhi lists as one of the four great influences in his life, raised the question which will be raised again and again if there are to be free men, "How does it become a man to behave toward this ... government today?" And he went on to comment, "I answer that he cannot without disgrace be associated with it. I cannot for an instant recognize that political organization as my government which is a slave's government also." The American people "must cease to hold slaves and to make war on Mexico though it costs them their existence as a people.... There are thousands who are in opinion opposed to slavery and to war, yet who in effect do nothing to put an end to them; who, esteeming themselves children of Washington and Franklin, sit down with their hands in their pockets and say they know not what to do, and do nothing; who even postpone the question of freedom to the question of free trade.... I think that it is not too soon for honest men to rebel and to revolutionize."

In 1944 G.B. Shaw published his book, *Everybody's Political What's What*. In discussing the question of general strike versus conscientious objection as a means of bringing government officials to the point of seeking peace or stopping war, Shaw observed that:

... The social organization of such conscientious objection is the only method now available for preventing a war. ...

... The conscientious objector does not starve himself; he asserts himself in the practical form of a flat refusal to fight. And if he is numerous enough, there will be no war. ...

... A majority of objectors is not necessary: an organized minority could stop war as it stopped Prohibition in the United States. ...

One may question that a minority could stop war, but certainly one cannot question that disobedience both to military service and to payment of taxes for war would reveal to the state that a segment of the population cares enough to pay a price for peace. Wide-spread resistance to war preparations and the willingness of resisters to face imprisonment would have to be taken seriously by the state and ultimately would have a profound effect on American foreign policy.

The action of Norbert Wiener a year ago is worthy of observation, for this one scientist has had a profound effect upon the thinking and action of many men in the States and abroad. Norbert Wiener, one of the outstanding mathematical analysts of our time, a professor at Massachusetts Institute of Technology, published in *The Atlantic Monthly,* January 1947, a letter which earlier he had addressed to the president of a great aircraft corporation who had requested of him the technical account of a certain research Wiener had conducted during the war. Professor Wiener's indignation at being asked to participate in rearmament less than two years after the war's end is typical of a growing sensitivity among many American scientists today. His conclusion is revolutionary and makes Norbert Wiener more than a scientist and more than an ordinary man: he has become a prophet. After stating that in the past scholars had made it the custom to furnish scientific information to any seeking it, Norbert Wiener pointed out that the bombing of Hiroshima and Nagasaki had made it clear to him that "to provide scientific information is not necessarily an innocent act, and may entail the gravest consequences." He therefore felt it necessary to reconsider the established custom of scientists to give information to any person who might inquire of him. He stated it had become perfectly clear to him that to disseminate information about weapons in the present state of our civilization is to make it practically certain that the weapons will be used, and in that respect the controlled missile, concerning which he was requested to give data, represented the still imperfect supplement to the atomic bomb and bacteriological warfare. He said that their possession can do nothing but endanger us by encouraging what he describes as the "tragic insolence of the military mind." Wiener's conclusion was this: "If, therefore, I do not desire to participate in the bombing or poisoning of defenseless peoples—and I most certainly do not—I must take a serious responsibility as to those to whom I disclose my scientific ideas.... I do not expect to publish any future work of mine which may do damage in the hands of irresponsible militarists."

Civil disobedience is not advocated as a cure-all, nor is it urged as an alternative to world government. It is not itself equal to the adjustment of social, political and economic displacements which have produced first depression and then dictatorship and war. Such adjustments are in reality the means of peace. But in our fear, when we behave as if the truth were not true, the real problem, the struggle to provide men with bread, beauty and brotherhood, has been relegated to a second place. Our fears have brought about an armaments race and until we have broken the vicious circle of this race with the Soviet Union, there cannot be attention, energy and money given to the basic causes of war and injustice. It is important to realize that such competition can be ended when the United States is willing to disarm completely. We have within us as individuals the responsibility and power to help achieve this task. We have the responsibility and the duty to make an effort to save the world from the curse of atomic war. We have the power to disarm the United States by one gun if we refuse to carry one; we have the power to take a gun from another if we refuse to pay for it by refusing to pay that part of taxes used for war.

There are those who will say that this is a futile, unrealistic and impractical course, but as we look through history we find that it is dependence on arms which is unrealistic. Every nation that has put its faith in violent force has sooner or later been overcome. Today we must face not merely the question, What will happen if we give up our arms? but we must face two other question: first, What will happen if we do not give up our arms? Then we must ask ourselves, Can we expect that others will be willing to give up their arms unless we do so first?

Edmund Taylor, formerly director of the Office of Strategic Services in India, and author of *Strategy of Terror,* has since published his book *Richer by Asia,* in which he describes his living in India and his contact with Gandhi and Asia. In discussing disarmament he points out that pending the establishment of one world it is our duty to try to persuade other nations to join us in extensive disarmament, but he is quick to point out we must not expect to be trusted or followed immediately, for too much suspicion has been sown for too many years. He is convinced that we must resign ourselves to seeing other nations insist on retaining some war-making potentialities, and he pleased if they accept any limitations at all. He then concludes:

> That leaves us the alternatives of retaining our own arms, or disarming unilaterally and announcing to the world that we will never under any circumstances resist aggression by force. The time may be near – if it has not arrived already – when we must seriously consider whether that is not the best thing to do, whether the evils which armed resistance, even successful, would bring on us would not be worse than any possible consequences of surrender.

In a very real way the American people sense that Edmund Taylor's question is a profound one. Men argue that violent force is the great protection of our democratic institutions, that in arms alone lies security. On this premise we pile higher and higher armaments and bases which are to provide us this much sought security. Consequently we have the world's largest air force, the greatest industrial output, fantastic weapons; we have naval bases circling the globe; we urge our scientists to find even more devastating weapons. Yet how do you account for the fact that the higher and higher this mountain of force rises, the deeper and deeper the fears of the American people become?

We have become so involved that Dr. Harold C. Urey, outstanding liberal scientist, in a quarterly publication, *Air Affairs*, recently came out with an article which conclusively proves what a frightened man he is. Failure to safeguard development and use of atomic energy, he believes, will inevitably lead to civilization-destroying war, and to head it off he concludes that the United States may have to declare war itself "with the frank purpose of conquering the world and ruling it as we desire and preventing any other nation from developing more weapons of war." He reveals the extremity of the proposition by adding, "This is a possible course of action; it's one that I can't contemplate with any pleasure but one which may be a strict necessity."

Indeed, only a miracle can save us, and that is the miracle of opposing injustice everywhere, first of all in ourselves; it is the miracle of depending upon the power of good to overcome the power of evil; it is the miracle performed when we no longer believe that Satan can cast out Satan. In the book, *What Can We Believe?* an exchange of letters between Dick Sheppard and Laurence Housman, English poet-dramatist, there appear the following statements:

> I don't believe the rise and fall of empires, however good and great, is decisive for the coming of God's Kingdom on earth. The Fall of the Roman Empire must have seemed at the time the biggest possible disaster for the advance of civilization in the then-known world. But was it?
>
> Most nations die, I suppose, because of their sins; but if one nation died because of its righteousness, as the Christ of history died on the cross, what a wonderful New Incarnation that would be to prove, and what a wonderful new faith for the troubled nations it might give rise to, it might convert nation-worship back to Christianity, again.

We cannot convert nation-worship back to Christianity again unless we care enough, unless we can believe that man is in apprehension like a god, unless we are able so to revolutionize and to discipline ourselves that those who behold us exclaim of us, "In action how like an angel!", unless like Jesus and Gandhi we attain that spirit which makes it possible for us to stand with arms outstretched, even unto death, saying, "You can strike me, you may destroy my home, you may destroy me, but I will not submit to what I consider wrong; neither will I strike back." Many will question the practicality of such a course, but has not the life, the work, the death of Gandhi demonstrated in our time that one man holding fast to truth and to non-violence is more powerful than ten thousand men armed?

Yet even though failure should seem certain, the faith we profess demands allegiance. But how are we different from the heathen if we strike back or submit to unjust demands and laws; or what have we left to protect if in the process of defending our freedom we give up both democracy and principle? How can we love God, whom we have not seen, if we cannot, in time of crisis, find the way to love our brothers whom we have seen?

Selected Internet Writings
by *Hugh Hollowell*

Editor's Forward

Neither Hugh nor I recall precisely how we met each other, but we suspect it's through a mutual friend. This friend is an atheist who likes to poke at Christians, and he probably noticed that Hugh and I sound rather like one another. I was a divinity school geek frustrated by pervasive elitism. Hugh had committed to beginning a relational ministry with the homeless population in Raleigh.

In the years since then, Hugh has been an inspiration to me, and being exposed to his real-world relational ministry has grounded my academic theologizing. On the day my bride and I walked down the aisle in front of our family, Hugh was ejected from a city park for the crime of serving biscuits to his friends. As of this writing, Hugh's Love Wins Ministries has become a unique hub of genuine Christian compassion and a striking prophetic voice.

The following writings are drawn from various internet publications, but primarily the Love Wins blog. They provide an overview of the confrontations, struggles, and insights from this ministry in the image of Jesus. They challenge each of us to see how our privillege prevents us from living truly into Jesus' call for our lives, and they reflect the day-to-day vulnerability of a Christ-like love.

Selected Internet Writings

Who Sinned That These People Are Poor?

There are people who work in inner-city ministries that teach job skills. Or have after-school programs or keep kids off drugs.

That is not my story.

I run an organization in Raleigh called Love Wins Ministries, where we pastor and work with chronically homeless people. These are not the people in line at the soup kitchen or in the shelters. These are the poorest of the poor—folks who live under bridges and sleep in dumpsters. People who smell of urine and mumble to themselves as they walk down the streets. A lot of times, these people do not get better.

I don't get a lot of success stories. But I do know an awful lot about hardcore urban poverty.

As a result of my work, I speak to a lot of groups about our work, and one question always comes up in the Q and A afterward. So today, I am just going to focus on that question: "Why are these people poor?"

I will answer that question in a minute, but first, I want to talk about Jesus.

Incidentally, if you ever want to get the guy in the seat next to you on the airplane to shut up, answer any of his questions with exactly that sentence: "I will answer that question in a minute, but first, I want to talk about Jesus."

In the 10th chapter of Luke is the story we call the Good Samaritan.

We all know this story. It is a Sunday School, Vacation Bible School story. When I was a kid, we did it on flannel graph (I am showing my age there...you probably saw it on *Veggie Tales*). There, up on the orange flannel background, was the victim, lying by the side of the road. The scripture tells us he was "set upon by thieves". In the neighborhoods I spend time in, we would say he got jumped.

On our flannel graph, to the far left of the man we see the priest, very elaborately dressed, looking very pious (he is doing God's work, you know...), on his way to the temple, having passed by the man. Behind him we see the Levite, a pious layman, also on his way to the temple...he is in a hurry too. It might be his turn to be a greeter that day, or maybe it's his turn to read the scripture during worship. And there, kneeling by the cutout of the victim, we see the Samaritan, cradling the victim in his arms.

Then the Sunday school teacher would say "Which person should we be?" and we would all scream "The Samaritan" and the teacher would say "good job" and give us a sucker and we went home. And that is about as far as we ever go with this story, even if we have reached an age where we no longer get a sucker after being taught about the Bible.

But for a minute, let's not pretend we are the Samaritan. Let's pretend we are the one who got jumped. We are laying there in the ditch, oozing blood.

Today, we are the victim.

I know if I am the victim, I only have one question: "Why me?"

We know virtually nothing about the victim. Jesus gives us nothing here. We do not know if he was a good man or a bad man. We do not know if he was pious or apostate, rich or poor, stingy or generous.

Why me?

We don't know.

We don't know, and we don't like that. We people of faith do not like to admit when we do not know. We don't like that at all.

About a year ago, Tanya was walking back to the rooming house after having a fight with her boyfriend. It was late at night, and to get there, she had to cross Martin Luther King Blvd, which has five lanes.

Like I said, it was late at night, and on that section of MLK, the street light was burned out. And Tanya was wearing dark clothes.

The drunk driver never saw her. He hit her dead on, ran over her and drug her now dead body about 300 yards. He said later he thought he had hit a dog.

I preached her funeral, and I said the sort of things one says at a funeral, but inside I was screaming: "Why God? Why Tanya?"

The church did not have any really good answers in that moment.

The reporter on the TV said Tanya was just in the wrong place at the wrong time.

Personally, I think that reporter was, in that moment, quite Jesus-like in her theology.

We like to see our prosperity, our good family, our happy lives, our full stomachs as signs of God's favor, as evidence of our doing "the right things".

But if that is the case, then I have a few questions:

Why did I grow up in a house with parents who loved me, who passed on a work ethic and taught me how to dream, how to set goals, how to love? I had nothing to do with it—it just happened. I was in the right place at the right time.

Why did my friend Danny grow up in a house where his mamma's boyfriend beat him with a fan belt, where his mom had to sell her body to survive after Daddy went to jail and where the only male role model in his life was the local pimp? He didn't pick that life. He was in the wrong place, at the wrong time.

When it comes to the economically poor, you need to realize you are not better than these people—you are not smarter, you are not more in God's favor, you are not more virtuous. You aren't better, you are just better off.

More questions:

How would your life have turned out if you had to steal food in order for your little sister to eat? If you had to go to school three days in a row in the same clothes? If you had to sit on the porch in the cold while your momma is 'entertaining' men for money so you can eat tonight? How would that have shaped your views on sex and intimacy?

There are all kind of reasons that people are economically poor, and it seldom has anything to do with their salvation, or their walk with God, or their destination after their death or whether they said some prayer.

Last spring, I was invited to a small group meeting a local college ministry puts on in order to talk about Love Wins, to see if any of them wanted to volunteer. I thought I was the main event, but they told me they had to do the Bible Study first.

The passage was the story of the rich young ruler, who comes to Jesus for advice, and then Jesus tells him to sell everything he has and to give it to the poor. The people in the small group were having a tough time with this.

After hearing that story read, a young guy in the room—richer than 80% of the planet, born the predominant race and the most privileged gender in the wealthiest country in the world—the very epitome of a rich young ruler to the majority of our planet—it was then that this kid said, "I think the important thing to keep in mind is to have a balanced view. After all, God gives us our possessions for a reason, and—"

It was then that I lost it.

"Hold on," I said, "God didn't give you your possessions. You have those things because you paid money for them. You had money to spend because you are employed. You are employed because you are well educated and look trustworthy to employers, both benefits of growing up white and male and inheriting a culture built on stolen land with the labor of enslaved people."

You would have thought I drop kicked a kitten across the room.

Look—I have a congregant who lives in a car. And at night, when its 25 degrees and she is shivering and shaking and wanting to turn the car on for heat but knowing she does not have the money for gas—all the while crying out to God and praying for warmth...but no warmth comes.

So if you tell me that God has given this rich young ruler in that overheated living room his possessions while leaving my friend in the car to shiver, I call shenanigans. Because if that is true, then you are saying that God loves this kid more than he does my friend in her car. Or more than he does the 80% of the planet that lives on less than $10 a day.

You are not better than they are. You are just better off.

Hear what I am not saying. I am not saying poverty is not caused by sin—I think it is. But I know a guy who used to work for a textile plant where they made t-shirts. We demanded cheap shirts, so they closed his plant. I won't ask for a show of hands today asking who is wearing a shirt made overseas—I know I am. But if you are, you and I are complicit in this man's misfortune.

Yes, poverty is a result of sin—but it is the sin of the deacon in your church who works at the bank and that approved those mortgages he knew were sketchy. It is the sin of ignoring our fellow man while we obsess over *American Idol*. It is our sin that allows us to grow obese while 17 million children go hungry here in the US.

It is our sin, not theirs.

Once after I spoke somewhere, I had a pastor come up to me and said, "If poverty is not caused by the person's sin, then what do we as people of faith have to say to it?"

In the 9th chapter of John, Jesus heals a blind man. Maybe you know the story?

As he walked along, he saw a man blind from birth. His disciples asked him, "Rabbi, who sinned, this man or his parents, that he was born blind?" Jesus answered, "Neither this man nor his parents sinned; he was born blind so that God's works might be revealed in him."

The disciples are a lot like us. They want to know why this problem exists. They want to get down to the root cause. And, being religious people, they think the root cause has got to be this man's sin.

Jesus does not seem to get too caught up into root causes. Jesus knows that the blind man was just born in the wrong place at the wrong time. But, he says, that God's work can be revealed in this man, as a result of this man's condition.

Maybe that is the answer for us, as people of faith. Not, "How did this happen?" But, "As a result of this, how can God's work be revealed?"

How can God be glorified in this moment?

The apostle Paul tells us that we are the body of Christ. The work the resurrected Jesus does in this world happens through our hands.

When Jesus walked the earth, he did not hunt for root causes—instead he touched the sick, fed the hungry and brought good news for the poor.

As the physical embodiment of the resurrected Jesus, we should do no less.

Love as a Force for Good

This was a blog post published February 14th, 2014.

His name is Keith, and yesterday was his first day to come to 707 West Jones. He was new in town, and was staying at the shelter, and someone had brought him to us.

Now, yesterday was far from a typical day for us. Most of our staff was snowed in at home, the downtown soup kitchen was closed, and the whole city was shutdown because of the snowstorm.

But it was Keith's first day, and on the best days, it can be hard to understand what we are doing there.

We don't have a security guard. We don't have a metal detector. We don't have security cameras, or an ID requirement, or even a scheduled mealtime.

We do have a warm building, plenty of chairs, and a pot of hot coffee of variable quality. There is a bathroom you can use, and a washer and dryer you can share with other folks. And you can have a conversation and be treated like you are human and feel like you are, as we like to say in my tradition, made in the very image of God.

If you spent the night before in a typical homeless shelter, that can be confusing indeed.

So Keith had lots of questions.

But one of them was, "Why is it called Love Wins?"

So I told him we had this crazy idea that if you treat people like people, then they act like people. And that we had learned that what people who are experiencing homelessness really need is a place to belong, not a place to tell them what to do. So we have worked to create that place.

A bunch of the guests were listening. Charlie was nodding, and he chimed in.

"They really care about us here. Like today—the other places we could go are all closed. But Hugh here walked across town to make sure we had a place to be today. He didn't get paid extra for that—he did it because he cares about us."

Mike always has something to say, so he said it.

"Here, I can be me. I get to help out. I get to contribute. They don't care that I was once in jail, here I get to answer the phones and help people."

I agreed. And then I told Keith that here, we think everybody deserves grace, so it doesn't matter what you have done before, and it doesn't matter where you came from and we don't care what your past looks like. All that matters is that you want to be here. And if you do, we want you here.

Roger said, "This place is safe. And as long as you keep it safe, you can stay here. The only people who are made to leave are the ones who make it not safe for other people. But even they get a second chance tomorrow."

Then I said, "Keith, the short answer to your question about why we call it Love Wins is, because, we believe it does. We believe that Love is what makes the world work, and when we show Love to each other, it makes the world better. And if we want the world to be better, we have to work at loving each other. And we can't love each other if we don't get to know each other."

Keith stared at me for a second, then he smiled.

"By getting to know each other, we are making the world better. I like that. I like that a lot."

Then he said, "What can I do to help?"

We get called naive a lot. We have been told that this work is impossible to do without an armed guard at our building. We have been told that if we let people make decisions for themselves we would end up with total anarchy. We have been dismissed as saints, and we have been dismissed as idealists.

But what we really are is just a bunch of people, some of us housed and some of us not, who really, really believe in Love as a force for good. For whom Love is not a quaint concept to be trotted out with heart candies and images of Cupid, but as the motive force of the universe.

So, today on Valentine's Day, when the world celebrates Love, know that you don't have to quit celebrating it tonight at midnight. You can embrace it. You can use it to make the world better.

My new friend Keith is excited about that. I hope you are too.

Making Things Right

This morning, I received an email, thanking me for our work, and the sender mentioned, "After all, there but for the grace of God go I."

This is a pet peeve of mine, actually, so I posted the following to Facebook:

> When you say, "There but for the grace of God go I," what you are really saying is, "I have God's grace, and they don't."
>
> Which, I assure you, is not true. So, uhhm,—don't say that.

Don't get me wrong. I know that isn't what the writer of the email meant. But that is exactly what the writer said—the literal meaning of her sentence. That person, except God's intervention, or protection, or providence, could be me.

But if that is true, then you are assuming God has withheld those things from the person you are talking about. Otherwise, according to the logic of the statement, they would be like you.

So don't say that.

It would be more kind, and accurate, to say, "I am lucky to have not had to deal with the circumstances that have led them to where they are."

It is a quaint phrase, like, "The Lord helps those who help themselves," that reinforces our popular theology—that we are somehow favored by God in a way others aren't. And even if we don't actually believe God dispenses grace to some and not to others, we have heard it so often that it sounds right, sorta, so we use it in conversation.

But we shouldn't. For not only is it bad theology, it is bad sociology, too.

Because the reason you are not homeless, for instance, has much less to do with God's grace and more to do with the parents you were born to, the family that raised you, the values you were passed on, your race, gender and sexual orientation, and, most importantly, your relationships, both current and past. Any of those are reasons for becoming homeless.

I am fully aware that someone with a high view of God's sovereignty (God's being in control) could make the case that God does, in fact, decide who is homeless or not. But that then means God also decides who went to Auschwitz and who did not, or who got HIV and who did not, or which Haitian got to die in the earthquake.

God desires us to make things right for those whom have been left behind, not for us to pronounce judgments relative to how much God's grace has caused them to be there.

So, how about we work together on that?

Loving The Unloveable

This email went out to our list of supporters and interested folks on July 29th of 2010. We send something like this out most months.

Dear Friends,

When I met them several years ago, they were homeless. She had delivered five children, all of whom had been taken by the state. He was a crackhead living off her food stamps, who made spending money by turning tricks for the white-collar types that cruise the homeless camps looking for sex.

He has several kids by different women. She has a two pack a day habit. They had a baby together – his family was fostering that kid for the state while they "got things under control". Then they found out she was pregnant. Again.

Luckily (!) about this time, they were on a city bus that hit a car. As a result, they got a small settlement. They paid a year's worth of rent on a place infested with fleas & roaches & moved in just in time for her to deliver the baby. The state let her keep this one.

They still had no money, no job. They had food stamps & whatever church they were stringing along for help that week. He was still turning tricks & she was selling her food stamps and WIC allotment. Apparently, the state was impressed by their industry & let them have custody of their other child, who is now three. The last time I was over there, the kid was watching a VHS tape of New Jack City & eating a cold hot dog while a roach ran across his foot.

Last week, I get a phone call the day before I go out of town. He ran off with the neighbor, with whom he has been having an affair. The neighbor is HIV positive. And the lease on the apartment runs out at the end of August.

Her mental health caseworker & I talked to her for hours, encouraging her to file for child support & get a restraining order. She said she will. While I am out of town, he moves back in with her. And why not—it's almost time to get food stamps again. It's hard to blame her—the thought of being alone with two kids has her terrified.

Loving these people is not easy for me. It is easy for me to say that they are where they are because of the choices they have made, or their moral failures, or whatever. But if I only love people who are lovable—well, even terrorists do that.

My Evangelical friends complain I don't talk enough about my faith in these letters. Well, understand that the only thing that keeps me answering the phone when she calls is my belief that she is valuable to the God I profess to believe in. And the only reason I am not filled with total despair for those babies is the assurance found in the ancient prayer that one day it will be "on earth as it is in heaven."

But until that day comes, I don't know anything to do but to try my best to love them, even when it is not easy. And to pray really, really hard.

They could use your prayers, too. Truth be told, so could I.

Love Wins. Always.

Lying to God

I have to tell you—I hate being lied to. I hate being played. I think we all do—no one likes to feel taken advantage of. In fact, this is one of the most frequent reasons people tell me they don't want to get to know the poor.

I am not about to say it does not happen—it certainly does. If you do this work long enough, you are going to get lied to. And by long enough, I mean, about 15 minutes.

You will hear stories of starving Grandmothers, of impending illness, of needed prescriptions, of lost paychecks and stolen backpacks—all of which can only be solved by a cash infusion, given directly to them.

Or you hear the same story from three people, all of whom are involved, and it is three very different stories. Usually with the person telling the story being the offended party.

There are all sort of reasons and explanations why this happens (most of it has to do with us and what we are doing) which I will talk about later. Today, however, I want to recommend a spiritual practice I have engaged in when I get played.

Think about the person who played you. The one who lied to you, who tricked you, who used you.

Think about your hurt, the pain you feel, the humiliation, the anger.

Got it?

Now, replace the offender with yourself. And replace you in the story with your favorite image of God.

Do you ever lie to God? Not reveal all your true motives when you talk to God? Promise God one thing, and then fail, and then try to hide the failure, or feel ashamed of how it did not work out?

I thought so.

I wonder if God feels the pain, the disappointment, the anger, the frustration that we do. Or maybe God, being God, feels it much, much more than we do.

And yet, the Christian story is that God is unending in the pursuit of relationship with us, that God is without boundary in love and that, despite our best efforts to create distance from God, will seek us out like a lost sheep, ignoring everyone else to focus on us.

Loving peope who are hard for us to love give us the opprotunity to try to love as God loves. After all, if we only reach out to love those that can love us back, even terrorists and white supremacists do that.

Deliberate Inefficiency or What Is This Project Called

This morning, I get on my bicycle at 8:45 and ride through the cold crisp air to meet Jim at the CVS to pay for his hypertension medication. He was introduced to me yesterday at our regular Sunday Morning Breakfast.

He and I were to meet at the CVS at 9:00am. By 9:30, I gave up on him, but only after standing in the cold for half an hour. That Jim was not there when we agreed to meet is no reflection on his character, per se. When you are homeless, time is a fluid concept. He got out of the shelter at 7:00 or so this morning and so it is quite possible he sat outside the CVS from 7:30 until 8:50 and then gave up on me.

Or maybe he found someone to hand him $4 cash yesterday after we talked. Or maybe he forgot.

In any event, there are countless ways to have made the project called "Get Jim some drugs" more efficent. Off the top of my head:

- Have a volunteer take him yesterday to the 24 hour pharmacy and pay for his drugs.

- Have a $5 CVS giftcard in my pocket

- Agree to meet him this morning at the shelter and take him to the pharmacy.

- Develop a prescription drug program.

- etc.

Any of those would have been more efficent and, in fact, more effective at the project called "Get Jim his drugs".

But that is not the project I am working on.

Instead, I am part of a project that could be called "Let's Get to Know Jim". And all relationships involve deliberate inefficency.

When you meet a friend for lunch, you do not go to the place that promises you the most efficent souce of high quality calories—instead you go to the place that makes hanging out with your friend the easiest. Things like quality of food, how fast the kitchen is and even cost take a back seat to things that make it easier to spend time with your friend. You are not working on the project called "Get Maximum Calories at the Best Price". You are woking on a project called "Hang out with Mike over Food".

So, the project called "Get to Know Jim" took a hit this morning. It cost me a half an hour in the cold and fleeting frustration. And occasionally, on days like this, I am reminded why the projects other people are working on are the ones they are working on—because the relational way is hard and inefficent.

That does not mean it is wrong, however.

What We Mean When We Talk About The Homeless

"I don't know how to talk to the homeless."

About once a week, some well meaning church person will tell me this. It is usually after they read something I wrote or heard me speak about how the problem of homelessness is, at it's core, a relationship problem.

Sigh.

Well, we can start by not talking about "the homeless". To me, "homeless" is a class descriptor is an othering term. It presupposes the idea of the other, that somehow, the person who is homeless is different from you.

For example, if I asked you for advice on how to talk to "the blacks", you would be aghast. You would (hopefully) patiently sit me down and explain to me that you talk to black people the same way you talk to white people—that we are the same sort of people.

The reason we talk about "the homeless" as if they are a different sort of creature than we are and we treat them as if they are a different sort of creature than we are is because, well, we believe they are a different sort of creature than we are.

But, if we are people of faith, we have a problem. Because the biblical story won't support that notion. The Jesus story tells us that love of our neighbor is the equivalent of our love for God, and in the story of the Good Samaratin, Jesus defines our neighbor as anyone who is in need, regardless of the social boundries that divide us.

We are the ones who need saving. And until we see that our concern for the "homeless" is as much about us and our need to be liberated from our privilege as it is them and their need to be liberated from their oppression, we won't get anywhere at all.

How To Not Be Taken Advantage of By Panhandlers

The number one question I get asked by well meaning Christian folks who want to "help the homeless" always centers around panhandlers and being "taken advantage of". I will tell you how to avaid being taken advantage of by homeless and panhandlers. In fact, how to quit being taken advantage of by anyone.

You ready?

Give up ownership of what you are giving away.

If I give you a sweater for Christmas, and you take and swap it for a toaster, did you take advantage of me? No, because when I gave it to you, I gave up ownership of the sweater.

If I give you money for your birthday, and you buy video games with it, even though you need a new shirt, you did not take advantage of me, even if you did make poor choices.

Likewise, if you give a panhandler a $10 bill, and he buys a beer with it, he did not take advantage of you. He took the gift you gave him and exercised his free will to buy what he wanted to buy with your gift.

When you gave it away, you gave up ownership. At that point, the only way you can be taken advantage of is if you somehow feel that you still have rights over that money. Which means that you think you have rights over the person spending the money.

Which, quite frankly, says a lot about you.

Look, I am not saying you should necessarily give panhandlers money. In fact, I talk a lot about this issue here and here. But I am saying that much of what passes for concern about the wellbeing of the panhandler is in fact our own issues of control.

Dave and Communion

The first time Dave came to chapel, he was pretty tentative.

Frank, a regular attendee, had pretty much drug him there, and Dave was looking a lot like someone who had been drug there.

He was fine before the service started, but when the prelude music started, he bolted for the door and sat outside, chain smoking cigarettes. Frank offered up Dave during prayer request time, saying Dave had a long history of drug abuse, and that while he is sober now, his family had pretty much disowned him. And because his family is heavily involved in the church, Dave does not do church well.

When Frank said that Dave did not do church well, there were three or four "Me eithers!" shouted from the rest of the congregation. One of them may have been me.

In any event, after the benediction, Dave wandered back in and joined us for the potluck dinner we had scheduled for that day.

I figured we would never see him again.

The next week, in come Frank and Dave, five minutes before the service starts. Dave sits down, opens a hymnal and manages to stick with us through the first song, at which point he heads for the door and chain smokes the rest of the service.

The following week, Dave makes it until after prayers of the people, but when I start in on the ancient words of institution that begin communion ("On the night he was arrested, the Lord Jesus took the bread..."), Dave is gone.

The fourth week, he sits all the way through the words of institution. Then I say what I always say:

> There are a lot of different theories in the church about who is allowed to take part in communion. But here, we take the position that this table isn't my table, or even the church's table, but that this table belongs to Jesus. And at Jesus' table, everyone gets to eat.
>
> So here, we don't care what you have done, or what your past is like, or if you've been baptized or not. All that matters here is that you want to eat at Jesus' table. If you do, then you can take communion with us.

The line forms in the middle, and one by one, folks line up to accept the bread and dip it in the cup. Dave is the last in line.

"Can I really take communion?," he whispers as he approaches me.

"Of course," I say, as I hand him the bread.

Dave takes it and dips it in the cup, smacking his lips as he devours the juice soaked bread. Then he wanders back to his seat and weeps silently as I pronounce the benediction. And before we're done saying amen, Dave is out the door.

On Monday, Dave pops by the office.

"You know what I did last night," he asks. "I wrote my mom."

"Really? How long has it been since you talked to her?," I ask.

"A long time. Maybe 20 years. Anyway, I told her that for the first time in years and years, I had been to a church and had taken communion. I thought she would want to know."

I bet she did. And I thought you might want to know, too.

The Gift of Tears

Several years ago, I was speaking at an event. It was a large secular audience, so I gave my mostly secular talk. In that talk, I mentioned I run a faith based organization. I also used the example of gay marriage as a way that relationships change how we feel about "the other". That is really all I said about gay marriage, or homosexuality or really, anything about my own faith.

When I got finished with my talk, I made a beeline for the bathroom (nerves, you know). I'm standing at the sink, washing my hands when a guy walks in. He stands just inside the door and looks at me for a few long seconds, making me a bit uncomfortable. Finally, he walks over to me.

"Are you gay?," he asks.

I tell him I'm not.

"But gay homeless people—you help them, right?"

I tell him I do.

"And you're a Christian, right?"

"Right."

He looks me dead in the eye and says, "I did not know you could be Christian and help gay people."

Over the next few minutes, standing in that bathroom, he tells me how his family has ostracized him because he came out to them. How they are very religious and because of them, he no longer wants anything to do with the church.

"I hate the church. After everything they have done to me and my friends, I can't stand their hypocrisy and their self-righteous attitude."

I told him I did not blame him a bit. He asked if he could hug me. I said yes.

In that bathroom, with tears in both our eyes, he hugs me and says thank you for being willing to help everybody, including gay people. He turns and walks for the door.

Hand on the door, he turns back and says "You know, it's strange. I hate the church. You can't pay me to go back there. But I really miss Jesus."

Then he turned, pushed through the door and was gone.

I think about that guy a lot. When I catch flack for helping and loving everyone without preconditions, I remember him and the gift of his tears drying on my shirt as I walked out of that bathroom. And I remember that while he hated the church, he missed Jesus.

The Sounds of Silence

Today, people died at the finish line of the Boston Marathon when two explosions went off.

I was sitting at my desk when the news came in, a steady stream of links from my various social media contacts. As the total of people affected by the carnage rose, I felt bile rising in my throat, finally erupting as tears as I sat and wept.

After years of working in the inner-city, pretty much nothing shocks me anymore—except the things we humans do to each other. There are no classes you can take to prepare for this, no magic words your minister can utter (which is doubly sad when you ARE the minister), no making sense of the horror that people are dead because of sudden, planned violence.

The social web is buzzing with commentary and analysis – folks trying to shed some light, to uncover some meaning.

There is no meaning to be had. There is no light, except that we bring with us.

On days like this, the only wise thing to say is nothing, which is often a good thing to say, and sometimes a good thing to do.

And mourn in the sounds of silence.

Do I Deny the Resurrection?

Occasionally I get emails demanding to know my stance on a particular piece of "historic orthodoxy". People wonder about my view of hell, or who I think Jesus was or if I think there will be a second coming. Because of the controversy over Rob Bell's book (which happens to have the same name as our ministry, Love Wins), this has only increased.

To tell you the truth, I think it is a bit funny. After all, I run a ministry for homeless people. Perhaps it would be more appropriate to ask my views on homelessness? But I digress...

So, to answer the title of this entry—do I deny the resurrection of Christ?

I can do no better than to quote Peter Rollins on the subject.

> Without equivocation or hesitation I fully and completely admit that I deny the resurrection of Christ. This is something that anyone who knows me could tell you, and I am not afraid to say it publicly, no matter what some people may think...
>
> I deny the resurrection of Christ every time I do not serve at the feet of the oppressed, each day that I turn my back on the poor; I deny the resurrection of Christ when I close my ears to the cries of the downtrodden and lend my support to an unjust and corrupt system.
>
> However there are moments when I affirm that resurrection, few and far between as they are. I affirm it when I stand up for those who are forced to live on their knees, when I speak for those who have had their tongues torn out, when I cry for those who have no more tears left to shed.

As you might expect, this does not calm the questioners down. They accuse me of not understanding the question. I understand the question perfectly well. I think they are the ones who do not know what they are asking.

So let me be even more clear:

The ancient story is that the most powerful government the world had ever known, Rome, had done the worst thing it could imagine to this man, Jesus. They beat him and killed him by the most brutal means at their disposal. Yet and still, the last words on his lips are reported to be his asking God to forgive his killers. On that Friday, the powers of the world said "No" to Jesus and the Kingdom of God he was preaching. If the tomb was empty on that Sunday morning long ago, that was God's "Yes" to Rome's "No". If the tomb was empty, then love overcame power and vindicated Jesus. It means that Jesus was right—the Kingdom of God is at hand, and we are invited to live in it.

If I swear allegiance to this Kingdom, where apparently the dream of God is that it be on Earth as it is in Heaven, then that has implications for how I live. If I pledge allegiance to the USA, it means I should not sell secrets to China. If I pledge allegiance to the Kingdom of God, then I cannot see how I can lend aid and support to the powers that oppose it, such as consumerism, militarism, class disparity and xenophobia.

If I act hateful, or in fact, less than loving to my neighbor, I have denied the resurrection just as surely as my selling state secrets to China denies my allegiance to the USA. I can wave a flag all day, but if I am acting against my country, you can hardly call me a patriot. And I can believe whatever you want about what happened that Sunday morning, but if I am not using what power I have to help God bring the Kingdom into fruition, to help make it on Earth as it is in Heaven, I don't expect you to call me a Christian.

What I Believe

I get emails questioning my orthodoxy all the time. For example, about a year ago, I was asked if I denied the resurrection of Jesus, and I replied. I have learned, however, that answering critiques does nothing to calm them down. Witness, for example, the comments on that post.

Lately, the emails have started back. Do I believe this, or that or the other thing. Virgin birth, historical resurrection, Genesis 1, the book of Job.

Sigh.

So, let's try this again. Here is what I believe...today.

I believe:

- That action is to belief as 19 is to 1.

- That faith without deeds is not faith at all, but superstition.

- That people are worth fighting for.

- That the problems of the world are, at their core, relationship problems.

- That when people ask "What can we do to end homelessness," what they really mean is, "What can we do to end homelessness and not change anything about us."

- That you can replace the word homelessness in the previous sentence with almost anything and the statement will still be true.

- That when you ask for help and people say, "I will pray about that", you had better start looking for Plan B.

- That it is not we who wait on God to act, but it is God who waits on us.

- That no one is going to care about your dream as much as you do. This does not prevent them from having opinions as to how you are doing it wrong, however.

- That folks who ignore you in your struggles will flock to you when you are successful. And then they will be hurt when you question their sincerity.

- That to follow the Jesus path will look like failure to the world that watches you.

- That, when measured in terms of impact on the world around them, the average church is indistinguishable from the average book club.

- That a lot of church people will be pissed off at that last statement.

- That some of them will be pissed off that I said "pissed off", and wish I would just talk about hell or something.

- That people who love that I fight for the rights of homeless people but wish I would shut up about the rights of women or the LGBT community do not understand either me or my work.

- That atheists contribute more financially to my work than do Evangelicals. (Actually, this is a fact.)

- That to ask whether evangelism or social justice is more important is the same as asking whether it is more important to send doctors to medical school or to heal people.

- That when there are two people groups, and one people group has more of something—power, money, privilege, resources, etc.—the onus for changing that discrepancy lies on the group with more, and to do less than that is less than Christian.

- That Jeremiah probably did not get invited to a lot of parties, either.

- That most Christians are indistinguishable from the culture around them.

- That I take anti-abortion people much more seriously when they have adopted a couple of kids.

- That the best critique of the bad is the performance of the good. As a result of this, I believe that if you want to know what I believe, you probably ought to just watch what I do.

Sexual Assault, Cold Nights and God's Plan

At 23, most people her age are very conscious of their appearance, but Stephanie's wardrobe consisted of thrift store finds and cast offs, leaning heavily toward stretch pants and sweatshirts that advertised events she had never seen and places she would never visit. She was a heavy girl, perhaps 250 pounds and her greasy, stringy hair only served to accentuate her poor skin. Because of her weight, she more shuffled than walked and her head was always bowed, seeking not to offend, avoiding eye contact.

The first time I met her, she was in line for food in the park. She shuffled along, mumbling thanks, eyes on the ground. Over the following months, I tried to engage her but whether it was my being a male, or her inner demons, it just was not happening. Like a dog that had been struck once too often, she flinched at contact.

When there was an open bed, Stephanie would stay at the woman's shelter, but more often than not she had to make other arrangements. On cold nights, she would trade sexual favors in exchange for a warm bed. To pick up spending money, she would trade sex for money—very little money.

Because of her weight and mental issues, often the promise of a warm bed was revoked, or the money not paid after the oral sex had been given. Several people later told me Stephanie was often sexually assaulted and raped, unable to resist her attackers.

The last time I saw her was on a Thursday in early November. It was inordinately cold that day, with a sharp, piercing wind. Stephanie shuffled down the sidewalk, huddled down into her jacket, oblivious to my wave, ignoring me when I called.

Stephanie made it into the women's shelter that night. There she could sleep; secure in the knowledge she was safe. In her sleep, Stephanie died of complications from sleep apnea. At age 23, she was another statistic of life, and death, on the streets.

I told Stephanie's story in a talk I gave at a church luncheon. When I finished, they prayed fervent prayers that Stephanie would be at peace in the loving arms of Jesus. They prayed that those who injure and molest women like Stephanie would be caught and punished. They prayed for God's kingdom to come and for shalom to rest on our city.

At the end of the talk, a lady came up to me, obviously moved by my story. Then she asked me the question I dread most: "How could God allow this to happen to Stephanie? Was this all part of God's plan?"

If you spend much time working in the inner-city, you try not to ask yourself that question—not because you don't know what the answer is, but because you do. And if you tell people the answer to that question, they get mad at you, and they call you names, and they don't invite you back.

What I wanted to tell that lady, but did not, was God did have a plan to take care of Stephanie; God's plan was us.

I wanted to tell her that it is not we who are waiting on God to act, but rather it is God who is waiting on us. I wanted to tell her that what Stephanie really had needed was not this lady's prayers but a safe place to sleep at night. What I wanted to tell that lady, but didn't, is that it is very obvious that we have the resources to help invisible people just like Stephanie but we simply lack the will to do so.

I did not tell that church lady any of that. But I wish I had.

The Small Stuff

Last Saturday, I was in Moore Square when William ran up to me. I have seen William around our hospitality house at 707 West Jones a few times, but he tends to keep to himself. He would make himself some coffee, or maybe grab some cookies and to the chapel and just sit. Occasionally, he would doze off.

"Man, I am glad to see you," he tells me. I brace myself for the bus pass or lift somewhere I am almost certain he is about to ask for. He surprises me.

He tells me how, over a year ago, he lost his construction job in a round of cutbacks. There was a little unemployment money, but when that played out, he lost his apartment. The next six months were a blur of friends' couches, periodic stays at the shelter, and more than a few nights on the street.

And then the depression came.

"I just could not get 'with it', you know?"

I assured him that, as someone who struggles with depression, I do get it.

He continues, "So, I came around Love Wins. And I would go to the labor pool in the morning, and not get sent out. And I would be all down, and then I would come to Love Wins, and I would feel better."

"But last week, man, last week was the worst. I didn't get sent out for days. I was really thinking about killing myself. I just felt like I couldn't go on."

"So, Thursday, I didn't go to the labor pool. I just came to Love Wins, and I sat in the chapel and prayed. I prayed hard. And then I would rest, and then I would pray again. And I decided I wasn't ready to quit."

"So Friday, I went back to the labor pool, and they set me up with a six month ticket! I am working for the next six months!"

He then practically knocks me down with a bear hug that came out of nowhere.

"Man, I don't know what I would have done all those days if I couldn't have come to Love Wins. You guys saved my life!"

We all want to do something big to change the world, when sometimes what is really needed is a warm cup of coffee and a quiet place to sit.

A lot of our work is small stuff—stuff like making sure the coffee pot is full, or that there is enough bread, or that the toiletry bins are full in the bathroom. Not sexy at all.

But because all those things happened, William had a place to go when he wanted to end it all. And he felt loved enough to face another day. And none of that was small to William.

The longer I do this, the more I am in awe that I get to do this.

Clothe Yourself in Righteousness (But First, Get Naked!)
by Magdelene Harrison

Editor's Note

The church frets extensively about "losing the young people". The response is often to look at new styles of worship, new programs, and alternative approaches to fellowship. Among the "young people", there is a general consensus that it is preferable to be "spiritual, but not religious", and that the church does not have much to offer except an expectation to tithe and petty church politics. This is not helped by church apologists, who tend to miss the point that being in community is not its own sales pitch.[1]

In light of that conversation, I am including this essay from Magdalene Harrison. Magdalene is a product of a kind of "spiritual but not religious" upbringing. As she recounts it, she was not so much raised in a religious tradition as trained in comparative religions. Thoughtful, deep, loving, and spiritual, she has everything a child in that upbringing might need, yet she finds value in exploring her tradition and laments how such a broad upbringing makes it hard to find depth. In a single essay, she both revives a long-dormant symbol within Quakerism as well as makes the case for tradition in a postmodern world.

---

[1] Take Rachel Held Evans, writing for CNN's "Belief" blog on August 2nd, 2013: "And in a world where technology enables millennials to connect only with those who are like-minded, baptism drags us—sometimes kicking and screaming as infants—into the large, dysfunctional and beautiful family of the church." That's not exactly an enticing or even positive description for those who find dealing with people—including oft-dysfunctional and incomprehensibly different others—to be a hassle.

Introduction

It's a bright spring day, full of promise and new cherry blossoms budding on the trees lining the curbs and sidewalks of my neighborhood in West Philadelphia. It's the kind of day in which seemingly everyone is inspired to go outside. The streets swell with all manner of people—walking to the farmers' market, riding their bikes to the park, playing with their children at the playground, eating at the many restaurants lining the avenue. On a day like this, I know I can't go more than a few steps without seeing the familiar faces of acquaintances and close friends alike—not to mention my Quaker community and a number of my spiritual elders. But on this particular day, when everyone practically glows with satisfaction, I'm distracted by feelings of dread. My stomach feels like it's dropped out of me, and my arms are shaking slightly from adrenaline. I can't quite tell, but I think I might want to die. However, I press on. It's time. I walk down the two flights of stairs to my front porch on the busy corner of 47th and Baltimore Ave. Standing on that porch, on the edge of throwing up or passing out, I take a deep breath. In. Then out. Again: in. Then out. As I breathe, I feel myself reach out to God, asking her to be with me, to help me feel her presence. In. Then out again.

Now I imagine that I am inhaling the peace and power that comes with that Presence, closer than our breath. In. Then out again. Now I start to feel light and can see the sunshine as if for the first time today. I'm calm. I breathe in. I exhale. Slowly, I step down to the sidewalk, surrounded by people. Then, I let my bathrobe fall until my skin feels the air and the eyes of all the people in the street. I am standing completely naked.

But I'm calm.

Chapter 1

The Importance of Symbols

Would you do this if the Spirit wanted it of you?

Although I have never actually gone out in my neighborhood in the nude, I like to believe that I would if I were led,[1] just like the early Friends who at times went naked in public.

...

...

(Just wanted to let that sink in for a minute in case this is the first time you've heard this.)

Yes, the early Friends went nude in public. They called this act "going naked as a sign," which was never done for enjoyment (as you might have done at Quaker camp when you were a kid). We have to imagine that as embarrassing and awkward, and even terrifying as it might feel to go naked in the streets of Philly, it would be a pittance compared to what a 17th Century Friend would have felt. In public, they did not even regularly bare their *arms* regularly, much less their arses! Nakedness was so supremely scandalous in the presiding culture that going naked as a sign was a radical exploit, enacted out of deep faith and trust in the communal sense of God's will. When is the last time you or I did anything as personally challenging out of faithfulness to Spirit?

This deeply transformative and empowering faith of those early nude-y Friends intrigues for just that reason. I don't just want to tell myself that I would carry out a leading as ground shaking as they did; I want to *know* that I would, with all the certainty of a Friend that has been completely transformed by my relationship to the Divine. However, when I look closely at myself, I am not convinced that my faith is as strong as the Quakers that came before me. This troubles me deeply. I know it troubles others too—but to our credit, not only do many of us find this troubling, many of us also mourn our own personal deprivation of this the earth-shaking (earth-quaking?) spirituality that is so glaringly absent from the lives of most modern Friends. We know what we are missing, and we are hungry for it. I believe this is an excellent place to begin. It is the place I find myself continuously returning.

But how to go a step further, beyond the hungering? Many of us have had conversations about the troubles of being a Quaker these days—we little guidance in finding our way on the spiritual path and no language to conceptualize the inner transformation that we have been taught to expect of ourselves. We have to look to other places, like Buddhism or modern psychology, for a coherent description

---

[1] When Quakers talk about "leadings" or "being led", we mean to imply that we believe God is guiding us to some action.

of the inner-life. For example, have you ever used the word "ego" when describing an inward process? I know I do all the time. But this word is not from the religious tradition of which I was Convinced.[1] As a high school senior, I chose to "get married" to Quakerism, with the belief that if I went deep with it even through challenging times then it would take me to places I could never get to by "dating around" with a multitude of faiths. This vow inspired me to not give up on our tradition, thinking, "Ah, I'll never find enough here.", but rather to maintain fidelity, pursuing my theory that with some archeological digging, I could find some of the precious tools we've lost. That's what this writing is all about—here is the result of my archeological exploits, and the very exciting tool I found, namely, the symbol of Nakedness.

As a modern Liberal Friend (raised by a Quaker father and a Mystical ex-Catholic mother), I will be forever grateful that religious creeds and spiritual practices were never shoved down my throat. At the age of seven, my meeting (an upper-middle class suburban N.P.R. meeting of the first order[2]) trusted in my own wisdom enough to not answer my questions with indoctrinating dogma, but to instead ask me, "What canst thou say?" This taught me to trust my own discernment, my own inward guide, something that most seven-year-olds are discouraged from doing, which shaped me in what I like to think of as positive ways. However, Friends are starting to see that this policy of guiding through non-guidance has also done a great deal of damage to us, both individually and as a community.

Individually, our dogmatic non-guidance leaves it to each Friend to reinvent the proverbial wheel of spirituality alone. Perhaps this begins to explain why we lose many Friends as they grow up. After all, it doesn't matter whether or not they hang around with Quakers because they'd have to make up their own beliefs and spiritual practices either way, right? As I see it, our current modes of sharing our religion and spirituality ensures that the only people who stick with the Society are the extremely desperate,[3] the extremely creative,[4] the extremely lucky,[5] and the extremely ambivalent.[6] Okay, so there are others, too, like the optimists, the nostalgics, blessedly naïve, and so on...I have probably still left some people out, and have painted a bit of a bleak picture, but I am not here to be another fellow back-patter. The picture is actually bleak; for, as far as my studies have shown me, there is nothing Quakerly about contenting ourselves with business as usual.

---

[1] The Quaker lingo for conversion is "convincement".   [2] The definition of an "N.P.R. meeting", more or less approved by an un-minuted consensus of N.E. Liberal Friends, is a monthly meeting in which National Public Radio is referenced in worship at least as often as Jesus, and probably more so.   [3] "Desperate" (like myself), as in, they are so desperate to understand something about Quakerism that they will probably end up dedicating a lot of their life and enormous sums of debt studying the religion that was intentionally kept from them over the course of their 10 years of Sunday School. (Sound familiar? Or am I projecting?)   [4] "Creative" as in the kids who are creative enough to invent their own practices and interpretations of how to *do* Quakerism, leaving them satisfied enough to continue onward, attending when it suits them.   [5] "Lucky" meaning the kids who are lucky enough to have been nurtured by an elder on the sly or a fabulous spiritual camp community, such that they have tasted enough of the fruits of the faith that they know they are in the right place.   [6] "Ambivalent" as in, ambivalent enough about their spiritual lives and/or religion in general that they are glad there is not clarity around worship, tradition, practice, and so on and thus are comfortable with business as usual.

We profess to be Friends of God: to stand in the Light together, to be a beacon on the hill, a fellowship of disciples, to live the gospel order. If we truly want this, as we profess to, then we are not doing enough.

The modern inability to communicate central aspects of our spiritual communities reinforces an isolation that seems antithetical to a religion centered on communal experience. My favorite example of this is our "fellowship" or coffee hour where we usually mill around and follow up on committee business or make small talk about anything but our spiritual lives. In part, I guess this is because it can feel awkard to be so vulnerable with one another, but in large part it is also because we barely know how to talk about such things. But, as we have learned from experience, if we never talk about the inward life, it is difficult to develop it. Without any concept of what is possible for a life of faith, can we imagine it? Without any forewarning of the perils of following Spirit, will we be prepared? Without any open acknowledgement of our most transformative inward experiences, can we really know one another? this type of information—the spiritual wisdom and experience of those around us—is critical to our ability to foster and endure the spiritual experiences that formulate powerful faith in one another and ourselves.

A central aspect of this problem with communication is a shortage of commonly shared spiritual tools—as in language, metaphor, and symbol. Surprising as it may be, early Friends had no shortage of symbols and metaphors that they used in their religious and spiritual lives. Were they decorations for the meetinghouses? No, but they were symbols nonetheless. In fact, our forebears were wholly immersed in a rich symbolic universe that they all shared, enabling them to establish a unified conceptualization of such things as their relationship to the Divine, the challenges and rewards of coming into intimate communion with God, the nature of humans, and so on.[1]

At the 2008 Young Adult Friends gathering at Earlham College, I had the good fortune to attend a workshop lead by Michael Birkel about the letters written between early Friends. What I remember most clearly was a letter written by Margaret Fell, which to my Bible-ignorant mind, appeared to be nothing more than a poetic letter with lots of lovely imagery. Then, to my great surprise, Michael showed us how each line, every image, was actually a reference to a particular biblical passage, and thus every line not only had its basic meaning in the context of the letter, but another layer of significance stemming from its biblical context. Incredibly, Fell could assume that her reader would understand the multi-layered significance of her words and images. What's more, this was par for the course in early Quaker communications.

The symbolic universe of the early Friends was almost entirely drawn from the Bible. When I say "universe", I mean that their minds were full of shared stories, images, words, and so on, which they used to understand and interpret their world such that they created a kind of universe of their own. We can also think of it as

---

[1] Steve Angell, my professor at Earlham School of Religion would probably curse the day he passed me in his class if I didn't clarify that actually, from year one, Quakers were never truly unified in their conceptualizations of such things, but rather were *more* unified in their conceptions than we are today.

a language. In his book on spirituality and language, Harvey Gillman confirms, "Sharing language is a part of belonging. We might say that each religion has its own language; even that each religion is a separate language...Christianity is a religious language in which certain truths are mediated to the world, through key stories, myths, concepts, images, and metaphors".[1] Likewise, Quakerism is also its own religious language in which we express our truths to one another through shared stories, words, symbols, metaphors, etc. Either way, scholars have found that, "a shared language and symbolism is known to promote connection, integration, and intelligibility" within communities.[2] Since Liberal Friends have all but done away with our traditional shared language, we mostly borrow from mainstream culture or other religions, which undercuts our connection, integration, and intelligibility.

Might an example help? I mentioned the term "ego" earlier. While there is nothing inherently wrong with using this term, consider the following scenario, in which many modern Liberal Friends have found themselves. You are talking to two other Friends about spirituality when one person uses the word ego, ostensibly referencing modern psychology. You respond by referencing a related practice you learned from Pema Chödrön, and the third person references some biblical story. Everyone wants to share their experience of relating to the divine, but you do not have a shared framework, and therefore cannot fluidly join one another in each other's processes. In order to do so, everyone would have to understand what you mean when you talk about your "shenpa", and you would have to learn what happens to Job, on top of reading Eckhart Tolle. That's a lot of hurdles for just one conversation, much less one of the most important conversations that can be had in a spiritual community! However, this kind of conversation has become so routine among Liberal Friends that we assume it is only a natural part of life, whereas in truth, it is a problem. Alternatively, if we had maintained some of our own particular language, how might this kind of conversation go differently? Might it lead our community to new and deeper places?

Now, beyond the issue of how shared language (or lack thereof) influences our ability to connect is this even more important consideration: the conceptual tools of language and symbols help us go places we could not get to without them. Heady stuff, right? Here, the influential 20th century theologian, Paul Tillich, can help. He argued that religious symbols, situated in their particular cultural context, open us to levels of spiritual depth and awareness that would be otherwise inaccessible.[3] Intuitively we know this; it is why many of us continue to seek such tools even when we do not find them in Quakerism. When we are so ignorant or afraid of traditional Quaker symbols that we are unable to utilize them, we reduce our ability to conceptualize our deepest experiences and in turn, our culture suffers the loss of both the symbols and the experiences.

One may wonder how I can claim that an experience might be lost, just because a word (or symbol) is.[4] Johann Goethe, a 19th century philosophical pioneer and early linguist, asserts that a religious symbol uses a particular form to illustrate a

[1] Page 50 of his book. See Works Cited.   [2] See Musser, page 490.   [3] See Musser, page 491.
[4] The works of Mircea Eliade and Michel Foucault come highly recommended when exploring the importance of symbol, metaphor, and language.

transcendent reality,[1] and, consequently, that transcendent reality becomes more concrete and accessible through its connection to the particular form. In other words, if we have language to describe a deep inward process, or a useful metaphor to represent that process, other people, who perhaps have never had that experience and never imagined it, can now conceptualize it in their minds. They can start to imagine what it might be like, prepare themselves for the process, or even actively cultivate the experience for themselves. On the contrary, if we have no clear ways to communicate such experiences (as in my hypothetical conversation above) then they are in effect less real for everyone, including the person who had the experience. This is where we find ourselves now.

Our Society is currently unable to speak coherently about our inward experiences of coming into intimate relationship with God. Early Friends did not have this problem. It is my sense that as our language regarding this pivotal inward experience became less and less clear, we gradually ceased to expect it of one another. Furthermore, even if Friends do still expect one another to be inwardly transformed by Spirit, we can hardly conceptualize what it is we are expecting, much less communicate about it. There are those of us who *do* want to experience an intimate and transformative union with God, but we have little guidance and no consistent manner with which to share our experimentation with others.

There are many ways one can go about solving this issue; my small way is to dig up some of the cool word-relics from our past. People talk about the "storehouse" of symbols. I imagine this as a kind of shed that every religion or culture has, full of all the metaphors they could ever want to use—metaphors that everyone is at least vaguely familiar with, which make sense in their cultural context. Having traipsed out into our proverbial backyard to check out our storehouse, I have to report that we have all but left it to rot, surrounded by the weeds of four hundred years of forgetting. The good news is that Friends used to have a huge number of symbols; there is a veritable two-car garage of a "storehouse". The other good news is that even if we forgot about all this stuff, it is still ours; all we have to do is dust it off and reclaim it.

---

[1] See Musser, page 490

Chapter 2

Naked with Friends

Of the symbols and metaphors I found while poking around back there, I've been most taken with the symbol of Nakedness.[1] This is not just because I think it's funny or fascinating (although I do think it is), but because it is particularly useful—we are in dire need of it. However, in her book, *The History and Significance of Quaker Symbols in Sect Formation*, Kathleen Thomas found that "Quaker phraseology today reveals no instances of 'naked' or 'covering' as metaphors"[2] even though Nakedness appears to have been an especially important and potent symbol for early Friends.

Consider the many symbolic acts various Friends were led to do as a message to the wider society: refusing to doff hats, wearing plain dress, wearing plain dress, wearing undyed clothes, riding a donkey into town, making shoes in a pulpit, burning instruments in a square, and so on.[3] Although many of these acts made Friends targets of real physical danger, sometimes leading to death, it is unlikely that any made the actor as vulnerable or humbled (read: humiliated) as going naked as a sign, and yet many Friends did it anyway.

As no scholar of the public perception of nudity in seventeenth century England or Colonial America, I cannot claim to know the true significance of publicly flaunting oneself in the nude, but the normative clothing (which left a *lot* to the imagination), the scandal caused by the nakedness, and the fact that public nudity seems to have been preserved for purposes of punishment[4] all lead me to the conclusion that getting down to one's skivvies was a greater personal trial

---

[1] I capitalize Nakedness for two reasons: first, I read so many Quaker tracts from the 1600s, in which every key word is capitalized, that I lost track of whether or not this is okay for contemporary writing; the second reason is that I want to differentiate "Nakedness" the religious symbol from normal nakedness, in the same tradition of capitalizing "Truth" when we mean it in the deeper, godly sense.   [2] Page 151.   [3] Quaker spoken word poet and musician, Jon Watts, is a great resource for these stories.   [4] Such as when men and women alike were stripped down and publically whipped. Ironically, I have come across a few accounts in which a Friend went naked as a sign and it was so upsetting to the public that they took them into custody, tried them for their "crime", and then, as punishment publically *stripped them*, tied them up, and whipped them, such as the case with Lydia Wardel around 1665 in the American Colonies, as recorded in Joseph Besse's *Collection of the sufferings of the people called Quakers.* After being tried for going naked as a sign, "the poor young Woman was stript, and tied with her naked Breasts against the Splinters of the Posts, and sorely lashed with twenty or thirty cruel Stripes" (page 232). A bit of a mixed message, eh?

than, say, keeping on one's hat. But let's not take my word for it when we have first hand accounts of "going naked as a sign".[1]

Imagine: one morning in 1672, Robert Barclay awakes (probably dressed in silly ruffley white PJs) and instead of lying around in bed thinking about whether or not the dog needs to go out, or if he needs to take the kids to school, he gets a leading. It's the kind that seems to come out of nowhere and implants itself in your mind like a ferociously invasive weed. This morning's leading? To go naked in the street as a sign to the people. The leading was agony to old Bob. But, like any good Friend, he brought it to his community for help in discernment and in the end, surrendered to it. He explains:

> The *Command* of the *Lord* concerning this thing came unto me that very *Morning* as I awakened, and the *Burden* thereof was very *Great;* yea, seemed almost insupportable unto me (for such a thing, until that very moment, had never entered me before, not in the most remote Consideration). And some, whom I called to declare to them this thing, can bear witness how great was the *Agony* of my *Spirit,* how I besought the *Lord* with *tears,* that this *Cup* might *pass away* from me! And this was the end, to call you to *Repentance* by this *signal* and *singular Step,* which I as to my own Will and Inclination, was as *unwilling* to be found in, as the *worst* and the *wickedest* of you can be averse from receiving, or laying it to heart.

What he is trying to say here is that this leading was god-awful: he was no more comfortable with it than anyone else might be. Yet his faith was steadfast, so he did it anyway.

Our next account is from Solomon Eccles, who earned some notoriety (and brutal punishment) by performing various extreme symbolic acts. In his awesomely titled tract, *Signs are from the Lord to a People or Nation, to forewarn them of some eminent Judgment near at hand,* he states, "I can truly say this, That I have strove much, and besought the Lord, that this going naked might be taken from me, before I ever went a Sign at all; but the weight lay upon me still, and...I had given up to go and was obedient." Thus, we see that even one of the most extreme early Friends shared Barclay's reticence. By most accounts, the Friends who received these leadings felt strong personal resistance, and it is often noted that such immodest behavior was contrary to their nature. The most remarkable part: they did it anyway.

Regardless of how uncomfortable it was for Friends to go naked as a sign, many heard the call to do so. Although there are no conclusions as to the exact number of Quakers who bore the burden of this leading, it was recorded as happening on

---

[1] It should be noted the "going naked as a sign" included many levels of nudity, such as wearing nothing but sackcloth. These days, we might think that sackcloth is an entirely different situation from bearing a birthday suit, but Richard Baumen, in *Let Your Words Be Few,* describes that going naked as a sign "involved appearing in a public place—the streets or market of a town, or a religious gathering—unclothed, though it is not always clear just how unclothed; some were stark naked, some wore modest coverings about their loins, others wore certain essential undergarments or sackcloth; but by the standards of the period all were naked." (page 88)

both sides of the Atlantic, over a few decades and beginning earlier than 1652.[1] As has already been noted, both men and women went naked, which strikes me as surprising for the times. The sign was enacted in churches, markets, town squares, the homes of priests and important men, Westminster Hall, courts, seminaries, and so on:[2] basically, anywhere people were deemed to be acting out of harmony with God.

Apparently Quakers going naked as a sign became so common (or at least infamous) that in 1661, a man named William Lowther wrote to the Secretary of State claiming, "In all the great towns, Quakers go naked on market-days through the town"[3] and later one scholar went so far as to say, "[t]here seemed to be a general emulation as to who should outstrip the rest,—and many persons went about the streets of London in all the nudity of nature."[4] It's a wonder we never learned about this in First Day School(!), especially considering that this was not just a group of rogue Friends, unchecked by their community. Rather, going naked as a sign was a widely discussed phenomenon that was acknowledged by Quaker leaders, who were even known to defend it, since the act was regularly attacked by critics of this new sect. Records of these defenses or "apologies" were written by Friends such as William Penn, Robert Barclay, George Fox, and Thomas Story.[5]

An antiquated history book describes Story as "an English Friend who had travelled in America. He seems to have been a moderate man, and to have condemned some of the extravagances of the Ranters..."[6] In other words, he wasn't full of malarkey (as my pops would say). It is on record that one time a "strict and rich Presbyterian" began to condemn the Quaker acts of nakedness, attempting to find a sympathetic listener in Story. To his surprise, Story responded with such a compelling and articulate defense of going naked as a sign, it deserves to be quoted at length:

> I answered, that whatever God had, at any time heretofore, thought fit to command in particular cases, is consistent with him still; and we read in the Holy Scripture, that the Lord commanded *Isaiah,* that great and evangelical Prophet, to *go and loose the sackcloth from off his loins, and put off his shoe from his foot; and he did so, walking naked and barefoot. And the Lord said, Like as my servant Isaiah hath walked naked and barefoot three years, for a sign and wonder upon Egypt and upon Ethiopia, &c.* Now, though this nakedness was to be a sign of shame unto the unhappy subjects of the judgments denounced, it was not inconsistent with the Lord to command the sign; nor is nakedness any indecency in his sight, since every creature comes naked from his all-creating Hand: It follows, then, that it is possible some of the Quakers, and rational religious men too, as that Prophet was, might be commanded of God to such actions, and to a good end also, riz. To rouse the people of this nation out of their deep lethargy and self-security, into a consideration of their various

---

[1] See Thomas, page 48.   [2] See Dixon.   [3] Quoted in Penney.   [4] See Dixon.   [5] You may have never heard of Thomas Story, but apparently he was in cahoots with some of our favorite early Friends and well respected among them.   [6] See Higginson.

empty forms of religion, which they severally exercised, without the life of religion (divine love and charity one toward another), too much a Stranger, at this day, among all sects and names. And thou canst not therefore make appear, that those Quakers were not commanded of God to do as they did in that case.[1]

We can imagine that if Thomas Story, as characterized above, stood behind these words, then many others in the society who did not go naked also accepted the sign and, citing biblical precedence, believed it was inspired by Spirit. Because early Friends saw themselves as part of a community of disciples, it was understood that anything God asked of a prophet previously may also be asked of them, and furthermore, the biblical significance of the sign was relevant to their own time.

An especially noteworthy example of how Quakers related to the prophets was the life of William Sympson, who started as an average guy but took on an extensively radical witness. In regard to going naked, George Fox described Sympson as the type of person "who never did these things himself".[2] Nevertheless, eventually Sympson became "something of a specialist at going naked"[3] after being led—in the manner of Isaiah—to go naked as a sign for three years all around England. Fox later testified:

He was obedient unto the heavenly command, and often ventured his *Life* and it was *given up:* who many times did receive *many stripes upon his naked body* with Thorn Bushes, so that when his *service was done,* Friends were forced to pluck the Thorns out of his flesh: But he was carried over all by the *mighty power of God.*[4]

Can you imagine? Going naked as a sign for three years!? And in blustery ole' England? Going back to my original question, is your or my faith so fired up with the power of Spirit that you or I could do something like this?

Whatever your answer, it is apparent that these folks had something to say and were not afraid to say it, but what was the message exactly? Wool is scratchy? Corsets are constricting? One scholar of Quaker symbols notes that the images of "'[n]aked' and 'covered' were used by [Friends] to describe both good and bad states".[5] For example, when Friends went naked their nudity could represent either the shameful state of lacking virtuous covering, such as Spirit's guidance, or the ideal state of having rid oneself of whatever separates one from the Truth.[6] Clothing then represented either that which obscured the truth, or the protection and power that God bestowed upon the faithful, which was thought to 'cover' them. Thus, going naked as a sign was meant to be a kind of radical eldering[7] for the viewers, calling their attention to their own need to be stript of the worldly and clothed with godly virtue.

When I first learned of this practice from Max Carter at Guilford College, he taught that the symbol fell out of fashion because this ambiguity of representing

---

[1] Quoted in Southey.   [2] Quoted in Dixon.   [3] See Bauman, page 89.   [4] Quoted in Penney.
[5] See Thomas, page 150.   [6] See Bauman, page 90.   [7] "Eldering" can be understood as the Quaker practice of holding others accountable to acting faithfully.

both desirable and undesirable states which hindered its effectiveness: the public didn't get it. It's likely that he's right in that onlookers would have been confused by the symbol's apparently contradictory meanings. But the early Friends' use of "Nakedness" in their communications reveals a fully developed sense of the symbol's meaning, complicated though it may have been, which leads me to believe that the act of going naked was much less ambiguous for them than for their non-Quaker audience.

There is a difference between Nakedness as a symbol and "going naked as a sign". The latter only corresponds to the symbolic act of literally going out in public *physically* undressed. Some scholars believe that this act was unpopular and of little import. On the contrary, the act is important because of the significance of *spiritual* Nakedness—the deeply transformative *inward* process of becoming spiritually Naked with God.

Now, I just spent a number of pages reviewing early Friends' use of Nakedness in terms of the public act. While this is good stuff and ripe for the imagining, going naked as a sign was actually a minor aspect of the Quaker use of the symbol. In fact, early Friends talked about nakedness a *lot*, even as a central theme in their writing. To give you an idea of its prevalence, consider that the *Digital Quaker Collection*[1] has over two hundred publications using the term "naked", a number of which include the phrase "Naked Truth". This phrase could refer to integrity (or conversely, deception) in day-to-day life, such as with conversation, preaching, business, or political dealings. However, even in these circumstances, the term "Naked Truth" usually pointed towards a deeper level of integrity or consistency with God's will. Then, as is still true, there was a difference between truthfulness or integrity in daily matters and living with integrity in regards to the bigger picture of what God intends for the world. For example, one could tell the "naked truth" by being honest about the worth of their goods, but this is small peanuts compared to living the "Naked Truth" by discerning how Spirit intends for one's own life to be an expression of the Kingdom of God. Quakers were pretty sure the latter of these two options was the more meritorious, ya heard?

Remember earlier, when we established that just about every symbol in the Quaker storehouse goes back to the Bible? So here's a little exercise: think of the Bible and think of Nakedness. One thing that comes to mind...? Bingo: Adam and Eve. Indeed, early Quaker writings seem to suggest that for them, the meaning of Nakedness went right back to the creation story: to the way that God made us and how we fell out of line with that original holy union of wills. Nakedness, being a central theme of Christianity's (and by extension Quakerism's) origin myth, can thus be understood as a charter symbol, or a symbol that helps define our reality, with fundamental implications about life and how to live it.

To get a sense of how the early Friends' perspective on Nakedness related to Adam and Eve, let's take a look at Creation and the Fall through the eyes of some of Quakerism's most honored: Isaac, George, and Margaret. Assuming we are familiar with the part where God makes humans and sees that they are good, Isaac Penington offers us a good place to jump in—the fall from that goodness. He

---

[1] Earlham College's online collection of transcribed works by early Friends.

explains that humans were created as good, but also with the "capacity" to make decisions without listening to God; i.e. we were given free will; "though [Adam] had no inclination in him not to depend [on God]...yet there was a capacity of so doing: before which capacity the tempter laid his bait". We all know that Adam and his pal Eve decided to take that bait, making their own decisions without consulting God. Fox describes the next part of their story in this way, "after man and woman had transgressed the command of God, and fallen from his image...the first covering which Adam and Eve made after transgression, was made of fig leaves... So here they came to see their outward shame and nakedness; who had fallen from the image of God that covered them; and therefore they went to cover the outward shame."[1] Ahh...so here is the origin of all this clothing and covering! Fox confirms that we only became aware and ashamed of our nakedness when we stepped out of line with God's will. Then, in a pitiful attempt to hide this mishap and protect ourselves from the scary feelings of shame, we began to clothe ourselves.

Penington relates how this choice felt for Adam and Eve. He claims, "Thus was [Adam] taken in the snare of misery, and brought to that loss which all the sons of Adam lie groveling under to this day, when the Lord at any time awakens the sense thereof in them." Thus, Adam and Eve userd their God-given free will to resist listening to God and the choice made them miserable. Early Friends maintained that this is still true, that we have the power to act out of line with God's will, but on a deep level we suffer for it, especially when it is brought to our attention.

At this point, it is important to note that neither Fox, nor Penington paint a picture of humans as inherently sinful, nor that it is *necessary* to hide from God. Margaret Fell even argues, "as the Apostle testifies, *1 John 3:* whosoever is born of God doth not commit sin, for his seed remaineth in him, and he cannot sin because he is born of God."[2] Thus, early Friends understood that our ability to act out of line with God (i.e. our free will) is still part of our goodness in the eyes of God, even though we mostly choose to feel bad about it. This unnecessary shame and fear then leads us to remove ourselves even further from God and the Gospel Order by hiding our Naked Truth, or our true selves, from everyone, including God. For example, every time we make some misstep and refuse to acknowledge it or get defensive, we are actively stepping away from faithfulness and the way of the inward Christ. We're hiding ourselves behind fig leaves. The problem is, all our bundling up does not actually ameliorate the problem. To do that, we'd have to start right where we were, face the fear and shame of admitting our missteps, strip away whatever we were using to avoid or obscure the bits of us we don't like, and in our nakedness invite God to cover us once more and thus return to our original state of unity.

This was something that Friends experienced in their own lives and also wanted to share with the wider society, though not always in the most inviting terms. In the following passage, Margaret Fell, who referred to nakedness quite a bit in her writing, calls others to join her in the process:

[1] See George Fox's *Works*, volume 8, pages 256 to 257. [2] See Margaret Fell's *The Standard of the Lord Revealed*, 75.

[C]ease from your abominations, and outward profession of forms and colors without the life and power and purity of truth itself, for...all your covers are too narrow; the woe from the living God is to them, and all coverings, which are not with his pure Spirit, are to be rent. And though ye may seem fair on your outside, this will not hide you; He who searches the heart and tries the reins is come before whom all secrets are bare and naked.[1]

Here Fell adjures us to surrender all that distances us from Spirit, to our original state of being simply naked and good. This is partly something we need to do actively, but if we are unable to do it on our own, God will assist us by showing us the places that need to be transformed. God will help us whether or not we find it pleasant. Think of undressing. It is kind of like leaving our socks on accidentally, or maybe even on purpose because we think feet are gross. Then, God calls our attention to the socks by shining a sort of spotlight on them. And, if we're not totally ready and able to take them off, God will help us, even if we'd prefer to keep them on. Fell's last line is a warning that even though we might think we look good before God, if we are secretly still wearing some socks—concealing part of our heart—God will know.

If we imagine the process of exposing our Naked Truth this way, wherein our coverings may be ripped away from us, leaving us frightened and ashamed, it probably doesn't sound too appealing. And we're not just talking about socks. The coverings we are talking about losing or having stripped away are all the things we think we are; all the adjectives we use to describe ourselves, the environment in which we live, the people with whom we interact. One example of this we've seen recently in the U.S. has come about with our widespread economic changes. Consider the many people who always defined themselves as affluent, successful, or hardworking and then found themselves out of a job, losing their homes, and without the possibility of retirement. These types of changes force people to either grasp firmly to an outmoded understanding of themselves or to get in touch with the deeper Truth of who they are and what they are here to do.

Fox prescribes this nakedness for those of us who want "heavenly, saving wisdom and knowledge" to order us "in the affairs and service of God". For Friends who seek this, Fox explains that we cannot find it in the world. The world can only provide us with rags, these shoddy garments (i.e. all that we have, do, say, and believe that is not full of Spirit), "must be cast off, and trodden under foot by the spirit and power of Christ; which power turns you to Christ, who clothes all his sons and daughters with his heavenly fine linen, which will never wax old."[2] Thus, we should take heart! Fox assures us that if we submit to Spirit's will, we won't end up naked, cold, vulnerable, and more than a little embarrassed, but rather clothed by God Herself in garb that is way more sumptuous and comfortable than anything we could find ourselves—and I'm pretty sure it doesn't only come in Quaker gray.

---

[1] See Margaret Fell's *Brief Collection*. Punctuation added.   [2] See George Fox's *Works*, volume 8, page 192.

In a section of his writings titled *Naked Truth,* Isaac Penington describes The nature of this spiritual clothing. He asks, "What is the white raiment which the soul is to be clothed with, without which it is naked in God's sight and the sight of the truly discerning...?" He ultimately answers his own question, calling it the "raiment of Christ". Since he probably wasn't claiming we'll all end up sporting "Jesus is my Homeboy" t-shirts, let's explore this a bit. Quakers traditionally understood "Christ", the "Christ Light", or "Christ Spirit" more or less as a person's capacity to live reconciled with Spirit; in other words, Spirit + Human = Christ.

So, if we understand our new clothing to be our Christ-selves, then all this disrobing and redressing represents a process wherein we cease showing off all the ways we have distanced ourselves from Spirit (in other words, our "ego") and instead represent ourselves as the pure vessels for Spirit that we Truly are. To do this, we must strip away all the layers of socialization and let go of all the not-God we have in our lives, which covers us. This leads to a time of being fully bare before God and others—freckles, moles, and all. These blemishes represent our unfaithful parts, such as our violent or hurtful tendencies, our addictions, our pettiness, etc. This nakedness is embarrassing and scary (so vulnerable!), but when we take the risk to get to that state, we give Spirit the opportunity to cover us again, this time with the characteristics of Divine reconciliation such as Power, Love, Courage, Peace, and so on.

Hence, Nakedness is not merely the process of struggling and stripping down, but also finding deeper happiness and the wellspring of life. However, even though the end was sweet, for early Friends the shame and pain were just as real and thus were central to their use of nakedness as a symbol. We too should maintain this tension so that we will not be misled, thinking the process will be easier than it really is. So, remembering the difficulty, let us continue to explore the more enjoyable aspects of coming into right relationship with God.

In the next passage, Penington shares what it is like after we have become naked before God once more. He claims, "And most happy is he who knows the issues of death stopped, the issues of life opened, and whose spirit is naked and open before the Lord, for life to spring up in him, and the issues of life opened, and whose spirit is naked and open before the Lord, for life to spring up in him, and issue forth through him at its pleasure." It is to this final stage that Friends referred when they appealed to others "to be clothed in righteousness".

The appeal was both a sharp call to accountability to give up broken ways and a loving invitation to something much sweeter than business as usual. Isaac Penington further describes his experience of this promised raiment as follows:

> I am by God's love, by his grace, by his mercy, by his goodness, by his power, by his wisdom, by his righteousness, by his holiness, which he of his own good pleasure communicateth, and causeth to spring in me, and filleth and clotheth me with, as [s]eemeth good in his sight.

Here Penington does not just say that he feels God's love, grace, mercy, goodness, power, wisdom, righteousness, and holiness, but that his sense of his own existence *is mediated through God.* If I wrote a comparable statement about my own existence, it would look more like, "I *am* society's structures, cultural practices, historical processes, familial patterns, and my own motley collection of survival techniques." What would your statement sound like if you took an honest look at yourself? On a deeper level, I actually believe that my be-ing abides in Spirit, but that is not the reality I am most in touch with, nor the life I usually feel I am living.

Chapter 3

Modern Day Stripping

Inspired by the lack of Spirit in my life, I have often wondered what made the radicalism of the early Friends possible. If their witness only happened because they were all particularly extreme characters, then that is no help to me nor other extremists. However, these passages suggest that their powerful faith was not merely a factor of personality, but a consequence of their relationship with God. This means it is available to me too; the strength, fulfillment, steadfastness, righteousness, and energy that endured prison, beatings, and wide societal change is still available to us even now. This claim is not theoretical; I think it's true. As we excavate our most beautiful and useful words and symbols, such as "Nakedness", we can begin to use them in our own faith-lives by interpreting our experiences through those symbols. I experienced the power of this in my own life.

A few years ago, after dropping out of Guilford[1] on a Spiritual Leading, I felt God pushing me to radically alter the way I had oriented myself to the world. During times of reflection, such as waking up in the morning or walking down the street, my attention was repeatedly brought to parts of myself that were difficult to face: how I interacted with people, how I felt about myself, how I presented myself to others, and so on. During this excruciating and extended process, a friend of mine, who was learning about early Friends and their spiritual lives, told me the term "Spiritual Nakedness" and briefly explained that early Friends had used it to describe their inward experience with God. Soon afterwards, in one of those quiet moments when Spirit was working on me, I felt as though inwardly I was stripped down—exposed and vulnerable before God. Outwardly, I could do nothing but splay out on the floor and sob my sorry eyes out. It was devastating.

However, in that moment, I also remember feeling connected to my religious forebears and a sense that my experience was integrating, rather than fracturing. Although this powerful experience was disturbing, I at least had a conceptual framework with which I could interpret what was happening to me. Knowing that others had survived something similar and that it seemed to work out well for them was comforting. If I had not heard of this tradition, what would this pivotal spiritual moment have been like for me? I imagine I would have felt more confused, isolated, and afraid, lacking both the interpretive framework for the experience and the sense of communal connection.

But there is more. The process of getting Naked is not confined to esoteric spiritual experiences nor existential crises like the one I described above. I like to think of myself as a practical theologian, so if something doesn't seem tangible or practicable, I'm not on board. Luckily, I've been working with this symbol and its connected inward processes long enough that God's finally clued me in on ways it

---

[1] *[Guilford College is a college founded and supported by Quakers located in Greensboro, North Carolina. —ed.]*

can be used as a practice, rather than just a framework to understand a passive experience.

Recently I was living in another country for a time, pursuing an entirely separate Leading from this work you read now. As I was there, I intended to document my spiritual process. As I attempted to describe what was happening with me, I couldn't help but use the language of Nakedness. As so often happens, being immersed in another culture and location forced me to reconsider how I thought of myself.

Usually, I just go along living my life feeling more or less satisfied and self-assured, but suddenly, I couldn't communicate with others, so people I met could not get to know me in the way I'm accustomed. I couldn't participate in the activities with which I identify myself. I couldn't make the jokes that I would make at home. I couldn't share my spiritual or religious life. I could not even dress the same. With every layer of my life shifted and no adequate way to express myself, I felt my "self-hood" shaken to the core. All the things usually associated with me, Maggie, were no longer relevant.

So who was I? In that moment, I realized how truly "clothed" we are. All those things with which I identify myself are not eternal, and are therefore just constructs of my society, my family, my culture, and so on. At the highest point of desperation, I called my sweetie at the time and lamented over the nothingness or meaninglessness that was "me". Wisely, he assured me that those things were never me anyway, and that it is actually a great gift to be able to see that. Furthermore, I was not lost. If I could let go of those things I used to define myself, and avoid replacing them with new ones, then I would find the Eternal.

We can do this at any moment.

In that moment, I didn't remove enough layers to reach that Eternal self—the Inward Christ—but I believe that was because I wasn't really opening myself up to Spirit or the "Searchlight" which surely would have exposed me. Even though we can do this "undressing" at any moment, it is something that we have to choose to do. If I look at my life and ask myself, "Would I be this way or do this thing if I had been born in a different century? What if I had different parents, or was another gender?" and the answer is "No" or "Probably not", then I know that this is just a construction, a thing that is not of Spirit, not Eternal. It is up to me, with the help of Spirit, to do the work of letting it drop away from me.

There are also other ways to get Naked. I can tell people my Truth. When walking down the street, I can let myself cry, laugh hysterically, or dance around like a weirdo. When I feel myself getting defensive because it would be too scary and vulnerable to say, "I feel hurt", I can let that defensiveness drop and experiment with sharing my real feelings. I can tell the stories of my life that feel too scary to share with others. I can openly admit my weaknesses and my growing edges. I can be real with my power and my strengths too, overcoming any insecurities or fears that I'll be seen as conceited. These examples are more day-to-day Truths, but as we uncover the less revelatory layers, we make way for sharing ever more profound Truth.

And, there is more. One of the best parts about the symbol of Nakedness is that we don't need to go back to the history of symbol or its biblical roots;

Nakedness is something we know intimately from our own experience and context. Who isn't familiar with the potential embarrassment of bare-assing? Even those lacking inhibition around nudity still probably wouldn't want to go naked in their meeting house or someone else's church. Thus, the symbol works even without thirty pages of discussion. However, with a little bit of education, we can *also* use the added layers of meaning that come from the symbol's connection to Genesis and the early Friends. So, tell your f(F)riends! Get the First Day School teacher in on it. Think about William Sympson next time you take off your clothes. Try using the symbol in your prayers or in a meditation practice. But most importantly, GET NAKED and prepare yourself for the righteousness that will follow.

Post Script

You may have noticed that I breezed over my personal story, which is a bit ironic since the whole thing is about exposing our Truth. In part this is because I am no expert at getting Naked and/or allowing God to Clothe me. In my explorations of the spiritual life, I have found that maintaining consistent spiritual practices is *integral* to a steadfast, powerful connection to the Divine. I have high hopes that "getting Naked" can become a regular Quaker spiritual practice again.

I've only started to do this for myself and that's mostly thanks to the encouragement of those closest to me who challenge me to look seriously at myself and to continue growing in hard ways. Without their help, I'd mostly be too scared or overwhelmed to do the work, because let's face it, when we stop thinking of the Light as some touchy-feely fairy-godmother-type energy, but instead as a Searchlight that shines on the parts of us we try to hide, it's scary as hell (especially if you're from a family like mine, where admitting you are wrong is something you may never live down).

That said, I intend to go back to this practice for the rest of my life, and pray for the courage it demands. Join me. Let's start living like Friends of Truth. Let's see what happens in our lives and the wider world when we do so.

At the very least, it's likely to be more exciting!

Conclusion

Christianstory

All of these texts have, in one way or another, sought to lay out a vision for living a life of faith. They each and all call us to move beyond debates of doctrines and into the realm of life. In many ways, they are not theological texts, because they do not treat faith as an object of debate and discussion. The life of faith is not the goal, but the starting point.

Each of these texts, each in a different way, are inviting you to take up your role in the story embodied by Christ. One of the great tragedies of the modern world is that our stories are relegated to academics and entertainment. Yet television, blockbusters, and hit book series demonstrate the enduring power of stories to transform the world and the way we see it: consider how people can recognize the meaning behind "a glitch in the Matrix" or a reference to "Hogwarts". These are just the most obvious and commercial examples of how you and I speak in stories.

We speak in stores because stories are the way that we make sense of our life. Telling these stories is the way we bond to each other. These stories have the power to motivate huge masses of people to get together in giant conventions for the sole purpose to meet and bond with others who share the same stories. These stories have tremendous power, and that power goes underappreciated by everyone except the marketting and entertainment industry.

Stories are the fundamental building block of all of our thought. Developmental psychology has shown that when we are infants, our first inkling of complex thought is not a rational analysis of experiential cases. We are not born scientists. Rather, our first inkling of complex thought is the ability to comprehend a simple story with the most basic of plots: one character is on the scene, it does something to another character, and then both characters have changed.

At first, the only character we understand is ourselves, and the only other "character" is our perspective: we move our eyes and the perspective on the world (and, hence, the world itself) shifts. Soon, we conceive of outside forces: a ball rolls along and hits another, and the first ball slows down while the second starts rolling. While empirical ideas of "cause and effect" are still beyond our capability to comprehend, the world is already full of stories even as infants.[1]

Once we have managed to make some sense of our world through stories, we then use our stories to create relationships and to communicate in those relationships. Your personal sense of how a story flows and how storytelling works reveals your culture and shapes what will engage and inform you. Social boundaries are drawn and enforced by the stories we tell and the way we tell them.[2] Learning to love others means learning to appreciate their stories and their storytelling.

---

[1] For more on the psychological research behind this claim, as well as an insightful critique of various popular assumptions about how humans work, see Peter White's *Psychological Metaphysics*. [2] For more on this and citations to research backing the claim, see Ruby Payne's *A Framework for Understanding Poverty: A Cognitive Approach*.

To love the stories of others, we must first be comfortable with our own stories. Sometimes we have chosen our stories, and sometimes our stories have chosen us. Wherever their origin, our stories constitute us. Being intentional about the stories that constitute us is as essential as being intentional about the food that constitutes us. For the authors in this anthology and its editor, Christianity has provided the constitutional stories necessary for growth and spiritual strength.

Although some hyper-conservative portrayals of Christianity may try to limit it to only one story, the reality is that Christianity provides many constitutional stories. The Bible is predominently a series of stories, all of which are wrapped up in the story of Israel and culminate in Jesus Christ. Christianity's history also has many stories worth drawing into your identity, either as virtuous exemplars or as dire warnings. The community of faithful exist in order to tell these stories, and each community also carries with it local stories of wise elders, young radicals, and difficulties that were overcome through tenacity and faith. These stories make people laugh and cry and draw the community together into something more than a happenstance gathering of individuals. To be a Christian is to have faith in these stories and the community they engender.

Through this anthology, I have sought to give you new stories to supplement those that you may have picked up before. All the authors here gave you the grand narrative of the revolutionary Jesus: in the words Tolstoy puts into the mouth of Christ, "You have tried the other law for thousands of years; now try Mine, which is the very reverse."[1] Through social mandates, inner life, and interrelationship, the core story of Christ is one of an invasive and contagious faith whose grounding is love. More academic readers may have noticed that esoteric systematic theology is largely absent from these witnesses: for these followers of Christ, the moment's pressing need is so overwhelming that the abstract questions are largely irrelevant. If there is a doctrine, this is it: be God's plan in the present; have faith in God's plan for the future.

We should hear and tell all these stories again and again, and we should live and relive them again and again. We need these stories to constitute us, so that when we have an opportunity to be like these people and live into our own story, we know that not only *should* we take the opportunity, but we *can* take the opportunity. We can take risks, be vulnerable, and live into God's calling for our life. We can do it—after all, others have done it before us.

These stories are important to know: our stories constitute us, but more than that, our stories are our destinies.

---

[1] If you have not gathered by now, let me be very explicit: "the other law" is not Judaism or Torah; rather,"the Other Law" is the law of militarism, conquest, brutality, and savage independence.

I love to tell the story of unseen things above,
Of Jesus and His glory, of Jesus and His love.
I love to tell the story, because I know 'tis true;
It satisfies my longings as nothing else can do.

(Refrain)
I love to tell the story, 'twill be my theme in glory,
To tell the old, old story of Jesus and His love.

I love to tell the story; more wonderful it seems
Than all the golden fancies of all our golden dreams.
I love to tell the story, it did so much for me;
And that is just the reason I tell it now to thee.

(Refrain)

I love to tell the story; 'tis pleasant to repeat
What seems, each time I tell it, more wonderfully sweet.
I love to tell the story, for some have never heard
The message of salvation from God's own holy Word.

(Refrain)

I love to tell the story, for those who know it best
Seem hungering and thirsting to hear it like the rest.
And when, in scenes of glory, I sing the new, new song,
'Twill be the old, old story that I have loved so long.

(Refrain)

www.ingramcontent.com/pod-product-compliance
Lightning Source LLC
Chambersburg PA
CBHW051821040426
42447CB00006B/308